D0597166

332.6
OPD

JUN   2008

Farmers Branch Manske Library
13613 Webb Chapel
Farmers Branch, Tx 75234-3756

THE
WORLD
IS YOUR
OYSTER

ALSO BY JEFF D. OPDYKE

The Wall Street Journal. Complete Personal Finance Guidebook
The Wall Street Journal. Personal Finance Workbook
Love and Money: A Life Guide to Financial Success

THE
WORLD
IS YOUR
OYSTER

The Guide to Finding
Great Investments
Around the Globe

JEFF D. OPDYKE

CROWN BUSINESS
NEW YORK

Farmers Branch Manske Library
13613 Webb Chapel
Farmers Branch, Tx 75234-3756

Copyright © 2008 by Jeff D. Opdyke

All rights reserved.
Published in the United States by Crown Business, an imprint of the Crown
Publishing Group, a division of Random House, Inc., New York.
www.crownpublishing.com

Crown Business is a trademark and the Rising Sun colophon is a registered
trademark of Random House, Inc.

Library of Congress Cataloging-in-Publication Data

Opdyke, Jeff D.
The world is your oyster : the guide to finding great investments around the globe /
Jeff D. Opdyke.
p. cm.
1. Stocks—Handbooks, manuals, etc.   2. Investments, Foreign—Handbooks,
manuals, etc.   3. Portfolio management—Handbooks, manuals, etc.   I. Title.
II. Title: Guide to finding great investments around the globe.

HG4527.O63 2008

332.6—dc22   2007036718

ISBN 978-0-307-38104-0

Printed in the United States of America

Design by R. Bull

10 9 8 7 6 5 4 3 2 1

First Edition

To Amy, Zach-man, and Coley—
my own string of pearls

CONTENTS

THE
WORLD
IS YOUR
OYSTER

INTRODUCTION

Oysters in a Dishwasher

Every adventure begins with an inspiration.
This adventure was inspired by a dishwasher.

In the fall of 1995, I set out to become a global investor, convinced that limiting my investments to the U.S. stock market, though certainly home to some of the world's truly great corporations, restricted the opportunities to profit from the growth of companies building the products, selling the goods, and providing the services responsible for the economies expanding beyond America's shores. After all, more than 320 of the Fortune Global 500 are based outside the United States, and tens of thousands of smaller companies never show up on radar back in America. As such, overseas existed opportunities unavailable at home on the New York Stock Exchange or the Nasdaq Stock Market. Overseas traded the stocks of local companies most Americans never heard about — in places most Americans rarely considered.

I am not a professional investor. Nor am I a mutual-fund manager, hedge-fund trader, or research analyst. I am a journalist — an average investor, with access to the same tools available to every other average investor, namely, the Internet and an e-mail account. And I am convinced that as great as the opportunities are in America, they are not the only opportunities the world provides. I am convinced that the U.S. dollar, despite its supremacy and global reach, is not the world's only worthy currency. That conviction, in turn, compels me to seek out opportunities in stock markets far removed from New York City.

At the time this adventure begins — 1995 — international investors had no Lonely Planet guide to going global with your greenbacks; no Fodor's guide to the stock exchanges of the world. Stateside brokerage firms offered no real options either. Those that would transact in foreign stocks either demanded large purchases to justify their effort, or marked up the price of the stock sharply to cover their costs for trading overseas and converting dollars into whatever local currency the transaction demanded. Neither option appealed to a small-time investor unable to trade multi-thousand-share blocks and unwilling to pay usurious up-charges.

No, if I wanted to go native — that is, if I wanted to trade as the locals do, on local stock exchanges, in local currencies — I'd have to bushwhack the trail myself.

So I did, ultimately opening accounts over the years in New Zealand, Australia, Hong Kong, Singapore, and Canada that, combined, provide access to more than a dozen stock exchanges. In more recent times, I have begun to explore accounts that will allow me to own shares directly in places such as Vietnam, Egypt, the Middle East, and Eastern Europe.

And now the obvious question: Why?

Think back to Wall Street in the 1990s. U.S. stocks were rocking, the Standard & Poor's 500-stock index seemed incapable of disappointing. Stock-market profits flowed freely, barbershops became centers of investment counsel, and "playing the market" grew into a game that anyone could win. The U.S. indices racked up double-digit gains seemingly yearly and seemingly with little effort, some years posting returns of nearly 40%. And here's the irony: Not once in that decade did the S&P 500 top the list of the world's best-performing stock markets. In 1995, the year the S&P posted a monumental total return topping 38%, Switzerland moved up nearly 45%. Two years later, when the S&P notched an equally impressive 34% showing, Turkey put up a 118% gain. In 1998, the S&P's otherwise muscular 31% surge shriveled next to the performance registered by South Korea, which lit up the tote board with a 141% return.

The current decade is little changed. In 2003, when the S&P bounced back from three consecutive years of bear-market losses with a 29% gain, Thailand improved by 145% while Australia, Austria, Brazil, Canada, Denmark, Germany, Greece, Israel, New Zealand, Spain, and Sweden — among others — all powered ahead with gains of between 50% and 115%. When the S&P eked out a tiny, single-digit return in 2005, more than 40 other countries' stock markets performed better, led by Egypt, which roared ahead 161%.

The fact is, the U.S. stock market, as measured by the S&P, has *never* led the list as the world's top performer. In years the S&P flagged, any of a variety of other markets flourished. And in years the S&P flourished, any of a variety of other markets flourished more.

America, thus, is not the only land of opportunity. To find more of what the world has to offer, you must, like Australia's native Aborigines, set off on a walkabout, a journey of exploration. That, then, is the reason behind *The World Is Your Oyster*. Just as you need a little guidance crossing borders when you travel, so too do you need guidance when crossing borders as an investor. As traveler or investor, dangers and opportunities abound; you just have to know where to go and how to get there and what to be on the lookout for once you arrive. Thus, consider this guidebook your travel companion for buying and selling stocks around the world.

Other books make a great case for investing globally, but then tell you how to size up U.S.-based mutual funds or U.S.-listed foreign stocks as your investment options. That's akin to telling you how much fun it is to fish . . . then setting you loose on a koi pond. This is not that guidebook— though we'll certainly address in an early chapter the various ways to own foreign investments within the confines of the U.S. markets if you don't yet feel comfortable enough to wire thousands of dollars to a brokerage firm you've never heard of, in a country you've never visited.

This guidebook takes a novel approach: that individual investors want their money to interact directly in local economies, bypassing Wall Street altogether. As such, this guide dispenses the practical advice you need for finding the overseas brokerage firms willing to work with you; how to fund the account; the oddities you'll encounter with the way foreign companies report their financial results; the tax issues involved with owning accounts overseas; the challenges of being so far removed from your investments; and how to research and track the companies you buy and those you might want to buy.

This book will teach you about the risks of owning assets denominated in foreign currencies — everything from the geopolitical risk of governmental actions to the effects of currency fluctuations. It will detail in easy-to-understand language why currencies ebb and flow in relation to one another, how that affects your investments, and how to convert dollars to yen . . . and back again. Don't fret, though; currency conversion isn't nearly as complex as it might seem — plus, I'll take you to the websites that will convert the numbers for you instantly.

Inside you'll also learn how, and why, to tie a foreign bank account to a foreign brokerage account — a necessity for several reasons, not the least of which concerns dividends. Trust that your foreign shares are much more likely to pay a dividend than are your U.S. holdings, and trust that the bank teller down the block will look at you with the most dumbfounded expression when you ask if the bank can convert into dollars a dividend check denominated in Thai baht, even if that bank is a huge global institution in New York City or Los Angeles that offers currency conversion services to its customers.

You'll also find a chapter each devoted to China and Turkey, a case study in how to think long term about overseas profit potential, how to find and research companies in a foreign land, and the inherent risks you face once you leave home.

The best part: You don't need a passport. You can own the world from the comfort of home — no matter if home is a financial capital such as Boston, or the capital of trout fishing: Cotter, Arkansas. Regardless of where you live, these days you can buy and sell stocks from Tokyo to Cairo, Auckland to London to Shanghai, in the middle of the night, wearing your pajamas.

The message here is that for all the attention afforded Wall Street and its storied history, and despite the U.S. stock market's vaunted position as the world's preeminent financial marketplace, American stocks are simply not the be-all, end-all to investing. The New York Stock Exchange may in fact sit upon an island, but it's surrounded by a wide, wide world of investment opportunities unrelated to America.

That's what I went looking for in 1995—and found a dish-washer . . .

Fisher & Paykel is not a company many Americans knew about in the mid-1990s. However, as the maker of kitchen and laundry appliances it was a leader in its home country, New Zealand, and was a growing presence in Asia, where people have been increasingly moving into middle-class ranks, ushering in a ravenous desire for the same Western conveniences—i.e., electric dishwashers—enjoyed by consumers in industrialized nations. Investors specifically searching for consumer-oriented Pacific Rim companies likely to benefit from Asia's multi-decade economic expansion would likely stumble upon Fisher & Paykel (rhymes with Michael).

Yet even if they did, Fisher & Paykel was not a stock investors could easily buy in America circa 1995. To own Fisher & Paykel shares at the same price New Zealanders paid required transacting on the New Zealand Stock Exchange, nearly 9,000 miles (as the crow flies) from the New York Stock Exchange. Accomplishing that would necessitate a local bro-kerage account, funded with New Zealand dollars.

Equipped with a slow laptop computer and an even slower dial-up Internet connection, I trolled the Web for several weeks, dispatching e-mails to brokerage firms Down Under, asking if they might accommodate an American investor. Most responded with courteous missives informing me that they couldn't. A few never replied.

One—just one—welcomed me: New Zealand's now-defunct Ord Minnett Securities, where a local broker helped me open an account via e-mails and applications faxed across 17 time zones.

"All that remains," he ultimately wrote, "is wiring your funds" to a particular account number, routing it through a particular bank . . . on the other side of world . . . to a country I've never even visited.

Eagerly I complied.

Then heard nothing.

For days.

My enthusiasm waned; worry swelled. Was my trust misplaced? Had this seemingly affable broker really opened the account? Might he have just pocketed my thousands of dollars, assuming I'd never track him down, given the vast distance separating us?

Four days later, the notice arrived by fax: The broker, who had been out of the office for several days, had received the money, had funded the account, and had purchased for me shares in Fisher & Paykel and another company, a brewer, Lion Nathan Ltd., as I'd requested. And, he informed me, the sum of money I'd wired into my account was precisely 10 New Zealand dollars too few. On my very first overseas transaction, I had muffed my first currency conversion.

"But no worries," he wrote. "I'll cover that cost for you. Welcome to New Zealand."

With that, I was an international investor. A financial globetrotter.

Certainly, you don't have to cross borders physically with your money to gain international exposure. You can own mutual funds and exchange-traded funds (ETFs) in America that hold foreign securities—and there are many. Or, you can buy any of the hundreds of American depositary receipts, so-called ADRs, the U.S.-listed shares of foreign companies such as Sony, Toyota, British Airways, and Nokia that trade on various exchanges in the states. Or, as some investors do, you can buy shares of big, U.S. multinational companies such as Coca-

Cola, Wal-Mart, Citicorp, and even Starbucks, expecting that their presence in foreign markets will translate into meaningful exposure to overseas economies in your portfolio.

All those strategies are worthwhile, and we will explore each. Yet while certainly convenient, such strategies lack purity. All too often, buying international mutual funds, ETFs, and ADRs in the United States means owning the biggest companies in a country or region, companies — again: Sony, Toyota, British Airways, Nokia — that already are large, well-known global corporations. That's not necessarily bad, but there is a problem: Large, well-known global corporations typically already have a sizable portion of their business tied to the U.S. consumer, making them as much a bet on America as on local economies. The same holds for multinational American firms. Sure, they generate bushels of sales overseas, but they are first and foremost American companies, more often tied to movements in the U.S. economy and the U.S. stock market.

No, to profit from expanding local economies requires owning the small- and medium-sized companies intimately tied to those local economies, and that rarely have ties to the U.S. marketplace. And the way to own those companies is to invest directly in their individual home markets — in essence, to send your dollars packing.

When I first ventured overseas in 1995, that effort took time. Today those opportunities are easier to pursue and as convenient as trading stocks in America. Opening brokerage accounts and bank accounts in such places as Hong Kong, Singapore, Australia, and even Vietnam is generally no more difficult than ordering a book from an online retailer. With widely available high-speed Internet access, you can download account applications from brokerage and bank websites and, often, scan the completed document into your computer, attach it to an e-mail, and dispatch it to the other side of the globe in seconds. Wire transfers make funding an account equally easy, and online trade execution means you can exchange shares in Eastern Europe before New York's awake, sell on Sydney's open just as the American markets close, and trade through the night, if you wish, from Jakarta to Cairo.

As for researching and tracking foreign companies you own or might want to own . . . well, consider this: Ten years ago, when I opened that account in New Zealand, researching companies required nothing more than a slow Internet connection and e-mail. I'd sit in my office for an hour or two after work, plugging phrases such as "South Africa and brewery and shareholders" into a search engine, trolling for beer stocks on the Johannesburg exchange. The next day it would be "banks and Scandinavia," searching for financial firms in Norway and Sweden. I'd search for hometown newspapers with online content in places such as Auckland, Wellington, and Queenstown, New Zealand; or Sydney, Melbourne, and Perth, Australia, reading the local business section as a way of unearthing publicly traded companies and their business operations. To those that seemed promising or merely interesting, I'd shoot an e-mail to the company's investor-relations department, requesting the most recent few years' worth of annual and semiannual reports, which would dutifully arrive a few weeks later in the mail.

Today that process is magnitudes easier and faster, if only because the quantity of information available on the Web has exploded exponentially. Almost all public companies — in some of the most random countries — have a presence on the Web these days, and annual and semiannual reports are often available right there on the home page, easily downloaded, so that there's no more waiting on the mail. Research in various forms is available all over the Internet, ranging from brokerage firms, independent research houses, and financial websites to blogs, industry trade associations, the world's various stock exchanges, and the individual companies themselves. Each of these options can provide a wealth of investor-friendly information, as well as links to other useful sites.

Only one tool remains missing: the definitive guidebook to help you navigate your way from one country to the next.

Until now, that is.

Turn the page — the journey begins. . . .

CHAPTER 1

POSTCARDS FROM THE EDGE

Five Reasons to Go Global

Why go global?

When all is said and done, the answer defines this book.

Why, indeed, go to all the effort of putting money to work in places outside your home country when an abundance of opportunities to invest in some of the world's finest public companies exists right here in the fruited plains of the U.S. stock market? After all, in the world of 2007 more than 5,100 public companies carried the Made in America label, including some of the biggest, globally branded firms — McDonald's, Coca-Cola, General Motors, Wal-Mart, Exxon, and Boeing, to name but six. Own such companies and some portion of your money is at work in Asia, Europe, the Middle East, Africa, and elsewhere. A Pakistani buys lemon-and-spice-flavored fries for lunch at a Mickie D's in Karachi, and you profit. An Argentine buys the family's household supplies while shopping at the Wal-Mart Supercenter in Mendoza, and you profit. The United Arab Emirates' flag carrier, Etihad Airways, orders five Boeing 777 jets, as it did in September 2004, and you profit. Sure, such transactions are infinitesimal on your individual account. Yet spread across millions and millions of global transactions, those infinitesimal slivers of profit mass into real dollars over time.

And here in the states, you're not limited to just American companies with global tentacles. You also have access to a few thousand foreign companies whose stocks are listed in various American markets. Many of these foreigners carry names equally well regarded stateside: Honda, Vodafone, Air France, and Unilever, among them. Indeed, you can collect a vast assortment of so-called American depositary receipts, the U.S.-traded shares of foreign firms, from dozens of nations (including Malawi, the Dominican Republic, and Sri Lanka) without ever leaving American shores. Moreover, you can trade these companies' shares through a U.S.-based brokerage account as quickly and easily as you do American icons such as Apple Computer and Microsoft.

Venturing abroad, then, would seem an entirely unnecessary, if not extravagant, exercise.

Only it's not.

The world has entered an age increasingly absent the financial barriers that once derailed the flow of investment dollars across borders. U.S. companies today buy competitors in Germany; British companies buy in America; those in Japan cross into South Korea. U.S mutual funds, hedge funds, and pensions routinely invest a large portion of the money they manage in stock markets all around the world. And today we individual investors — the mom-and-pop investors, as Wall Street calls us — can ship our money off to work in far more locales than we've ever had access to. Good reason exists for doing so: Those 5,100 companies that are Made in America represented just 10% of the roughly 50,000 publicly traded companies listed on the world's various stock exchanges in 2007. Ten percent. In that context the American market, despite its prominence globally, seems a fairly constrained investment universe.

Certainly, many of the world's publicly traded companies aren't worth the effort. They trade in countries racked by war or political corruption or both; they trade on stock exchanges so small that you assume unacceptable trading risks, particularly when stock prices are falling; they exist in countries where you face limitations or restrictions on repatriating your money whenever you want; their corporate governance, assuming it exists, is questionable at best, leaving your investment in great jeopardy. Some are still owned in large part by various government entities and have about the same profit-making incentive as did those old Soviet collective farms. Managers aren't running such businesses to benefit private shareholders so much as they're running a business to preserve their job by keeping some lethargic, bloated, bureaucratic government agency content.

Vast numbers of others, however, are strong, viable, entrepreneurial companies, or those with decades of profitability in their past, trading in long-established markets, in long-stable countries with a long history of sound securities regulation. They sell proven products and services, with immense and expanding prospects to continue growing their business at home and abroad. Their corporate governance is robust and their managers and executives awake each day trying to make the company a little bigger and a little better for themselves and their shareholders.

The only "not" on their list: a presence in the USA.

If you want to own these companies — and there are very good reasons why you should — you have to go to them, because they're not coming to you.

Think about it in terms of, say, Japan's culinary staple, miso soup. You can shop your local hyper-super-megamart just around the corner from home and, though the store has thousands of items for sale, you're not likely to find two key ingredients: the miso paste itself and packets of bonito flakes, from which comes the soup's base. While the American hypermart will assuredly offer a few Asian selections along one-quarter of an aisle — if that much — it generally doesn't stock all that you need to cook up many of the truly authentic dishes. For that you'll need to shop at the Asian market on the other side of town, where the grocer stocks all the ingredients you need, commonly multiple selections in various quantities and quality grades, all the genuine brands sold back in the motherland.

Plus, the Asian grocer's prices are frequently lower, since for the hypermart these are specialty items worthy of a marked-up price, whereas for the grocer's clientele, local Asians, these are everyday staples. And the locals are not about to overpay for everyday staples. Sure, the transaction across town takes more effort and more time, and you risk not being able to read the label and may even struggle to communicate with the shopkeeper. But the Asian grocer can answer your questions, point you toward a better product, and offer tips on how the locals really use the ingredients.

All in all, you're better off shopping where the locals do — despite the added sweat in doing so.

Grocery markets and stock markets aren't so dissimilar. For all the companies you can buy on the American hyper-megamart of stock exchanges, so many more that you might want to own are simply unavailable where U.S. investors typically shop. Though thousands of 7-Eleven convenience stores populate North America, for instance, you had better operate from a brokerage account with access to the Tokyo Stock Exchange if you want to own shares of the Japanese company controlling the chain — Seven & i Holdings Co. Want to profit from China's rapidly expanding market for home ownership? Better have an account in Hong Kong to trade China Vanke Co., a Shenzhen-based residential property developer in major Chinese cities. You'll need the ability to trade stocks in Milan if you want to own the leading tour operator — Gruppo Ventaglio S.p.A — that Italians call on when they're planning a holiday.

And why would you care to own the leading tour provider in Italy . . . or a Japanese convenience-store operator . . . or a Chinese property developer? That answer goes to the soul of this book — to what it means to be a global investor: People the world over do exactly the same things we Americans do, they just demand their services and products from local businesses that cater to and profit from local needs. Just as we Americans like to vacation, so, too, do Europeans; in fact, each August it's as though the entire continent is on holiday. Whether it's Italians tanning on a Sri Lankan beach, Norwegians sunning on a ship trolling the Greek isles, or Brits jetting off to splash in the waters off the Balearic Islands, the cumulative billions of euros and pounds they're spending are pooling on the bottom line of publicly traded companies in their homeland, not American firms.

Tens of thousands of foreign companies simply have nothing to do with America. They don't sell their products here, they don't operate stores aimed at U.S. consumers, they don't run their factories here. They don't power American homes, they don't fly their planes, book their hotel rooms, or run their overnight-delivery operations here. They don't provide services that Americans in large numbers seek. And their shares don't trade on any of the stock markets in New York City. They are homegrown, purposefully built to prosper in their local economies, and they purposefully choose to list their shares in their home market, where local investors know the brand. To prosper alongside these companies — to participate in those economies that businesses and consumers just like you are propelling outside the United States — you must shop where the locals do.

As such, that initial question — Why go global? — might best be answered with a rhetorical question: Why limit your portfolio to the single lot of consumers and businesses that exists in America — to just 10% of what the world has to offer?

Of course, within that answer lies the problem — that whole "going global" thing.

For the most part, Americans reflexively balk at things foreign. Sure, we'll buy a German car, and a Japanese DVD player, and a bottle of Chilean cabernet, but those products are so ubiquitous throughout every strata of American society these days that they seem as much American as they are foreign. Likewise with the German and Japanese and Chilean stocks that list in American markets. Though foreign by birth, they're an acceptable American investment because they trade in New York — and in dollars — giving them an air of respectability. Plus, trading on the New York Stock Exchange, we know from experience, is easy. Trading in Tokyo, Frankfurt, and Santiago? Well, that seems not so easy. And besides, it's not America!

As a nation, we simply aren't given to looking too far beyond our own shores to satisfy our interests unless it fits some national frivolity at the moment—say, a U.S. World Cup soccer victory on foreign soil even though the world's game isn't really a game we pay much attention to on the whole. Statistics bear this out: The Pew Research Center, a nonpartisan organization in Washington, D.C., that studies the attitudes and trends shaping America and the world, reports that between 1997 and 2002, only 20% of Americans traveled abroad, while only a quarter telephoned or corresponded with people overseas . . . and you have to wonder how many of those folks were hyphenated-Americans visiting and communicating with relatives back in their home country. Outside of New York City, Miami, and a very small lot of über-urban population centers in America, when is the last time you saw a currency-exchange booth around town? They're a common site across most of the world, even in some of the smallest, most remote towns and villages.

Here's another point of reference: When a foreign company uses its foreign stock to acquire a U.S. competitor, meaning it pays American investors with its own foreign shares, we Americans generally sell the shares of the foreign firm quickly, a stock-market phenomenon known as "flow back," in which the foreign shares flow back to the acquiring company's home market.

Part of our foreign aversion is our isolated geography; aside from Canada, Mexico, and some all-inclusive beach resorts in the Caribbean, we Americans have no peripheral recognition that other countries exist as anything more than vacation playgrounds, threats to our apple-pie existence, or enemy combatants during Olympic moments.

Part of it is our history; for much of the past century, America has served as the world's dominant force culturally, politically, socially, militarily, and financially, characteristics that have imbued Americans with a wrongheaded superiority complex, perhaps best expressed by a *BusinessWeek* article in 2000 that made the case for owning U.S. multinational stocks instead of foreign shares by announcing that "American companies . . . aren't likely to be bested by foreign rivals."

Really?

Apparently, that little ray of sunshine never made it to Japan's Toyota Motor Corp., which has been besting Detroit's General Motors and Ford Motor Co. for years. And what of all those defunct makers of American electronics in an age when high-quality South Korean and Japanese brands fill store shelves and lead the sales rankings? Or all the long-dead and dying textile makers on the East Coast, losing ground to global players who produce the same or better quality at cheaper prices? Or what about the oceangoing shipping companies? Hang out around ports in Long Beach, California; Seattle, Washington; and Newark, New Jersey, and take note of the names stenciled on the cargo containers and ships' hulls: All the biggest players are based in northern Europe and Asia. Even cartoons have lost out to Asia, as any cursory amount of time in front of Cartoon Network will bear out. Cartoon production for America, meanwhile, is now big business in India, home to the world's second-largest entertainment industry, Bollywood. The upshot of our red, white, and blue mentality is that we mistakenly view the U.S. dollar as largely the only real currency, we mistakenly view U.S. companies as largely the only real innovators, and we mistakenly assume that U.S. markets represent the world's beacon of economic freedom (the reality: in 2006 we ranked ninth, behind leader Hong Kong and nations such as Singapore, Ireland, Denmark, the United Kingdom, and even Estonia).

Part of it is that we're not schooled in world affairs beyond noting our participation in certain wars, leaving us ignorant in a global context and out of step with much of the rest of the planet, since most countries are surrounded by various neighbors, some belligerent at certain points throughout time, and what happens just beyond the border has historically been relevant for any number of economic, military, and self-preservation reasons.

Basically, as Americans it comes down to this: Unless it affects us directly, we tend not to care what transpires over there.

That's unfortunate. Because what happens over there can be very profitable for your portfolio back here.

It just takes opening your eyes to the opportunities that exist beyond America. So, let's start this book by examining the five reasons you might want to go global with your greenbacks. . . .

WHY GO GLOBAL, REASON 1: BECAUSE YOU CAN.

History is destined to record 1989 as a watershed year for freedom. Soviet citizens in early spring voted for the first time ever in parliamentary elections that unseated many Communist party officials, what the government newspaper *Izvestia* welcomed as a new era of "the dictatorship of democracy." In late spring, democratic-minded Chinese students occupied Beijing's Tiananmen Square, marking what has been described as the greatest challenge to the Communist state since China's 1949 revolution and spurring, in some part, today's expanding freedoms awarded to Chinese citizens and the country's economy. By late autumn, East and West Germans were hacking to pieces the famed Berlin Wall, marking the eventual end of Communist East Germany, the reunification of a divided nation, and the eventual fall of communism throughout the Soviet Bloc.

That year—1989—investors wanting to own stocks around the world had 56 markets to choose from. Combined, they offered intrepid globe-trotters access to fewer than 26,000 listed companies.

And today?

More than double the number of countries now operate stock exchanges, upon which trade the shares of those roughly 50,000 listed companies.

As economies have sloughed off the oppression of central planning and embraced capitalism in some form and its market-based logic, and as countries have cleaved apart to reemerge as multiple nations seeking capital to survive and grow, stock markets have germinated all over the globe, often in spots Americans don't consider unless some tragedy makes the evening news: Kazakhstan, Palestine, Macedonia, Sudan, Lebanon.

Wherever stock markets have opened, brokerage firms have sprouted, too, some with an online presence of some sort, many eager to assist foreigners, including Americans, in opening and funding a brokerage account. Some firms have no online trading access, just an online presence announcing their services and contact information. Dealing with those firms requires that you fax and e-mail your account application, as well as any buy and sell orders. But that's not much of a problem; that's the way my first account began — the one in New Zealand — and the way it operated for several years before it ultimately progressed to online accessibility.

Whatever the method of order transmission (online, e-mail, or phone), the fact is that as an American investor sitting in front of your computer in any U.S. city, you can open local brokerage accounts to buy and sell securities in markets in Canada, China, Hong Kong, Japan, Australia, New Zealand, Thailand, Vietnam, Malaysia, the Philippines, Singapore, Taiwan, Russia, Spain, Greece, France, Finland, Poland, Estonia, Hungary, the United Kingdom, Portugal, Egypt, and Botswana. Oh, and Tajikistan, too. And that's the short list . . . the *really* short list.

Now, you certainly have no need to fund a brokerage account in every country that cracks open a stock market. Although some of the world's exchanges are exceedingly large and busy, each day trading billions of shares worth tens of billions of dollars, other exchanges . . . well, not so busy, really. On an otherwise average Wednesday in early 2006, all of eight different companies traded on the Abidjan Stock Exchange in West Africa's Côte d'Ivoire. The cumulative value of all 3,091 shares that changed hands that day: less than $290,000, roughly on par with what Miami Heat basketball star Shaquille O'Neal earned for a single night's work on the hardcourt. Some economies, meanwhile, are just too small and too dependent upon one or two industries, putting them — and by extension, your portfolio — at risk if ever those industries falter. In some markets, the volume of shares that trade every day is so shallow that your dollars are at risk in the event a crisis erupts that inhibits your ability to sell your stocks quickly. This is what Wall Street calls an "illiquid" market. That's not likely to present a huge challenge on the front end, when you're buying shares, because you're generally not in a rush and, as an individual investor, you're generally not trading huge blocks of shares. However, getting out of a stock, or stocks, particularly in an emergency, can be difficult since not enough buyers and sellers exist to trade enough shares (the Abidjan Stock Exchange is a quintessential example of illiquid). The upshot of such a situation is that the price for the shares you want to sell may have to fall sharply before any buyers emerge, leaving you nursing potential losses before you can exit, or at least shrinking your profits markedly.

Events in Lebanon in July 2006 offer a sober example. After Hezbollah, a radical Islamic group based in Lebanon, kidnapped two Israeli soldiers, Israel responded with a sustained attack from land, air, and sea, which begat Hezbollah raining a battery of rockets onto northern Israeli towns — in essence an undeclared war that ultimately stretched on for weeks. Israel's attacks decimated Lebanese infrastructure, including Beirut's international airport; Israeli warships blockaded Beirut's harbor. Until the bombs and missiles began to reshape the Lebanese landscape, Lebanon was a fragile democracy rebuilding its economy after years of civil war. In the relative peace after that civil war, beachside Beirut had taken up the mantle as playground to the Middle East. Tourism was driving the nascent economy, accounting for an estimated 15% of Lebanon's gross domestic product, according to the United Nations.

The exchange of bombs between Hezbollah and Israel changed that, leaving in the lurch those investors who owned Lebanese shares as a way to benefit from the country's economic rebirth.

Blasts started tearing through Beirut on a Wednesday. By Friday's market close on the Beirut Stock Exchange, Lebanese shares as a group had lost 13% of their cumulative value—a painful, fast plunge. Worse for investors: The market's close that Friday was, quite literally, the market's close. Lebanese exchange officials clamped off trading the following Monday. Had you rushed to get out when news broke of the hostilities, fearful that maybe the Lebanese exchange would close, you would have sold into a free-falling market, rarely a wise notion since you have no idea what price you'll receive. Yet, had you waited, the unexpected closing of the stock exchange meant your opportunity to sell vanished, leaving you to sit on losses, wondering when the market might reopen and how much lower investors would price the shares when it did. Beirut ultimately reopened the exchange two and half weeks later, and Lebanese shares did indeed fall further, losing an additional 4% that day.

Beyond acts of war, some otherwise peaceable countries impose currency controls or limits on foreign investors' ability to own local stocks. As such, you might not be able to buy what you want to own, or, if you can buy it, you might not be able to repatriate your money when you wish. You'll uncover this through your research, which we'll delve into in Chapter 3, or by asking the firms you contact in the various markets in which you have an interest. China's currency, the yuan, was not freely tradable as of 2007 and you cannot own so-called Chinese A shares, which are priced in yuan and which account for the bulk of Chinese listed companies. (You can, however, own the relatively small lot of B shares, priced in Hong Kong or U.S. dollars, but much more on China in a later chapter.)

Meanwhile, in other markets the consumer class, or what exists of one, is too worried about the basics of day-to-day sustenance to funnel idle cash into discretionary purchases—much less invest in local publicly traded companies. Without a real class of individual consumers and investors to drive the economy and buoy a market, a local stock exchange is lopsided in its dependence on institutional investors, a notoriously fickle lot that, when it comes to emerging and frontier markets in particular, flits from one stock exchange to the next without warning and, sometimes, without any obvious rationale. Those paper profits you might accumulate in a tiny market like, say, Côte d'Ivoire can vaporize quickly if the institutional folks suddenly decide they must send their money to Azerbaijan because, for whatever reason, it's hip to be investing on the Baku Stock Exchange.

Then again, small can be lovely, indeed.

Despite a relatively large populace, Romania is not a European juggernaut. With per-capita income of roughly $8,400 in 2005, according to the *CIA World Factbook,* the Eastern European country ranks well behind such powerhouses as Croatia, Latvia, and Slovenia. Nevertheless, the wide boulevards and narrow alleys of old Bucharest, once deemed the Paris of the East, teem with fashionable clothing and electronics boutiques, and cafés spilling out young Romanians jabbering into über-modern cell phones. The country may not stand as the epitome of wealth, as defined by Western standards, but Romania exemplifies what emerging Europe is all about: integrating once-archaic and now increasingly dynamic economies into the maw of Western European modernity. And, in turn, it exemplifies what international investing is all about: owning local and regional companies intimately tied to local and regional economies as those economies expand.

Romania's stock exchange, housed in a tall, modern redbrick and glass structure on a leafy avenue in Bucharest, is young by most standards; it reawakened in 1995 after 50 years of slumber under a Communist blanket. The Bucharest Stock Exchange, however, reflects what can happen when the rest of the world catches on to a country's potential.

In 2000, Romanian leaders opened negotiations with Western Europe about the country's potential accession into the European Union. That year, the 114 companies listed on the Bucharest exchange traded at a combined price-to-earnings ratio of just 3.98 — blindingly cheap. Those shares also paid dividends yielding nearly 7.5%, an elephant-sized rate by dividend standards and sometimes, though not always, an indication that a stock or, in this case, an overall stock market is priced inexpensively.

By the end of 2005, Romania was no longer cheap. Investors had flooded in, lured by Romania's European Union push. That low price/earnings ratio for Romanian shares had soared to more than 35, while the market's overall dividend yield had dwindled to 1.5% — both fueled by rapid appreciation of stock prices driven by increasing investor demand for Romanian companies. That demand largely grew from the country's preparations for entry into the European Union in 2007, an accession that required Romania to strengthen its economy and banking, legal, and judicial systems, and put in place measures to help keep a rein on inflation and other economic nasties. The nation struggled with that along the way, as have many entrants into the EU. Nevertheless, an economy once stifled under central planning and Communist corruption improved, as did the financial, legal, and judicial systems, all of which ultimately make any country a relatively safer place for an investor. And when investors consider a country a safer place, or see the improvements in action, they generally move in to buy shares of local stocks. All that demand pushes stock prices higher, which in turn creates more demand from other investors who see stock prices moving higher in a country with improving fundamentals. A virtuous cycle.

Circling back around to the rationale that you should go global because you can, American investors looking for ways to participate in the emergence of Eastern Europe have direct, online access to Romania through multiple brokerage firms — just as they have access to a host of up-and-coming economies. We'll get into this more in Chapter 3, but here's one example of what's available when you seek your own global footprint: InvestorsEurope.com accepts U.S. investors and allows you to trade directly on stock exchanges stretching across Europe, from England to Latvia, Russia to Greece. It's one of the more encompassing brokerage firms for European trading, and provides access to parts of Asia as well.

Best of all, investors with a global appetite will find firms like InvestorsEurope in every region of the world.

WHY GO GLOBAL, REASON 2: OPPORTUNITY.

Consider this list: German auto giant Volkswagen; French retailer Carrefour, the second-largest retailer in the world behind a certain Bentonville, Arkansas, chain; Germany's global retailer Metro; British grocery chain Tesco, with food stores stretching from Ireland to Japan to California; Japan's Tokyo Electric Power; Swiss food giant every kid knows, Nestlé; French-based global electricity firm Électricité de France; German global energy firm RWE.

These publicly traded companies — most of which you've probably never heard of, save for Volkswagen and Nestlé — share two common traits: 1) They each reside amid the Fortune Global 100, the list of the largest companies in the world; and 2) you will not find any of these shares trading on the New York Stock Exchange or the Nasdaq Stock Market (as of 2007).

Many of the world's largest companies are simply not American, though they assuredly benefit, just as General Motors and McDonald's do, from selling their goods to consumers and businesses around the globe. Some are huge players in America itself, yet have no presence on U.S. stock exchanges. BMW AG is one. The iconic German car company — maker of the eponymous BMW autos, as well as the hip Mini Cooper and the posh Rolls Royce — generated nearly a quarter of its revenues in North America in 2006. But you have a long drive to find BMW shares; they trade on Deutsche Börse, the German stock exchange.

THEY MIGHT BE GIANTS . . .

America can certainly boast of growing some of the world's biggest companies. But it doesn't own the market for "large." Two-thirds of the 100 global firms, as measured by Fortune Magazine, *resided outside the United States in 2005:*

RANK	COMPANY	COUNTRY
1	Wal-Mart Stores	USA
2	BP	UK
3	Exxon Mobil	USA
4	Royal Dutch/Shell	UK/Netherlands
5	General Motors	USA
6	DáimlerChrysler	Germany
7	Toyota Motor	Japan
8	Ford Motor	USA
9	General Electric	USA
10	Total	France
11	Chevron Texaco	USA
12	ConocoPhillips	USA
13	AXA	France
14	Allianz	Germany
15	Volkswagen	Germany
16	Citigroup	USA
17	ING Group	The Netherlands
18	Nippon Telegraph & Telephone	Japan
19	American International Group	USA
20	International Business Machines	USA
21	Siemens	Germany
22	Carrefour	France
23	Hitachi	Japan
24	Assicurazioni Generali	Italy
25	Matsushita Electric Industrial	Japan
26	McKesson	USA
27	Honda Motor	Japan
28	Hewlett-Packard	USA
29	Nissan Motor	Japan
30	Fortis	Belgium/Netherlands

31	Sinopec	China
32	Berkshire Hathaway	USA
33	ENI	Italy
34	Home Depot	USA
35	Aviva	UK
36	HSBC Holdings	UK
37	Deutsche Telekom	Germany
38	Verizon Communications	USA
39	Samsung Electronics	South Korea
40	State Grid	China
41	Peugeot	France
42	Metro	Germany
43	Nestlé	Switzerland
44	U.S. Postal Service	USA
45	BNP Paribas	France
46	China National Petroleum	China
47	Sony	Japan
48	Cardinal Health	USA
49	Royal Ahold	The Netherlands
50	Altria Group	USA
51	Pemex	Mexico
52	Bank of America	USA
53	Vodafone	UK
54	Tesco	UK
55	Munich Re Group	Germany
56	Nippon Life Insurance	Japan
57	Fiat	Italy
58	Royal Bank of Scotland	UK
59	Zurich Financial Services	Switzerland
60	Crédit Agricole	France
61	Credit Suisse	Switzerland
62	State Farm Insurance Cos.	USA
63	France Télécom	France
64	Électricité de France	France
65	JP Morgan Chase & Co.	USA
66	UBS	Switzerland

67	Kroger	USA
68	Deutsche Bank	Germany
69	E. On	Germany
70	Deutsche Post	Germany
71	BMW	Germany
72	Toshiba	Japan
73	Valero Energy	USA
74	AmerisourceBergen	USA
75	Pfizer	USA
76	Boeing	USA
77	Procter & Gamble	USA
78	RWE	Germany
79	Suez	France
80	Renault	France
81	Unilever	UK/Netherlands
82	Target	USA
83	Robert Bosch	Germany
84	Dell	USA
85	ThyseenKrupp	Germany
86	Costco Wholesale	USA
87	HBOS	UK
88	Johnson & Johnson	USA
89	Prudential	UK
90	Tokyo Electric Power	Japan
91	BASF	Germany
92	Hyundai Motor	South Korea
93	Enel	Italy
94	Marathon Oil	USA
95	Statoil	Norway
96	NEC	Japan
97	Repsol YPF	Spain
98	Dai-ichi Mutual Life Insurance	Japan
99	Fujitsu	Japan
100	Time Warner	USA
	USA Total	*33*
	World Total	*67*

Shares for some of the large, global companies do trade hands in the United States in one of a few ways. Some, typically the large foreign giants such as British Airways and Sony, list their shares in the states as American depositary receipts, American depositary shares, or global depositary receipts — known, respectively, as ADRs, ADSs, and GDRs. Others, including Nestlé, trade as ADRs or, more often, as "foreign ordinaries" in the so-called Over-the-Counter market. These ordinaries are, literally, the same ordinary shares that trade back in the local market. However, the OTC market, as it's called, isn't your typical stock exchange. In fact, it isn't a regulated stock exchange at all; it's an unregulated electronic bulletin board where buyers and sellers post their interest in some particular stock, and where many of the safeguards of regulated markets don't exist. We'll delve into ADRs, foreign ordinaries, and the OTC market in the next chapter, but for now recognize that trading many of the foreign shares listed on the OTC — and even some ADRs listed on the New York Stock Exchange or Nasdaq — can expose you to far more risk than you'd face sending your money into some random company's home market where their today is our last night, since many of those stocks go days or weeks, or longer, without logging a single trade, vastly increasing your liquidity risk, or the risk that you can't get out of a stock at a price anywhere near what the shares trade for in the home market because there's a dearth of buyers stateside.

To profit from many of the world's great companies — or many of the world's most promising companies on their way to greatness — you have no real choice except to go abroad. That's becoming increasingly important as individual overseas markets reach such a level of sophistication and wealth that the local companies no longer need New York or London to raise capital. Local companies can, instead, stay home — and many are — to raise money on their home stock exchange. If you want the opportunity those shares might represent, well, you know your only option.

But there's another way to consider this idea of "opportunity." Many industries in the United States are played out. They've had their day. They're mature. Whatever growth they muster is single-digit, at best, or the result of cannibalizing whatever competitors remain. Auto companies fit this mold well. The American car and truck market is so saturated that to lure buyers carmakers resort to gimmicks such as 0% financing, employee discounts for everyone, and a constant barrage of television commercials touting huge markdowns on every major, minor, and theoretical holiday.

Cellular telecommunications serves as another example. The United States was a growth market at one point, particularly in the 1990s. But now seemingly everyone and their teenager has a cell phone or three, so to entice new customers, cellular companies give away phones for pennies with new service contracts, and they battle one another by offering a gazillion minutes for $19.95 a month or the ability to talk free to others on some specific network. Like carmakers, they rely on stunts to hook new buyers. To grow their businesses in substantial leaps, cellular companies have had to resort to buying one another, though ultimately that's nothing more than a one-time steroid shot, not organic growth.

Overseas it's a different world, particularly in developing markets. Local automakers and parts suppliers in places such as China, India, and elsewhere have tremendous growth prospects as those economies expand, in the process creating an ever-larger class of consumers able to afford their own car. That represents years of growth for auto dealers, local and regional tire makers, auto-parts retailers, and service-station owners, among others. In China, for instance, owning a personal car has become something of a health issue. Although public transit has historically been the transportation of choice in much of China, the SARS (severe acute respiratory syndrome) scare of 2003 has many Chinese rethinking their reliance on buses and subways. SARS is spread through proximity to an infected person, and packed city buses and subway cars are nothing if not proud examples of proximity. In many cases they're as close as you can get to intimate without a public display of affection. The Chinese suddenly see a personal car as their escape from a potential health crisis.

On a lighter note, the Chinese, particularly in urbanized centers such as Shanghai, see a personal car as a means to a leisurely end. Their car represents a way to flee their crowded towns on the weekend by driving to the beach or the mountains or the countryside for the day. They increasingly are doing that, and on publicly traded, well-built toll roads — some of the best roadways in the world — that trim multiple hours off the distance between locations. In short, there's organic growth galore in the Chinese auto market.

Likewise, cellular telephone companies outside the industrialized world face years of natural growth. In a March 2005 study, for instance, British telecom giant Vodafone, backed by the Centre for Economic Policy Research, a leading European economic research firm, reported that the fastest-growing market for cellular telephones was Africa, a place to which few U.S. investors give much, if any, thought. (This seems like a random study with which to be familiar, and it is. But it's the kind of study that routinely leads to investment ideas, and Chapter 4 details how to find such random pieces of otherwise highly useful investment dope.)

A few statistical points from that Vodafone study:

1) 97% of Tanzanians said they could access a mobile phone, though just 28% could access a landline phone;
2) 85% of small businesses run by black South Africans relied solely on mobile phones for communication;
3) 59% of businesses in Egypt linked mobile-phone use to greater profits, despite the added costs of the mobile service;
4) the most important statistic, perhaps: The proportion of Africans using cell phones averaged just 6% of the population.

You can quickly do the math in your head: the fastest-growing region for cell-phone use; less than 10% penetration;

great reliance on cell phones among consumers and businesses where service exists. The implication is obvious: an elephant-sized opportunity for African cellular telecom companies to expand their customer base and, in turn, their profits, which ultimately flows through to a fatter stock price for investors who recognize what exists outside of America.

With such data in hand, it's not terribly challenging to find publicly traded African mobile-phone companies. One such potential opportunity that pops up after about 45 seconds of searching: Orascom Telecom Holding S.A.E., an Egyptian cellular-phone firm that trades on the Cairo, Alexandria, and London stock exchanges, all accessible by U.S. investors. Orascom is not just an Egyptian investment, though. The company also links people with mobile service in countries such as Algeria, Tunisia, Pakistan, Bangladesh, and even Iraq, where the firm received the first cellular license in the country's highly populated central region. Orascom had 52 million subscribers as of September 2007—in a part of the world where the company's current footprint has more than 460 million people—and it expects to expand into other rapidly growing cellular markets as well, such as Saudi Arabia.

Orascom, a company considered world-class in its industry and one of the biggest players in Africa and the Middle East, represents the kind of opportunity you don't typically find stateside in otherwise high-growth industries that have matured. It does, however, represent the caliber of opportunity that is readily available for investors willing to undertake a financial walkabout.

WHY GO GLOBAL, REASON 3: GROWTH.

In 21st-century America, we have forgotten our roots.

We are accustomed to being the stock market to the world, the biggest kid on the block, because we've held that position for decades. We don't remember that, at one point, hard as it is to imagine today, the United States of America was . . . a developing country.

And one with a raggedy, risky little stock market.

To be more blunt and entirely politically incorrect about it, we were a third-world banana republic fraught with an abundance of risks for well-heeled European investors who nonetheless saw the promise of dramatic growth in America and her young, public companies. Those investors had to stomach political assassinations, a civil war, economic upheaval, legal and regulatory revolutions and gerrymandering that were not always investor friendly, stock-market manipulations, government scandals, and free-market meddling by corrupt politicians. The list is long, and it reads like the risk profile of some backwater nation.

Still, those Europeans dispatched their ducats to a developing nation holding great promise for growth. And look at the greatness that has come of it. Look at the wealth she has created.

The sole reason investors invest is to grow their greenbacks — or their pounds or pesos or Moroccan dirhams. Without question, American equity markets today offer wonderful opportunities to turn a few bucks into a modest — or major — fortune. As long as we continue to practice our brand of capitalism, that fact isn't likely to change.

Yet on a macro level, when you get past the individual companies and look at the U.S. market as a single entity, the law of large numbers comes into play. We are a mature market. We are the world's largest market and largest economy. The chance that either the Standard & Poor's 500-stock index or the Dow Jones Industrial Average, the country's leading stock-market indices, will double in a given year is slimmer than a malnourished supermodel. The chance that a small, emerging market like, say, Egypt doubles in a given year? Egyptian stocks did just that in 2005 (up 161%), and in 2004 (up 126%), and nearly nailed the trifecta with a 92% jump in 2003.

Smaller economies — and "smaller" doesn't necessarily mean "small," just smaller relative to the world's largest economy —

can move with greater speed because they're coming off a lower base, often a *much* lower base. Once investors sense that some particular economy is moving or is an up-and-coming economy for any of a variety of reasons, they want to own a piece of it by owning the local stocks, working on the logical theory that when a particular economy improves, the local stock market will run hotter as well, and as it rises, so, too, will rise the fortunes of the local companies listed on that stock market. In particular, professional investors — the mutual-fund managers, hedge-fund traders, and other so-called institutional players — flock to those companies most levered to the economic cycle. Classically, that includes banks; consumer-product firms such as brewers (the wealthier the populace, the more beer people drink—go figure); firms that provide building materials and services, such as concrete and glass makers; and infrastructure investments, such as airports, toll roads, utilities, and ports. If you're already in those markets when the pros come calling, the stampede can bulk up your portfolio like a growth hormone.

One example: In 2000 the Australian economy, like economies in many parts of the world, loped toward recession. Shares of Australia and New Zealand Banking Group Ltd., the leading bank in the region, traded for less than $10 apiece. Within a few years, however, the world began to realize the pressure China's rapid economic expansion was putting on just about every conceivable commodity. Investors plunged into Australia, a commodity-based economy, correctly expecting that China's commodity consumption would bolster the economy in the land of Vegemite. Banks are a natural beneficiary of an expanding economy, spurred by a flood of increasing deposits and rising demand for personal and commercial lending. By early 2006, shares of ANZ Bank, as it's known, surged toward $29, a nearly threefold increase in six years — equivalent to an annual return of roughly 20%.

Now, none of that is to imply that success as a foreign investor requires divining where on Earth the pros might next alight and hoping you get there first. Nor does it necessarily require concentrating cash in small, forgotten countries as likely to struggle through a bloody coup as they are to fashion a robust market-driven economy. On the contrary, as the Aussie example demonstrates, equal opportunities exist in large, long-established markets that, like the S&P or Dow, also aren't inclined to double in a given year—markets in places such as the United Kingdom, Singapore, France, and elsewhere. Good businesses, many of them small and, therefore, well off the radar screen of American investors, thrive not because of where they call home but because they make products a horde of consumers or other businesses want or need.

Products like, say, water.

True, in the age of nanotechnology, life-advancing pharmaceuticals, and the Apple iPod, water, clearly, is not the sexiest product on offer these days. As a technology, H2O makes the 600-year-old Gutenberg printing press seem thoroughly modern. Yet not far from the runways of Singapore's Changi Airport you'll find the corporate headquarters of Hyflux Ltd., which is taking lowly water to new heights.

You can't watch a National Geographic special without recognizing that vast stretches of the Earth thirst for clean water for drinking and hygiene and, increasingly, high-tech applications that are helping developing nations rush toward first-world status. Hyflux is answering nature's call.

That famous line from Samuel Taylor Coleridge's *The Rime of the Ancient Mariner*—"Water, water, everywhere, nor any drop to drink"—that's Singapore. The island-state for decades has slaked most of its thirst for fresh water by sucking it from nearby Malaysian rivers—ironic, given that Singapore is surrounded on all sides by water, though, to be sure, it's seawater. Enter Hyflux. The company developed a technologically advanced and efficient way to use that abundance of ocean. The water-technology company in 2005 opened the country's first seawater-desalination plant. By forcing seawater through membranes with microscopic pores, Hyflux strips out the dissolved salts, leaving drinkable water. Every day the company's plant produces 30 million gallons, 10% of Singapore's consumption.

That same year, 2005, Hyflux also broke ground on a similar facility in China, where the liquid needs of 1.3 billion people clearly surpass one plant. Indeed, China's Eleventh Five-Year Plan, set to run between 2006 and 2011, aims for heavy investments in water resources so that an additional 100 million people (more than one-third the population of the United States) will have safe drinking water. To do so, China will spend billions of renminbi (the Chinese currency, also called yuan) on municipal water-treatment plants. Hyflux will be a player in that gusher of cash. The company is also searching out opportunities in India and the Middle East, where water demands are legendary.

In essence: Build it and they will drink. And that's just what Hyflux is doing.

Thus, a company little known to U.S. investors is a global technology leader in a product with unquenchable consumer and business demand across the fastest-growing corners of the world. It's just not a global leader that trades on any major American stock exchange. Owning Hyflux necessitates an account in Singapore — one of the most developed markets in the world, and one of the numerous countries where brokerage firms welcome American individual investors.

OWN GOOD COMPANIES

It seems such an obvious truth — almost simplistic — like saying, "Don't forget to breathe." Yet too many investors think "global investing" and immediately become punters with a gambler's mentality. They "play" India because they hear outsourcing is hot; or they read about the drug Tamiflu as a means to potentially combat an avian-flu outbreak, so they throw a few dollars at the Swiss pharmaceutical firm Roche Holdings, hoping for a quick score, disappointed, though, when the stock doesn't pop up by $7 or $8, so they sell.

Investing overseas is no different than investing in America. You're buying a piece of a business, not a chance at a lottery jackpot.

Regardless of the home address, good businesses always win out — or at least they win out enough times to make that statement true enough. Certainly, you'll tap into your share of laggards and losers over time; everyone does, including professional investors with decades of experience. No matter the due diligence you put into the selection process, companies are vulnerable to the whims of life: decaying economic conditions, wrongheaded governmental policies domestically, global tensions, trade wars, military wars, embargoes, political elections, changing consumer trends, currency revaluations, rogue employees, generation-leaping technological advances. The list is long. Your control over any of these possibilities is precisely . . . nil.

Don't let any of those vulnerabilities dissuade you from venturing abroad, though; the same forces toy with U.S. companies constantly. Americans fear inflation, and stock prices go down. The Federal Reserve stops raising interest rates, and stock prices surge. Tiny, Seattle upstart Microsoft sees a vast potential for a computer operating system that technology giant International Business Machines shrugs off, and two decades later IBM operates in the shadow of the undisputed technology leader. Look back on the 9/11 terrorist attacks: airline and tourism stocks suffered mightily in the wake of an event few could predict. Recall the first Clinton administration and the efforts to reform health care: pharmaceutical stocks, in particular, tumbled on fears the reforms would inhibit drug companies' ability to price the medicines they engineer.

Today, Southwest Airlines, American Airlines, and Continental Airlines are still in the air. They struggled through terribly turbulent skies for a while, but they're flying and earning a profit. Merck, Pfizer, and Bayer are still ginning up expensive, blockbuster drugs. IBM refocused its efforts on areas outside the Microsoft halo and is highly profitable.

Stock-market turbulence is simply a fact of daily life for investors the world over, from the Goliath-sized markets to the Davids. It's nothing to fear. It's just another variable to factor into your buy, sell, and hold decisions.

Good companies the world over find a way to survive the unpredictable vagaries of business life that arrive with great regularity.

WHY GO GLOBAL, REASON 4: DIVERSIFICATION.

Let's say you own the neighborhood sandwich shop. Look at the menu: Your only offering is grilled chicken. But you grill a mean chicken, better than anyone has ever grilled a chicken, and, so, you notch a fair amount of success hawking just the one sandwich to a knot of sated diners every day. You're happy with your singular focus, and the eatery consistently generates profits.

And just when life seems grand, some charismatic goon pitching a food fad convinces a populace of perennial dieters that grilled chicken is lard in disguise. Or worse, an E. coli bacterial outbreak kills a dozen kids in your hometown and is linked to chicken. Suddenly, your fowl is foul, and your dreams of ruling the roost are Southern fried. Your chicken is yardbird-non-grata as gourmands who once flocked from miles around to baste their taste buds with your chicken now perch themselves well away. Sales plunge. Profits turn to losses as you struggle to keep your chicken shack aloft.

Oh to be diversified in a moment like that, when sales of Philly cheesesteak, tuna, and peanut-butter-and-jelly sandwiches are rocking the local restaurant scene.

The same concept is continually at play in the stock market. Look at your portfolio: Much of what you own are, likely, U.S. stocks and mutual funds that hold shares in nothing but U.S. companies. Nothing wrong with that, necessarily; this is

America, after all, and you instinctively know more about American companies and American stocks and trading in American brokerage accounts than you do the companies and brokers that ply their wares and services in, say, Hungary. Only natural, then, that your investment choices reflect your comfort zone. Nevertheless, when the U.S. stock market cracks or crashes, as it wants to do from time to time, your U.S.-centric portfolio is feeling like a chicken eatery during an avian-flu scare — that is to say, plucked.

Diversification is the necessary buffer.

Essentially, diversification divides your money among multiple investments. You can define those investments as asset classes (i.e., stocks, bonds, real estate, commodities, collectible coins); investment styles (growth stocks, value stocks, momentum stocks); a range of industries (medical, finance, technology, airlines, retailers); and company size (small, medium, large). Or, you can diversify geographically.

When you put money to work in foreign lands — particularly when your focus is the smaller, domestic companies and not the giant, multinational firms — you become a cog in another economy, subject to the actions of an entirely different base of consumers and businesses, economic cycles, and currency trends. That helps to insulate your American-centric, dollar-dominant portfolio against the ebbs and flows that stir here at home. The rest of the world simply doesn't move in lockstep with the United States. If our economy is cooling, or the Dow Jones Industrial Average is falling, European or Asian or Latin economies and markets may be rising, or at least holding relatively stable. If the U.S. dollar is weakening, then by definition other currencies are strengthening. With some of your dollars working in foreign markets, then, the entirety of your portfolio isn't under pressure.

Thus, just as you wouldn't want a menu built around a single item, you don't want a portfolio built around a single country. Because even if you diversify an American portfolio across asset classes and investment styles, industries, and company size, and, as a result, feel your portfolio is built to weather the inevitable storms, your only exposure is still just the U.S. market. And if the U.S. market tanks, then none of that diversification will matter all that much since your portfolio will labor to remain afloat as U.S. asset prices broadly sink in value. All of them might not tumble, but enough of them will that they'll drag down your overall account.

Oh to be diversified in a moment like that, when markets and economies elsewhere in the world are thriving, or at least holding their own.

Stocks aside for a moment, U.S. investors face another risk not many people think much about. Currently, your financial life is tied largely, if not exclusively, to the greenback—your salary, your bonus, your bank account, your home equity, and, probably, the vast bulk of your investments. Makes sense; you live in America, thus you earn, spend, and invest American dollars. Yet so much of what Americans buy isn't produced here anymore. We import many of the goods that define our daily life. All those goods we bring in from other countries — be it wine, cars, caviar, clothes, shoes, carpets, watches, whatever—were made and priced in whatever the home currency is. If that home currency appreciates against the dollar— that is, if the dollar buys fewer and fewer yen, yuan, baht, euros, ringgits, etc. — then the price of that product on the store shelves where you shop goes up. Nothing about that product changed; it's not new and improved, it's not bigger, it provides no additional servings. The only difference is that it takes more dollars to buy the currency needed to purchase the foreign product, and that shows up on the sticker price you pay. The upshot is that your income faces the risk of depreciating against the value of the goods you consume.

Managing the currency and single-market risk that you face means reducing your dependence on dollars and the movements of U.S. stocks. When you diversify into foreign stocks, you not only diversify across markets, you are, by extension, diversifying across currencies as well, since those foreign shares are priced in the local lucre. That provides a dual buffer: 1) When American stocks flag, foreign shares provide a potential counterbalance since their prices might remain stable or even rise in value, offsetting losses at

home; and 2) when the U.S. dollar weakens against other currencies, the value of your foreign stocks necessarily rises, even if the
share prices don't budge. That's because the foreign currency those
shares are priced in suddenly buys more dollars, in this case offsetting the rising prices of the imported goods you buy at home.
More on this in Chapter 5, Casa de Cambio.

This diversification stuff isn't just theoretical. There's
much academic science backing it. Reason 5, just below, will
explain this more, but statistics show that between 1970 and
2001, the standard deviation of the U.S. market by itself was
15.5 (standard deviation is a measure of volatility). The U.S.
market and the Europe, Australasia, and Far East (EAFE)
Index combined produced a standard deviation of 14.5, meaning a decrease in risk. And those are all large, developed stock
markets. Throw in the emerging and frontier markets and the
diversification is even greater. The clear message: Although
global stock markets may occasionally be linked in their movements, adding international stocks to a portfolio reduces the
overall volatility over time. It reduces your risk.

WHY GO GLOBAL, REASON 5: RISK REDUCTION AND RICHER RETURNS.

Though it seems contrary to logic, given that investing in
potentially volatile nations overseas would obviously tend to
enhance your risk, the practical reality of owning international
companies is that as part of an overall portfolio they actually
shrink your risk and inflate your returns.

The financial academicians call it "mean variance effi-
ciency" or "mean variance spanning." In plain speak the concept boils down to this very simple idea:

*When the economies of one or two or three countries are
flailing, the economies of one or two or three other
countries are riding high.*

Think of it as the "all your eggs in multiple baskets" philosophy, only from a portfolio perspective. By girdling the globe with your greenbacks, you're taking advantage of the inherent differences that exist from one economy to the next. Singapore, for instance, is an economy strongly propelled by electronic manufacturing, financial services, and the world's busiest seaport. A Western European economy such as Spain, meanwhile, thrives on service sectors such as retailing and tourism. Both in turn differ markedly from Chile, endowed with vast mineral wealth propelling the economy along South America's western spine. When you broaden your frontiers, you effectively protect yourself from downdrafts in a single market or particular industrial sectors. When the technology sector sank in the early part of the new millennium, Singapore, where disk drives and computer wafers are fabricated, felt the pinch. Conversely, Chile was feeling no pain amid a resurgent market for commodities, particularly copper, Chile being a world leader in copper production.

Consider this example from 2002: For the S&P 500, that was a decidedly nasty year, with the benchmark American index down nearly 23%. In other corners of the world, investors celebrated their good fortune.

2002 RETURNS

This chart, courtesy of Russell Investment Group, a Tacoma, Washington, financial-services firm, shows the annual return in 49 markets around the globe in 2002, a rotten year in many stock markets. Notice, though, that even in bad years there are often many winners. Notice, too, the wide gulf between those winners and losers. While you would have lost money in the United States and many other countries, you would have balanced out those loses in markets such as New Zealand, South Africa, and elsewhere.

COUNTRY	RETURN	COUNTRY	RETURN
Pakistan Index	154.0%	Portugal Index	−13.2%
Czech Republic Index	44.2%	Mexico Index	−13.3%
Indonesia Hybrid Composite Index	42.8%	China Index	−14.0%

Hungary Index	30.7%	Spain Index	−14.9%
Peru Index	29.1%	United Kingdom Index	−15.2%
South Africa Index	28.0%	Denmark Index	−15.6%
Thailand Hybrid Composite Index	27.6%	Venezuela Index	−15.8%
New Zealand Index	26.1%	Hong Kong Index	−17.8%
Colombia Index	25.4%	Chile Index	−19.8%
Austria Index	17.3%	Netherlands Index	−20.3%
Russia Index	15.7%	France Index	−20.8%
Korea Free Index	8.6%	United States Index	−22.7%
India Index	8.4%	Taiwan Index	−24.5%
Jordan Index	4.5%	Greece Index	−25.3%
Egypt Index	1.6%	Ireland Index	−26.2%
Poland Index	1.3%	Philippines Index	−29.0%
Australia Index	−0.3%	Finland Free Hybrid	
Malaysia Hybrid Composite Index	−0.7%	Composite Index	−29.9%
Italy Index	−6.3%	Sweden Free Hybrid	
Norway Free Hybrid Composite Index	−6.7%	Composite Index	−30.1%
Morocco Index	−8.4%	Brazil Index	−30.7%
Switzerland Free Hybrid Composite Index	−10.0%	Israel Index	−31.2%
Japan Index	−10.1%	Germany Index	−32.9%
Singapore Hybrid Composite Index	−11.0%	Turkey Index History	−35.7%
Canada Index	−12.8%	Argentina Index	−50.5%
Belgium Index	−14.2%		

Own just the S&P in 2002 and you lost big. On the other hand, own a taste of a few markets like, say, Pakistan (up 154%), New Zealand (up 26%), and Poland (up 1.3%), and the strength in those markets would have mitigated some of the losses in the United States. To see this in action, assume that at the beginning of 2002 you managed two $100,000 portfolios that looked like this:

Country	2002 Return		U.S. PORTFOLIO		INTL PORTFOLIO	
			Portfolio Allocation	Profit/ (Loss)	Portfolio Allocation	Profit/ (Loss)
		Beginning Value		$100,000		$100,000
United States	−23%		100%	$(23,000)	80%	($18,400)
New Zealand	26%		0%	$-	12%	$3,120
Pakistan	154%		0%	$-	3%	$4,620
Poland	1%		0%	$-	5%	$65
		Ending Value		$77,000		$89,405

The international portfolio, built with two otherwise small and volatile markets (Pakistan and Poland), cut your losses in the United States by more than half. In effect, it reduced the risk you faced in a U.S.-only portfolio and, in turn, improved your return. (Of course, this is just a simple example of what this concept looks like in practice. This is absolutely not a recommendation to spread your assets across the likes of Pakistan, where, in the current environment, there are too many exogenous risk factors in the country and the general region for an individual investor to control.)

Still, this risk reduction works because of something the pros know as "correlation," or how various objects move in relation to one another. Those objects can be different stocks, different assets classes (stocks vs. gold, bonds vs. commodities, whatever), or different countries' stock markets. Mathematically — and we'll keep the mathematics brief — correlation runs along a rather short scale stretching between +1 and -1, with 0 in the center. Perhaps a useful way to think about this scale and correlation, in general, is in terms of the local pub: Some people gravitate to each other and shadow each other around the bar all evening; they are positively correlated (+1) in that what one does, the other generally does, too. Some are like those ex-lovers who still frequent their regular haunts but always move in opposite directions for fear of bumping into each other; they are negatively correlated (-1). And then there are those who have no idea the other person exists, each moving about the bar randomly and totally indifferent to the other person's movements; they are noncorrelated (0), though through sheer happenstance their orbits might pass occasionally and they might even move in a same direction temporarily.

Apply that imagery to global stock markets and you have correlation mastered. Countries minimally correlated (those closest to 0) move about unaffected by another's actions. Countries highly correlated (those closest to +1) move increasingly in lockstep. Those negatively corrected (closest to −1), move opposite of one another, with one falling while the other rises. Graphically, it looks like this:

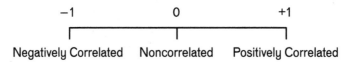

Correlation is relevant because even if you diversify across an abundance of assets to reduce your risk, your investments may actually be so correlated beneath the surface that when one is falling the rest of the pack is headed south, too. That's often the risk you find inside a portfolio built exclusively from the stocks of just a single country. With some exceptions, stocks in any one particular country generally move broadly in unison, though certainly some will move at a far greater pace and to a far greater degree than others.

For a portfolio to withstand the vicissitudes of market cycles here in the United States, you want a collection of investments that have a relatively low correlation to the happenings on Wall Street. I say "relatively" because almost every market in the world has some correlation to the United States. The daily action in New York imposes a heavy gravity on much of the world's financial markets. What happens during our trading hours often moves markets elsewhere. European shares, for instance, can be in the midst of a nasty morning sell-off after Asian shares struggled through a horrible day. But stocks in New York open their day on a high note because of some positive economic news or a string of strong earnings reports out of key companies in leading industries, and European stocks suddenly rebound in the afternoon while Asian stocks rally the following morning. Though such occurrences don't happen every day, they do happen with a certain regularity. As the old saw holds: When the United States sneezes, the rest of the world catches a cold.

In the 15 years ended Dec. 31, 2005, the correlation between European and U.S. stocks was 0.89, according to Ibbotson Associates, a Chicago investment-research firm. Even with emerging markets as a group, the correlation was 0.82. With such close connections it would seem that the world's markets so tightly orbit one another that you can't easily find those minimally correlated economies. To be intellectually honest, global stock markets have become increasingly linked, generally with the United States at the center of the orbit. Indeed, the correlation between the world as a whole and the S&P 500 was 0.97 between 2000 and 2005, according to S&P data. That's pretty much an-eye-for-an-eye territory.

Even the developing markets swing at times based on what happens in America. That truism about America sneezing was never more true than in May 2006, when rising interest rates in the United States spooked investors in emerging markets. Stock indices from Brazil to Russia to Indonesia tumbled hard. Still, on an individual country-by-country basis, relatively low correlations do exist. Japan, for instance, the world's second-largest stock market, shares a correlation with the United States of just 0.36 in terms of total return, or the price performance of the underlying stocks plus any dividends you receive from those companies. Austria was at 0.40; Iceland, 0.13.

OF BIG AND SMALL . . .

A vast gulf separates the U.S. stock market from that of, say, Venezuela, and it's not just the Caribbean.

The United States represents a so-called developed market, one of the largest, stablest, and most well-regulated markets in the world, while the Bolsa de Valores de Caracas, where only about 70 stocks were listed as of 2007, represents a developing market, or what Wall Street calls an emerging market. Vietnam, which launched the Stock Trading Center in Ho Chi Minh City in July 2000, represents a frontier market.

The distinctions between those three terms are pretty much what you'd expect just based on the words, but here are the technical separations:

Developed: These are the world's biggest markets—the United States, Britain, Japan, for instance—and by Standard & Poor's definition developed markets generally impose little or no controls on foreign investors, such as the ability to move money into and out of a country freely, or how much stock a foreign investor owns in any company, though in some otherwise developed markets, countries can limit foreign ownership in certain strategic industries, such as defense, communications, and sometimes finance.

Emerging: These markets often impose some sort of investment restrictions, such as limiting the amount of shares foreign investors can own, controlling the amount of capital that can leave the country, or displaying extensive government involvement in listed companies. As Standard & Poor's notes: The presence of "pervasive restrictions on foreign portfolio investment . . . is a sign that the market is not yet 'developed.' " The list of more than 30 emerging markets includes the likes of China, South Africa, Russia, Brazil, Chile, and Saudi Arabia, among others.

Frontier: These markets tend to be even smaller and more illiquid than emerging markets. Corporate and stock-market information is often sparse. The more than 20 markets in 2006 that fit the frontier label include the likes of Bulgaria, Bangladesh, Kenya, and Ecuador.

CATEGORY

DEVELOPED	EMERGING	FRONTIER
Australia	Argentina	Bulgaria
Hong Kong	Brazil	Croatia
Japan	Chile	Estonia

Countries		
New Zealand	Colombia	Latvia
Singapore	Mexico	Lithuania
Austria	Peru	Romania
Belgium	Venezuela	Slovenia
Denmark	China	Slovakia
Finland	India	Ukraine
France	Indonesia	Botswana
Germany	South Korea	Côte d'Ivoire
Greece	Malaysia	Ghana
Iceland	Pakistan	Kenya
Ireland	Philippines	Lebanon
Italy	Sri Lanka	Tunisia
Luxembourg	Taiwan	Mauritius
Netherlands	Thailand	Namibia
Norway	Czech Republic	Ecuador
Portugal	Hungary	Jamaica
Spain	Poland	Trinidad and Tobago
Sweden	Russia	Bangladesh
Switzerland	Turkey	Vietnam
United Kingdom	Bahrain	
Canada	Egypt	
United States	Israel	
	Jordon	
	Morocco	
	Nigeria	
	Oman	
	Saudi Arabia	
	South Africa	
	Zimbabwe	

This separation between developed, emerging, and frontier has a risk element to it. Developed markets such as Britain, Germany, France, Sweden, Hong Kong, Singapore, Japan, Australia, and a few others are effectively no riskier than the U.S. market, as measured by volatility, which is a measure of risk. Between 1993 and 2006, according to investment-research firm Ibbotson Associates, the Standard & Poor's 500, and the

Morgan Stanley Capital International Europe, Australasia, and Far East Index (known as the EAFE, the Dow Jones Industrial Average of developed non-U.S. markets) were nearly identical in terms of their standard deviation, or how volatile the expected ups and downs are.

THE MORGAN STANLEY CAPITAL INTERNATIONAL EUROPE, AUSTRALASIA, AND FAR EAST INDEX

Known as the preeminent benchmark in the United States to measure international stock-market performance, the MSCI EAFE tracks the developed markets outside North America. This is what the index looked like at the end of 2005.

COUNTRIES REPRESENTED IN THE MSCI EAFE AND THEIR CONTRIBUTION TO THE INDEX:

COUNTRY	WEIGHT	COUNTRY	WEIGHT
Japan	25.6%	Finland	1.4%
United Kingdom	24.0%	Belgium	1.1%
France	9.3%	Singapore	0.8%
Switzerland	6.9%	Denmark	0.8%
Germany	6.8%	Ireland	0.8%
Australia	5.2%	Norway	0.7%
Italy	3.8%	Greece	0.6%
Spain	3.7%	Austria	0.4%
Netherlands	3.4%	Portugal	0.3%
Sweden	2.4%	New Zealand	0.2%
Hong Kong	1.6%	TOTAL	100.0%

THE TOP 50 SECURITIES IN THE MSCI EAFE BY SIZE OF COMPANY

BP	UK	E.ON	Germany
HSBC Holdings	UK	BNP Paribas	France
Toyota	Japan	Credit Suisse	Switzerland
GlaxoSmithKline	UK	BBVA	Spain
Total	France	BHP Billiton	Australia
Vodafone	UK	Allianz	Germany
Royal Dutch Shell A	UK	Unicredito Italiano	Italy
Novartis	Switzerland	Ericsson	Sweden

Nestlé	Switzerland	Sumitomo Mitsui Finc'l	Japan
Roche Holdings	Switzerland	Rio Tinto	UK
Mitsubishi UFJ Financial	Japan	Anglo American	UK
UBS	Switzerland	AXA	France
Royal Bank of Scotland	UK	Takeda Pharmaceutical	Japan
Sanofi-Aventis	France	Deutsche Bank	Germany
Royal Dutch Shell B	UK	Lloyds TSB	UK
Nokia	Finland	ABN Amro	Netherlands
Banco Santander	Spain	DáimlerChrysler	Germany
AstraZeneca	UK	Deutsche Telekom	Germany
Mizuho Financial	Japan	Honda Motor	Japan
ENI	Italy	Tesco	UK
Siemens	Germany	Canon	Japan
Barclays	UK	Société Generale	France
Telefonica	Spain	Diageo	UK
HBOS Group	UK	France Telecom	France
ING Group	Netherlands	BASF	Germany

Emerging and frontier markets are another matter entirely. In that same 13-year stretch, emerging markets were 65% more volatile than the S&P 500. And on an individual basis, specific markets can be even more unstable. Chinese stocks, for instance, were 1.6 times more volatile than the S&P, according to Ibbotson.

The key reason to know this is simply to recognize that just because you put your money to work internationally does not necessarily mean you're taking on an abundance of risk. If you confine your investments to developed markets—and that's not necessarily a recommendation—your portfolio is not substantially riskier because of it.

A QUESTION OF QUANTITY

Technically speaking, if you were to build a portfolio entirely blind to your country of residence and instead let the relative size of each nation's stock market determine how much of your portfolio you allocate to the United States and to the rest of the world, you'd be investing half your money outside of America.

At the end of 2005, the cumulative value of U.S. stocks stood right at 50% of the S&P/Citigroup Broad Market Index World Composite. Japan accounted for slightly more than 12%; the United Kingdom, a bit more than 10%. The remainder of your money you would have scattered about equity markets throughout the rest of the world, in pieces of increasingly small stature, such as Slovenia, which amounted to just 0.01% of the index.

Few people invest this way, of course, though it's certainly a legitimate strategy. Many indices, in fact, are built in similar fashion — blind to everything except the relative size of each company, country, or industry constituent in whatever group is being indexed.

According to the pros who design asset-allocation models, the right amount of global exposure falls somewhere between 5% and 40% of a portfolio — assuming you pay attention to asset allocation in the first place. Individual investors often don't, at least not dogmatically. There's nothing wrong with that approach, actually, so long as you're comfortable with the companies you own and the markets in which you own them, and you don't let any one company or any one market assume too large a position. After all, you're not investing in "exposure," you're buying pieces of a business and pieces of an economy in which you seek to profit. How much you have allocated overseas is generally an item several checkpoints down the list. It's not like you find yourself already holding 20% of your money overseas, only to stumble across a great company in Portugal that you can't buy because you're at your optimal allocation. Good companies are good companies. If it were me, I'd buy the stock in Portugal anyway, paying little heed to the fact that this new stake might push my foreign exposure to 23% of my portfolio.

Ultimately, how much you invest overseas is a personal decision based largely on how well you stomach the inherent risks of owning some particular stock, bond, or mutual fund in some particular country, including the United States. Only you know how comfortable you'd be with, let's say, 40% of your portfolio in Asia, for instance, just as a currency crisis wrecks markets from Tokyo to Kuala Lumpur. If your first inclination is to flee at all costs just so you can preserve some capital, then such broad exposure to the region was wrong for you from the get-go. Maybe with a smaller concentration you would just shrug at the hiccup, content with the companies you own, recognizing that they operate good businesses in growing industries and that they'll recover.

Determining how big a nut you're willing to stash overseas in general, and in any one country in particular, will evolve with your experiences investing directly in foreign markets. At the outset, you might be fairly cautious, uncertain of what you're going to experience and how you will really react to the volatility that is destined to occur. You might think you have the fortitude to gut out a wrenching downdraft in some market; it's easy to think you're bulletproof when no one's shooting. But you really won't know yourself until that market 12 time zones away tanks just when barkeeps around your hometown are announcing last call and you're wide awake and wired watching your stocks deflate online and fretting about all those lost dollars.

In general, the factors that go into determining how much exposure you should have to any investment in particular include the following.

• **Age**: The younger you are, the more risk you can accept. The older you are, the less risk you want to accept. The reason: If the risk you assume at a young age doesn't pan out, you still have many years to recover from the damage. When you're older, the recovery time is drastically shorter, likely impairing your ability to recoup what was lost. Either way, though, you will almost always want some exposure to international stocks, even in retirement. Your nest egg must generate the growth necessary to keep pace with your spending needs through the years, and you generally cannot expect a portfolio increasingly composed of bonds, as many retirement portfolios mistakenly are, to carry the financial weight of your retirement. Although you might be able to live off the income those bonds generate early on, you're not creating any growth necessary to compensate for inflation over time. In later years, that could leave you draining your account faster than anticipated, prompting you to curtail your lifestyle or risk running out of money before running out of sand in your hourglass. A diversified portfolio that continues to include stocks provides that necessary growth. International stocks, in particular, offer the diversification and growth opportunities mentioned above; they're not always correlated with U.S. markets, providing a buffer against bear markets in America; and they often grant you a sweetener in that many foreign companies sport dividend yields well in excess of what you traditionally find in the states, potentially boosting your retirement income.

• **Risk tolerance**: This is tied in with age, to a degree — the older you are, the less risk tolerant you're likely to be since recouping losses may be improbable, if not impossible, at some point. But it's equally an emotional issue, that gut-check question about how well you will sleep at night knowing a big slug of your money is invested in an emerging market where anything from a currency meltdown to an act of war to an unexpected coup could erupt. You'll find a plentitude of online risk-assessment quizzes by searching Google. Some are better than others. Rutgers University, the state university of New Jersey, operates a pretty useful quiz at www.rce.rutgers.edu/Money/riskquiz/.

• **Time frame**: This isn't just a factor for foreign investing; it applies equally to domestic stocks and stock mutual funds as well. If your idea of "long term" is a year or less, you shouldn't be in U.S. stocks, much less international stocks. (This does not apply to day-trading, but that's not so much investing as it is Vegas-style gambling, and you're unlikely to be day-trading on the other side of the world anyway.) Investments need time to work. You don't always know exactly where a company is in its cycle, and you don't always know what's next for an economy.

You can never be sure a political or corporate emergency won't erupt to entirely destroy your expectations. You should instead think in three- to five-year increments, and even longer if the companies are performing well. Stocks I own in New Zealand and Australia have, as of mid-2007, been part of my portfolio for nearly a dozen years; shares in Singapore and Hong Kong have been in the mix for nearly six years.

• **Need**: Do not invest in foreign stocks the money earmarked for a house or the funds you'll need to pay for a 15- to 17-year-old's pending college education. Do not invest money that you absolutely, positively must be certain will retain its value, regardless of time frame. All stocks carry risk, and certain types of foreign stocks carry a heap of added risk because of the country, region, or industry they're in.

DON'T DRINK THE WATER

If you've ever traveled anywhere outside of Western countries, you've no doubt heard that warning, lest you find yourself hunched over a foreign toilet—or a squat little hole in the ground—wishing you'd not tested your luck with that glass of tap water at the restaurant to soothe a tongue scorched by a spicy vindaloo.

Investing abroad has its risk of upset, too, and as a global investor you need to know exactly what you face venturing overseas before committing any money to any investment. Sometimes these risks are dangers that can drain away your investment; sometimes they are opportunities to move into a certain stock or country when others are reflexively running away without first thinking through their actions. There are essentially four broad risks, three of which you largely have little or no control over.

• **Geopolitical**: Terrorism is, perhaps, the quintessential example of geopolitical risk. Every time terrorists strike a building or a train, or threats of explosives close international airports, stock markets the world over tumble as investors rush to repatriate their money. The tensions on the Korea Peninsula are another example. If ever that demilitarized zone separating North from South is breached in a hostile way, stocks globally will dive on fears of nuclear reprisal. A less traumatic example: oil. If world oil supplies are ever choked off by war, acts of terrorism, or acts of economic intimidation, investors around the world will dump stocks — well, except oil stocks — and drive stock markets down because of worries over the likely result: a surge of inflationary pressures that radically higher oil prices will engender. The thing is, as the average Main Street investor, there's not much you can do to mitigate this risk. The best you can do is analyze the situation as it happens to determine if the risk is really to the companies you own, or if they're just sideswiped in sympathy. If the latter, the best course often is to sit tight, maybe even buy a little more, since the greatest profits typically accrue to those who knowledgeably wade in when panic has mispriced stocks across the board.

• **Country**: The Lebanese/Israeli conflict of 2006 serves as a good example of this risk. You can invest in a country — in this case, Lebanon — for all the right reasons only to see those reasons explode in a volley of mortar shells. Or maybe consider India, circa May 2006, where small investors dumping their shares to meet brokerage-house margin calls ultimately sparked a sell-off that sent the Indian market down as much as 22% in just eight days — this after India had been one of the world's best-performing markets to that point. Barely a month goes by that some individual country doesn't face some sort of crisis that spooks investors and sends local and maybe even regional stock markets reeling. And the country doesn't have to be a developing nation; developed markets get hit all the time, too, though the magnitude of losses generally isn't as dramatic. You can at times mitigate some of this risk by paying attention to economic and political conditions before you invest. In many instances, however, the sour situation (the bombs in Lebanon) erupts with no foreseeable warnings.

- **Currency**: Most of the globe's various monies ebb and flow in relation to one another every day in the world's largest investment market, the currency market. But sometimes geopolitical, regional, or country-specific events unfold that send the value plunging for the currency of the country you've invested in. In the late 1990s, countries including Russia, Brazil, and Thailand all had major currency woes that not only rocked their local stocks but also rippled through emerging stock markets around the world. Again, some of this you can mitigate by paying attention to what governments are doing with their currencies and the concerns they're voicing about their currencies being too strong or too weak, or the country's growing inability to service its debt. Some of it will happen entirely unexpectedly.
- **Company**: In late 2003, one of the biggest corporate accounting scandals in history erupted inside Europe's largest dairy company, Italy's Parmalat SpA. Accounting records indicated a hole in Parmalat's finances of about €14 billion; the company fell into bankruptcy and the shares were worthless (although a new, healthier Parmalat with newly issued shares rose from the ashes). Or take the case of Ireland, March 2005, when the biotechnology company Elan Corp. was forced to yank from the market its promising multiple-sclerosis drug, Tysabri, following the deaths of some patients. In the span of one day's trading on the Irish Stock Exchange, Elan shares plunged to €6.49 from an opening price of €20.40. Both of these instances exemplify company risk—the risk that an event specific to a single company undermines your shares. With some companies this risk might be something you know about beforehand, or it could be a surprise risk like that which Parmalat investors awoke to find one morning.

There is a fifth risk you face that might more appropriately fall under country risk or maybe currency risk. But because it overlaps both, I'll call it boneheaded-policy risk, for lack of a better term. Case in point: Thailand, December 2006.

Concerned about a rapidly appreciating Thai baht, the local currency, Thai officials decided to impose currency controls, announcing that foreign investors must henceforth lock up 30% of their foreign-exchange deposits for one year, interest free. Worse, investors who wanted to repatriate their money earlier than one year would face stiff fines. Investors the world over told Thailand just how stupid such a plan was: They grabbed their money and bolted for the exits immediately, sending stocks on the Thai exchange down 15% the day of the announcement. For comparison, a crash is universally defined as a one-day loss of 10%.

In the wake of crumbling stocks, Thai officials quickly retreated, effectively announcing, "Well, maybe not such a good idea after all, folks. . . ." Still, the damage was done. On the bright side, investors with an account that allowed access to Thai shares, and who recognized that the one-off, ill-formed, quickly overturned policy spoke to the clumsiness of Thai officials and not to the health or viability of Thai companies, saw the gaffe as an excellent opportunity to dive into the country and grab some short-lived bargains. Thai shares rebounded quickly.

Just to be entirely fair, although all of those risks are particularly germane to your money overseas, the reality is that the same risks are at play even with domestic, U.S. investments. Geopolitical happenings echo through Wall Street all the time (again, think: terrorist attacks and what typically occurs in U.S. stock markets); country risk is certainly apparent here whenever unexpectedly dour economic reports spook the market; currency risk is a factor as the U.S. dollar weakens against world currencies, shrinking your buying power, given that so many goods Americans buy are crafted overseas. You can't avoid company risk no matter where you invest in the world—just remember the world-class crooks who destroyed Enron, Adelphia, and WorldCom. As for bonehead-policy risk, we've got that aplenty. Think back, for instance, to the early 1990s when, in Bill Clinton's early days in the White House, the administration was intent on driving down the costs of prescription drugs, regardless of market forces. Pharmaceutical stocks tanked as investors fled in fear of government's heavy- and ham-handed policy—a policy that ultimately went nowhere, but gave savvy investors an opportunity to grab at rock-bottom prices major drug stocks that went on to double and triple in value over the intervening few years.

Whereas all those risks pertain to countries, currencies, and stocks directly, you also run up against a few other occasional struggles that deal more with the mechanics of managing overseas accounts. In one instance, a brokerage firm in New Zealand essentially imploded, leaving my stocks and cash frozen as regulators tried to unravel the mess. That process took several weeks, forcing me to find a new broker, which I did easily enough. But that meant I had to then alert various stock-custody firms in New Zealand and Australia holding various shares in my name to ensure that my stocks remained accurately tied to my new account. I had to open a new call account (basically, a bank account) attached to the new brokerage account so that dividends would flow in the appropriate direction.

In other instances you face a communications risk. Companies overseas often move relatively quickly on corporate matters, and though they dispatch all the necessary paperwork to shareholders, the time required for that paperwork to make it to you can mean that it arrives just days before—or sometimes days after—some corporate event takes place. Maybe that means you don't get to vote on a merger proposal; maybe it means you don't get to exercise stock warrants that were issued to you for some reason. In the latter case, that doesn't mean you'll lose out on any money; the warrants will often be sold for you and the money dumped into your account. But it might have been that you wanted to exercise those warrants to buy additional shares in the company at a below-market price, and now you can't.

Whatever the case, and no matter where you venture in the world, you will stumble upon the occasional obstacle to managing your money overseas. Expect it. Don't fight it. And don't fret about it. It's all a part of being a global investor.

But also know that such obstacles are all dealt with easily enough — even if you are 9,000 miles away — and that the potential profits far outweigh the potential hassles.

CHAPTER 2

OYSTERS AT HOME

Diversifying Globally Inside America

Not everyone is up for adventure.

Take my maternal grandfather; he spent World War II in the Marine Corps repairing bombers and fighter planes in violent locales such as Guadalcanal, often forced to ride inside the planes for various reasons — an on-the-job requirement that scared the bejeezus out of him each time. While raising me, he routinely announced that he would never board another airplane in his life — a promise he kept — and that his only interest in the rest of the world he'd fulfill upon his death. "I'll fly around once," he'd say, "see what I want to see, then head on up to heaven."

A lot of American investors share similarities with my grandfather — they want nothing to do with venturing anywhere beyond home for any of a number of reasons: fear of the unknown; fear of what they do know or at least think they know; currency conversion concerns; the challenges of researching companies located on continents far removed from North America; worries about potential political and regulatory changes that might upset an investment or an entire overseas portfolio. Military conflict.

That's OK. You don't necessarily have to pack your dollars off on an overseas adventure to benefit from global growth, though your opportunities in the United States are comparatively limited and not always as pure a play on foreign economies as you might assume. Still, if you're not yet comfortable with the requirements of investing abroad directly, or you never want to go overseas but do want the benefits of diversifying your U.S. investment and currency exposure, you have available here in the states several internationally minded investment options, including:

- U.S. multinational companies, such as McDonald's, Pfizer, Intel, General Electric, and many, many others that derive some or even the bulk of their sales and earnings from overseas operations.
- U.S.-listed foreign companies such as Swedish automaker Volvo, Germany's Siemens, Japanese electronics maker Sony, French dairy-food leader Groupe Danone, Mexican cement giant Cemex, and hundreds of others that tend to be multinationals as well, and which tend to be fairly well known in America. These are the so-called American depositary receipts, or ADRs.
- Several hundred international mutual funds that offer the ability to own stocks across the entire world, a broad swath of the world, a specific region, or, in some cases, throughout a single country only.
- A growing list of exchange-traded funds, so-called ETFs, that resemble mutual funds — though they trade like shares of stock— and give you exposure to the broader world, specific regions, or markets in individual countries.
- A vast selection of foreign-ordinary shares that trade in the Over-the-Counter (OTC) market, the same shares that locals buy in their home markets. But be warned, this corner of Wall Street can be far riskier than investing in the same company directly overseas.
- Access to foreign stocks listed on select foreign exchanges through some U.S. brokerage firms. Expect certain limitations, however, that can reduce the appeal of this alternative.

For investors who don't want to physically place their money in an overseas brokerage account, these are your options — and they're not necessarily bad. Many have posted excellent returns. Some of the mutual funds are run by some of the savviest foreign-stock pickers in the business. If nothing else, going global by staying at home can be easier than actually opening accounts overseas for several reasons:

- The global-centric investments that trade stateside do so in U.S. dollars and during U.S. market hours, so you have no chance to muck up a currency calculation, no need to transfer money overseas, and no depriving yourself of REM-sleep because you're placing orders in the middle of the night to buy some publicly traded palm-oil plantation in Indonesia, where it's already tomorrow afternoon.
- The foreign companies that list their shares on the New York Stock Exchange and the Nasdaq report their results in English and according to U.S. accounting standards, simplifying your research and eliminating any need to speak Japanese to figure out whether video-game maker Nintendo Co. reported strong or weak sales in the past year and how management sizes up the coming year. (This could change, as the Securities and Exchange Commission, as of mid-2007, was considering allowing foreign firms to report results according to International Financial Reporting Standards, or IFRS.)
- Dividends are paid in U.S. dollars, erasing any challenge you'd have — and you always have that challenge — converting into dollars at your local bank branch those rupiahs distributed by that Indonesian palm-oil plantation.
- Mutual funds and ETFs offer a fairly wide variety of options for owning investments in various corners of the globe, nixing the need for you to figure out for yourself where in the world to put your money to work, and which companies might be best in some particular market.

- The availability of foreign ordinaries in the OTC market, and the ability to buy directly on certain overseas exchanges through some U.S. brokerage firms, opens up an entirely different world, offering access to the small- and midsized foreign companies that either don't list or have no interest in listing their shares on the New York Stock Exchange or the Nasdaq.

For all of these reasons, especially the convenience of buying and selling stateside, U.S. investors began latching on to global-centric investments in the 1990s, coinciding with Wall Street's brokerage houses and mutual-fund companies increasingly touting the wisdom of including a taste of foreign stocks in a balanced portfolio for all the diversification and risk-reduction reasons mentioned in the previous chapter. Foreign-focused mutual funds, in particular, gained tremendous traction. During the decadelong span between 1995 and 2005, the number of foreign-stock mutual funds available in the states nearly quadrupled to more than 1,100, while the amount of investor money those funds managed jumped sevenfold to more than $515 billion—which, if measured in terms of national economies, would have made that stash the 17th largest economy in the world in 2005, just behind the Netherlands, just in front of Belgium. Some of that growth, of course, came from capital gains recorded on the stocks the funds held. After all, in those ten years, Finnish stocks nearly quintupled; Spanish stocks more than tripled, while South African shares nearly did so and Canadian and Australian more than doubled. Brazilian stocks increased almost eight times over.

Gains aside, investors pumped a ton of cash into U.S.-based, foreign-stock mutual funds over that same period. Actually, to be entirely precise, investors pumped 265,351.35 tons of cash into foreign-stock funds, that being the cumulative weight of the $242.33 billion of new money that flowed into foreign-stock mutual funds during the decade, according to AMG Data Services, which tracks mutual-fund statistics.

This gusher of cash, the rise in the number of international funds, and the growth of the ADR market speaks to the fact that even if we are still leery of going overseas directly, we are growing more comfortable venturing overseas, albeit by proxy. Still, that is putting a foot in the right direction.

So let's take a look at the various ways you can build your confidence as an international investor—or diversify your portfolio with overseas stocks—without forsaking the relative safety of America just yet.

U.S. MULTINATIONAL CORPORATIONS

Everyone has played with toys at some point in their life. So undoubtedly you know Mattel Inc.—America's toymaker. You likely grew up with Fisher-Price products as a toddler; moved on to HotWheels, Rock'em Sock'em Robots, and Barbie in your preteen years; and as an adult you might still play games such as Scene It?, Scrabble, and Outburst with friends and family. All carry Mattel's red logo.

While you're busy on family game night trying to convince your skeptical nine-year-old that the nonsensical "qwiznor" is in fact a word and that you get bonus points for using all your Scrabble tiles, Mattel is busy successfully hawking Scrabble and a toy-store's worth of fun and games to kids and their parents in more than 150 nations. The result: In 2006, nearly half of Mattel's $5.65 billion in worldwide sales came from overseas. That makes America's toymaker the toymaker to the world. And it means that if you own Mattel shares, you own a globally diversified business with a proven ability to appeal to kids and adults from Bangkok to Barcelona, Buenos Aires to Boston.

In short, you own a U.S. multinational.

Multinationals started as purely American brands, often decades ago. Through the years they've grown in size and expanded their reach to the point where their tentacles now coil out from America to touch businesses and consumers globally.

Perhaps the quintessential example is Coca-Cola. From a small pharmacy in Atlanta, Georgia, where the first glass of Coke fetched a nickel, Coke's distinctive beverage and shapely bottle is recognized throughout the world, and is available everywhere from Michelin-rated restaurants in Europe to every roadside refreshment hut from rural Saint Lucia to the brushlands of southern Africa. Coke products—including soft drinks, water, teas, coffee beverages, sports drinks, and juices (some 400 in all)—are sold in more than 200 countries, from Argentina to Zimbabwe, Yemen to Kyrgyzstan. The upshot: Coke's overseas sales in 2006 amounted to nearly 71% of the soda maker's $24.1 billion in revenues. Absent that global reach, Coke isn't so much teaching the world to sing as it is humming "The Star-Spangled Banner" alone and posting sales growth about as inspiring as a flat soda.

Or take maybe the most literal symbol of global span: airplane maker Boeing. Every two seconds of every day, a Boeing airplane lifts off the tarmac or lands somewhere in the world, flying passengers to some of the most random spots imaginable, in the service of airlines most Americans would never recognize—like, say, Nigeria's Bellview Airlines, flying 737s between that country's coastal oil-town of Port Harcourt and the industrial city of Douala, Cameroon. Although Boeing grew up in America, its success today depends greatly on its ability to sell airplanes around the globe. Jet sales certainly still occur in the states, and passenger traffic continues to grow domestically, yet the United States is the definition of a mature market, populated by a relatively small lot of long-established airlines and a few upstarts, and a well-established consumer class that isn't likely to grow exponentially in size.

The bulk of Boeing's commercial airplane opportunities thus exists overseas, particularly in developing regions such as China, Southeast Asia, the Middle East, Latin America, Africa, India, and Central Europe. In those locales, Boeing finds a different reality: hundreds of millions of consumers rapidly moving into the middle class and, as a result, increasingly flush with disposable income for expenses once deemed too luxurious — such as vacations that start by boarding an airplane. Airline travel is expanding at a far faster clip overseas than in the United States, and aircraft orders routinely flood in from developing-market air carriers ramping up the size of their fleets to keep pace with demand. One telling example: At the 2005 Paris Air Show, carriers from the Indian subcontinent — where new, low-cost airlines seem to emerge with the regularity of the monsoon season — placed orders for 145 jets from both Boeing and its Toulouse, France, nemesis, Airbus Industrie.

The result of all this global air-traffic expansion on Boeing: Nearly two-thirds of its commercial aircraft sales from 2000 through mid-2006 came from carriers that don't fly the American flag.

Because multinationals nurture deep ties to foreign markets, one school of thought among some U.S. investors holds that these big American companies are the best way to gain global diversification without assuming the variety of political, economic, corporate, and currency risks that you otherwise face when buying foreign shares directly.

There's some logic in that argument. A company selling goods overseas is not solely dependent on the U.S. economy. That diversifies and can stabilize sales and earnings. If sales of Coke products slow in the United States for whatever reason, then sales growth in Brazil, Egypt, and elsewhere can help keep overall revenues stable. Moreover, those sales and earnings are generally in foreign currencies. That buffers the company's bottom line during periods of currency upheaval. The net effect is that if Coke is generating 71% of its revenues by quenching the world's thirst, then at some point Coke's share price rises in value to reflect those richer profits. (Remember: A stock's price is nothing more than investors' cumulative perception of the worth of a company's profits, and as international sales fatten those profits, well, in effect, they ultimately fatten the stock as well.)

In 2005, the 30 companies that constitute the Dow Jones Industrial Average reported combined sales of roughly $2.3 trillion. Of that, their combined foreign sales amounted to about 40% of the total, or about $1 trillion. Some companies, such as computer-chip maker Intel, generated in excess of 85% of their sales overseas. Others recorded scant global sales. Below are the 30 Dow components and the impact that overseas operations exert on their sales:

COMPANY	TICKER	FOREIGN SALES*
Intel	INTC	85.4%
Altria Group	MO	79.7%
Exxon Mobil	XOM	75.7%
Coca-Cola	KO	70.8%
McDonald's	MCD	66.0%
Hewlett-Packard	HPQ	64.8%
3M	MMM	60.7%
DuPont	DD	56.4%
Procter & Gamble	PG	55.3%
International Business Machines	IBM	53.8%
Caterpillar	CAT	52.6%
United Technologies	UTX	51.5%
Pfizer	PFE	48.0%
American International Group	AIG	45.3%
General Electric	GE	44.9%
Johnson & Johnson	JNJ	43.8%
Citigroup	C	43.0%*
Merck & Co.	MRK	42.0%
Alcoa	AA	40.7%
Honeywell International	HON	35.1%
General Motors	GM	34.3%
American Express	AXP	32.4%
Microsoft	MSFT	32.3%
Boeing	BA	29.9%
Walt Disney	DIS	22.4%
JPMorgan Chase & Co.	JPM	21.4%
Wal-Mart Stores	WMT	19.7%

The Home Depot	HD	6.5%
Verizon Communications	VZ	3.2%
AT&T	T	0.02%

*Denotes % of foreign income, not sales.

The case can be even more compelling for multinationals such as Harley-Davidson. Harley's image defines the American ideal to much of the world — the freedom of mobility, wide-open spaces, and a bit of acceptable rebelliousness. That image helps explain Harley-Davidson's robust, non-U.S. sales. This is from a press release the Milwaukee motorcycle maker issued in July 2006, reporting its sales for that year's second quarter: "U.S. retail sales . . . grew by 8.1% and international sales increased by 17.3%."

On the surface, that's pretty good. Harley's international sales are growing at double the pace at home. Dig into that international sales growth, though, and you understand why U.S. companies are so eager to go global. While sales in established markets such as Canada and Europe increased that quarter by 13.4% and 15.6%, respectively, Harley's sales in what the company labels "all other markets" — South Africa, Turkey, Egypt, Saudi Arabia, Venezuela, Uruguay, China, and even Borneo, among others — expanded by nearly 34%. Now, the sheer number of cycles sold in those "other markets" was small — just 7,406 out of a total of nearly 197,000 Harley bikes sold — but that's sort of the point: Harley has a vast opportunity to sell even more motorcycles overseas, opening up for the company a potentially large and lucrative market that will pump up the bottom line far faster than relying on just U.S. growth alone.

Companies generally detail in their financial reports, particularly their annual reports, how much revenue and profit (the proverbial "top" and "bottom" lines) come from domestic and international sources. Some companies spell this out in the glossy part of their annual report up front; some offer the details in the back of the book in a section called "Geographic Information" or maybe "Segment Analysis." You'll know it when you see it — it's obvious for what it is.

If you want to base your international investment strategy on multinationals, there are a few ways to consider this. (For the record, the companies mentioned below are not specific recommendations. Rather, they are examples to better illustrate the kinds of companies you might think about.)

Established Pioneers: These are the American giants that first ventured overseas decades ago. Cincinnati's Proctor & Gamble, for instance, planted its flag on foreign soil for the first time in 1930. The maker of detergents, shampoos, over-the-counter medicines, and other daily-use products now sells its globally known brands in more than 140 countries.

Established pioneers are the U.S. companies with a broad international footprint, generating a large chunk of their revenues globally. Some are providing the everyday services and products consumers need, such as P&G. Others include food and beverage companies such as McDonald's and Coca-Cola; the tobacco giant Altria; and health-care names such as the eye-care company Bausch & Lomb or drug maker Baxter International. Even cosmetics have gone global; Avon Products, for example, in 2006 accumulated nearly three-quarters of its sales overseas. These are the established pioneers that are relatively stable investments because the products they sell — consumer staples — generate scads of global sales in good times and bad; consumers always need shampoo, food, cleaning products, medicine, etc.

Some established pioneers are more volatile because their products and services are not staples. Though they still generate boatloads of cash overseas, they are more susceptible to economic conditions, fickle consumer trends, or government spending. Technology companies fit this category, as do the big energy firms. Exxon's predecessor, for instance, first arrived in Saudi Arabia's oil fields in 1946, and today international sales amount to 75% of Exxon's top line. Computer-chip giant Intel, meanwhile, racks up more than 85% of its sales overseas.

The challenge for these pioneers comes in the form of a weak economy or tumbling energy prices. Intel struggles when consumers are not buying computers and electronics; Exxon feels the pain when oil and chemical prices slide. Other industries where the fortunes of established pioneers ebb and flow include companies that mine for metals or sell other types of commodities, and industrial companies selling the big machines that others use to build infrastructure or plow farms — Boeing, General Electric, Caterpillar, and John Deere.

When you buy the established pioneers, you're buying into proven, well-established global operations.

Modern Explorers: These are the young Turks that are relatively new to global growth and that are now making their mark overseas. Many of the companies that fit this group are specialty retailers or consumer-discretionary companies reliant on consumers spending dollars that aren't earmarked for staples. Modern explorers include the likes of Harley-Davidson and retailers such as Circuit City, Best Buy, The Home Depot, Starbucks . . . even Genuine Parts, a provider of replacement auto parts in the consumer market — a potentially nice niche to fill in places such as China, where car sales are gaining momentum. Some financial firms slip in as well. E*Trade, an online brokerage firm, has operations in several European and Asian countries and picks up roughly a tenth of its revenues overseas.

When you buy the modern explorers, you're buying in to the relatively early stages of a company's continued global expansion. Starbucks, the nearly ubiquitous American coffee-house, opened its first international store in Vancouver, Canada, in 1987, and by summer 2006 had more than 3,400 stores in 36 countries outside the United States. That sounds like a fairly large number. But the Seattle-based java juggernaut has more than 8,400 stores in its home country. Obviously the world is large enough to handle substantially more Starbucks-branded caffeine huts than you find in America. Indeed, the chain has stated publicly that its long-term plans call for 30,000 stores, with half outside the United States and many expected to be in China. So, Starbucks expects to brew up quite a lot of foreign sales, and while you might not be getting in on the ground floor of that global growth, you're certainly on one of the low floors.

That's not to imply, though, that the modern explorers don't suffer setbacks. Wal-Mart opened its first international store in Mexico City in 1991 and now operates in about ten countries. Yet in 2006, the world's largest retailer retreated from South Korea after failing to win over customers there; two months later it abandoned Germany for the same reason.

Now, all that said, the theory that multinationals are the best way to play foreign investing is not all that it promises.

Yes, multinationals can ring up sizable sales abroad. Yes, their earnings are plumper because of those international efforts. And, yes, shareholders ultimately benefit because those plumper earnings mean the share price is likely to move higher. All of that is fine . . . until Wall Street cracks.

You see, many of America's largest multinationals are components of the Dow Jones Industrial Average, or "the Dow," the iconic symbol of the American brand of capitalism. The math, then, is pretty obvious: If Wall Street, i.e., the Dow, is headed lower, by definition, then, many of the stock prices for the biggest companies in America — the *multinationals* — are generally headed lower, too. I say "many" because not all stocks move in tandem with the Dow; some rise even as the laggards drag down the entire average. We're back to that relationship I mentioned in Chapter 1 — correlation, or how asset prices move in relation to one another. Consider again that list of 30 Dow stocks. The movement in the share price of General Electric, for example, which picks up roughly half its sales overseas, was highly correlated to the overall movement of the Dow in the five years ended in October 2006. The same holds true for United Technologies, DuPont, Caterpillar, and IBM. In fact, over 5- , 10- , and 15-year periods more than 20 of the 30 Dow stocks have a correlation of 0.5 or better to the Dow itself.

CORRELATION TO THE DOW JONES INDUSTRIAL AVERAGE OF THE INDIVIDUAL STOCKS IN THE DOW AS OF 2006:

	CORRELATION		
COMPANY	**5-YEAR**	**10-YEAR**	**15-YEAR**
General Electric	0.78	0.75	0.73
Citigroup	0.78	0.73	0.67
American Express	0.77	0.72	0.66
JPMorgan Chase & Co.	0.75	0.69	0.64
United Technologies	0.74	0.65	0.62
DuPont	0.73	0.61	0.59
Caterpillar	0.70	0.59	0.57
American International Group	0.70	0.54	0.54
International Business Machines	0.70	0.59	0.54
Honeywell International	0.69	0.61	0.59
3M	0.69	0.60	0.58
Microsoft	0.68	0.56	0.56
Alcoa	0.68	0.57	0.54
Walt Disney	0.67	0.54	0.52
Wal-Mart Stores	0.65	0.59	0.59
Intel	0.65	0.56	0.56
Exxon Mobil	0.63	0.50	0.48
Boeing	0.61	0.53	0.51
The Home Depot	0.61	0.60	0.60
Hewlett-Packard	0.58	0.52	0.52
Verizon Communications	0.58	0.53	0.53
General Motors	0.57	0.56	0.53
Pfizer	0.57	0.45	0.45
AT&T	0.56	0.46	0.46
Johnson & Johnson	0.54	0.48	0.48
Coca-Cola	0.53	0.46	0.46
Procter & Gamble	0.52	0.43	0.44
Merck & Co.	0.46	0.46	0.44
McDonald's	0.44	0.42	0.43
Altria Group	0.33	0.32	0.33
Average	**0.63**	**0.55**	**0.54**

Fact is, although a company's financials benefit from international sales, the stock price won't always automatically benefit from that foreign exposure when the U.S. markets are broadly retreating — and that sort of defeats the purpose of the diversification you're looking for with your global investing. When all is said and done, Harley-Davidson is an American company, owned largely by American investors, who, when the American markets turn sour, tend to move out of the American stocks they own, largely indifferent to whether Harley's profits come from a Hell's Angel buying a Hog in southern California or a Japanese businessman posturing for his friends by laying down a few million yen for an American bike in Tokyo. International sales and earnings might help a multinational better weather the downdraft, but the chances are great that your multinationals will still feel the pinch of a falling U.S. market. Through the years, in fact, a number of academic papers have found what one called "weak evidence" that multinational stocks provide much diversification to a U.S.-based portfolio. U.S. stocks are U.S. stocks first and foremost, and they generally tend to follow the direction of U.S. markets.

To a degree, that weak evidence has, well, weakened somewhat in recent years as the movements of domestic and international stocks have been more aligned because stock markets and economies have grown closer. Some of that recent closeness is certainly just dumb luck, since much of the world was riding, in unison, an economic upsurge during a commodities boom that started in late 2001. At some point, economies will decouple again — they always do — and when that happens stock markets will not be as seemingly united as they were in 2005 and 2006. At that point, the correlation between various markets will revert to a more normal range, and foreign stocks and U.S. stocks — including multinationals — will no longer seem so unified.

Moreover, for all the exposure to foreign markets that multinationals do provide, they don't give you the same type of opportunities that are the hallmark of overseas investing:

opportunities in smaller, local companies that don't have ties to the American economy. U.S. electronics retailer Best Buy, for instance, bought into China in 2006, and China, with its geometrically exploding base of gadget-happy consumers, is certain to be a great market for electronics retailers. Yet China will always be just a part of Best Buy, whereas it will be everything to Gome Electrical Appliances Holdings (pronounced Go-May), one of the largest Chinese electronics retailers popular with the locals. When investors from around the world go in search of investments in China, they will naturally gravitate toward the local companies like Gome, not Best Buy. Because Gome is where the real opportunities lie as a global investor.

In the end, multinationals are certainly one way to own exposure to global markets — so long as you understand that they're not a pure play. A portfolio built entirely of multinationals won't have the same degree of diversification it otherwise would if you owned foreign stocks directly. Moreover, you have to accept that U.S. multinationals are more likely to ride the tides ripping through Wall Street than they are to track the stock markets in the countries in which they do their business.

DEPOSITARY RECEIPTS

When it comes to buying individual foreign stocks, American depositary receipts are where U.S. investors first look.

ADRs, as they're commonly called, are the body doubles of the stock market. They are faux shares of stock that stand in for the actual shares of a foreign company seeking to access the capital available in the United States and the cachet that a listing on the New York Stock Exchange — arguably the world's most prestigious — offers.

Take, for instance, British Airways, the flag carrier for the United Kingdom, and a brand name most people will recognize. The air carrier's shares trade in London, but U.S. investors have easy access to the stock in the states through British

Airways' ADRs that trade on the New York Stock Exchange. Those ADRs in turn offer owners a stake in British Airways' income stream, a share of any dividends paid, and a vote on corporate matters, just as with the actual shares in London.

Yet the ADRs are not the actual British Airways shares. Instead, they're a bit of financial jury-rigging designed as a mirror image of those London shares. The ADRs are tradable certificates, each backed by physical BA shares, which in turn are held in trust by a financial institution, such as JPMorgan Chase & Co. or the Bank of New York, both significant players in depositary receipts.

The NYSE is loaded with ADRs and similar investments known as ADSs (American depositary shares) and GDRs (global depositary receipts). In practical terms this trio is identical; in technical terms they differ slightly. An ADS is an actual share of stock that a foreign company has registered in the United States, while an ADR is a bundle of shares wrapped together in one security (more on that in a moment.) A GDR is an ADR of a company listed in multiple foreign markets, such as the GDRs of Russian airline Aeroflot that trade in Germany as well as the United States. For the sake of simplicity, we'll just refer to the lot as ADRs, since that's how investors generally know them.

This take on overseas investing — owning what is essentially a doppelgänger — has long roots in America. JPMorgan introduced the first ADR in 1927, allowing Americans to own a piece of famed British retailer Selfridges Retail Ltd. By the end of 2005, more than 2,000 foreign companies traded as ADRs in New York. Combined, that year those stocks traded more than 41 billion shares worth nearly $1 trillion.

MOST WIDELY HELD ADRS IN 2005

COMPANY	ADR SYMBOL	COUNTRY
BP plc	BP	UK
Royal Dutch Shell plc	RDS	UK
Petroleo Brasiliero (Petrobras)	PBR	Brazil

America Movil	AMX	Mexico
Cia Vale Do Rio Doce	RIO	Brazil
Teva Pharamaceutical Industries	TEVA	Israel
GlaxoSmithKline plc	GSK	UK
Nokia OY	NOK	Finland
Vodafone plc	VOD	UK
Total SA	TOT	France

For American investors, ADRs have some key benefits:

- You gain access to a relatively wide variety of foreign companies from scores of countries.
- The shares and any dividends received are paid in U.S. dollars.
- Certain ADRs — generally those listed on the NYSE and Nasdaq — must provide, in English, the financial reports that shareholders receive in the home market, and they must report their numbers based on Generally Accepted Accounting Principals, known as GAAP, the accounting standard U.S. companies use. This could change, though, as I noted earlier, given that the Securities and Exchange Commission is looking to allow foreign firms to use International Financial Reporting Standards. Either way, foreign firms with ADRs in the United States must report their finances based on some version of accounting standards that are broadly accepted in Western financial markets.

Foreign companies find benefits in ADRs as well, and they often want shares available in the United States for any of several reasons:

- **Access to capital**: New York is the world's largest capital market, giving foreign companies a means of raising additional cash when those opportunities might not be available to the same degree at home.
- **Increased global presence**: Many companies that list ADRs in the United States are global players to begin

with, and a listing in the world's largest market for stocks only enhances their profile among investors.

- **Customer outreach**: Sticking with the British Airways example, many ADRs, though certainly not all, represent companies that have a customer base in the United States, and a New York listing makes it easier for those customers to invest in the companies making the products and offering the services they rely on.

SPONSORED VS. UNSPONSORED

Though this is a bit inside baseball, you might as well know all there is to know about ADRs.

They come in two flavors: sponsored and unsponsored.

Sponsored ADRs have been listed on an American market by the company itself, and these ADRs carry the same rights afforded investors in the company's primary market. The Securities and Exchange Commission imposes on these ADRs the same regulatory reporting requirements that American companies must comply with, meaning the underlying company must report its financials to the SEC every quarter. In general, ADRs must be sponsored to gain a listing on the major U.S. exchanges or quoted on the Nasdaq system.

Unsponsored ADRs are listed without the involvement of the underlying company, and the ADRs do not necessarily carry all the shareholder benefits that the local investors have in the home country. Unsponsored ADRs are generally issued by depositary banks that see a demand in the U.S. market for shares of some particular company. These certificates have no regulatory reporting requirements with the SEC.

Because ADRs are generally not the actual foreign shares, they can be—and routinely are—packaged to make them more palatable to U.S. investors. Swiss shares, for instance, are notorious for triple-digit prices; that reflects the investment culture in Switzerland, where institutional investors, rather than mom-and-pop stock traders, typically play a dominant role in the market. With millions of Swiss francs to invest, institutions aren't paying much attention to the nominal value of a stock, and so they don't really care that the shares of, say, Merck Serono S.A., a global biotechnology leader based in Geneva, trade in Switzerland at more than 1,100 francs, or $887. (This quote was in early 2007.)

Relatively few individual investors in the United States, however, will pay that kind of money for a single share of stock. That's a key concern for foreign companies with a New York listing, given that individual investors play a significant role in the American stock market. Foreign firms know their U.S. shares must be priced to attract that mom-and-pop audience, what Wall Street refers to as the "retail" crowd. Generally, that means a price within a band between the mid-teens and roughly $50 to $75. And that requires packaging.

Knowing that U.S. investors would balk at the high-dollar price required to buy a single share, Merck Serono, when it came to America in the summer of 2000, structured its ADRs to represent just a fraction of a Swiss-listed share. Each Merck Serono ADR, therefore, equals just 1/40th of a share back in Switzerland. Stated another way, you'd need to buy 40 Merck Serono ADRs on the New York Stock Exchange to equal just one Swiss share. The result: While a single Merck Serono share fetched the equivalent of $887 on the Swiss Exchange in 2006, a single Merck Serono ADR in New York cost $22.15 at the same moment — 40 times less than the Swiss share.

Such packaging is common with ADRs. In some cases you're buying what amounts to fractions of a share, as with Merck Serono. In others cases you're buying multiple shares, as with Aluminum Corp. of China, for which each ADR stands in for 200 shares of stock. And in some instances, the ADRs trade on a one-to-one basis. Two websites useful for ADR research are www.adr.com (run by JPMorgan) and www.bnyadr.com (run by the Bank of New York). Both sites offer a bundle of data on ADRs and the underlying stock, and they provide search capabilities if you're looking to research a specific company, or trolling for companies to research in a certain country or region, or a particular industry within countries or regions.

If ADRs represent the international route you want to take, then pursuing strategies similar to those you might follow with U.S. multinationals isn't a bad idea. Many of the ADRs, in fact, are multinationals in their own right.

Examples of the Established Pioneers, those that are long-established global players, include companies such as:

SABMiller plc (South Africa/United Kingdom): More than a century old, this is one of the world's truly global beer makers, with 130 brands distributed in 60 countries from America (Miller) to Zimbabwe (Rhino Lager).

BASF (Germany): This global chemical giant has customers in more than 170 countries and production facilities on five continents.

L'Oréal (France): With 18 brands, the beauty of the world's leading cosmetics maker is that it sells 135 products every second to consumers in more than 70 countries.

Unilever (Netherlands/United Kingdom): Every day, 150 million people across 150 countries choose a Unilever brand. Some of the ones you might recognize here in the states are Bertoli olive oil, Country Crock spread, Dove soap, Hellmann's mayonnaise, Wish-Bone salad dressings, Slim-Fast, and Vaseline.

The Modern Explorers club, populated by companies relatively young in terms of global sales but which have fast-growth opportunities, includes ADRs such as:

Vodafone Group (United Kingdom): The first connection on what would become the world's leading mobile-phone network occurred on Jan. 1, 1985, with a call from a dock near the Tower of London to Newbury, where the British firm is based. Vodafone's cellular interests now stretch across 60 countries, including the United States, where it is part owner of — Can you hear me now? — Verizon Wireless.

Tesco (United Kingdom): One of Britain's leading food retailers, Tesco first crossed borders in the mid-1990s with stores in markets such as Hungary, Poland, and Slovakia. Now it has hundreds of stores in Thailand, Japan, and China, and in 2007 it moved into the United States with stores in California and Nevada.

Lan Airlines S.A. (Chile): The national airline of the world's longest country — 2,700 miles from tip to top — is rapidly becoming a South American juggernaut, with separate airline operations in Peru and Argentina and a flight schedule that stretches from Frankfurt, Germany, to Sydney, Australia. Lan is one of the fastest-growing airlines on its home continent, and LanChile, the flagship brand, has racked up a host of awards, including Best Airline in South America.

Dr. Reddy's Laboratories (India): Founded in 1984, this pharmaceutical firm was the first non-Japanese Asian drug company to list its shares on the New York Stock Exchange. Dr. Reddy's now sells medications across 100 countries.

As with multinationals, ADRs have some kinks, too.

Many ADRs, particularly those on the NYSE and the Nasdaq, are global giants in their own right — some of the world's biggest companies. Many have extensive ties to American consumers and businesses. The classic examples: Sony and Toyota. Both are arguably as much American as they are Japanese. Toyota, in fact, generates basically a third of its global auto sales here in the United States — greater American exposure, relatively speaking, than Coca-Cola. Such symbiosis with America's economy isn't necessarily bad; it can provide stability and growth opportunities that help drive a company's stock price higher over time. After all, with the world's wealthiest consumer population — and our penchant for spending — the United States represents The Prize for foreign companies that succeed in conquering American aisles.

Still, in trying to diversify away from the U.S. dollar or the U.S. economy, you're buying into companies that themselves are highly dependent on both. That's counterproductive.

And then there's also counterintuitive.

You'd think that a foreign stock, even if it is an ADR, would move based upon how the stock moves overseas. The local shares go up, the ADRs go up. The local shares go down, so go the ADRs. By and large, that generally is the pattern. But there's a chink in the chain. Two academicians — Stephen Foerster, from Canada's University of Western Ontario; and G. Andrew Karolyi, at Ohio State University — found in 1999 research published in the *Journal of Financial Planning* that foreign companies, once their shares start trading in the United States as ADRs, often begin to exhibit a modest increase in their correlation with U.S. market indices such as the S&P and a significant decrease in their correlation with the indices in their local markets. In short, Mr. Karolyi says, "they become more 'American' in their risk exposure." The reason: If the Dow Jones Industrial Average and the S&P 500 are in full retreat, investors reflexively sell off the stocks they own, generally indifferent to country of origin. At some point when all you see are red numbers on the CNBC ticker, a stock is a stock is a stock, regardless of its provenance. So shares of Toyota or Honda might be up on the day in Tokyo, but a broad sell-off in the states can have the ADRs slipping here.

As such, your foreign investment, while certainly foreign at the core, can act a lot more American than you might expect.

Like U.S. multinationals, then, ADRs can be a convenient way to add an international flair to your portfolio. Just be aware, though, that many of the ADRs you'll come across cast a broad shadow across the U.S. economy and can begin to move more closely with American stocks — both of which can undermine your international efforts.

FOREIGN ORDINARIES

I bought my first foreign stock in 1985. I was 19 years old at the time, and through a very small account at a discount brokerage firm, I placed an order (by way of touch-tone phone, mind you, not the Internet) to buy 100 shares of Wellcome plc, a British pharmaceutical company that, with its drug AZT, was the first to address the growing demand for medicines to fight what was then the newly worrisome AIDS virus.

Today, through all the drug-company mergers that have occurred, the Wellcome shares I once owned are buried within Britain's GlaxoSmithKline plc, one of the largest of the world's so-called Big Pharma firms. Glaxo's stock trades hundreds of thousands of shares every day on the New York Stock Exchange as an ADR. Wellcome, when I snapped up the shares as a teenager, traded far fewer shares each day in the United States and was not listed on any American exchange. My brokerage firm went trolling for the stock in the Over-the-Counter market.

The OTC, as it's known, is the catchall term given to a collection of different markets — the OTC Bulletin Board, the Pink Sheets, the gray market — where investors can access all manner of companies not listed on any of the major American exchanges. Most of the international stocks that trade in the United States trade in the OTC market, and most are known as "foreign ordinaries," the same ordinary shares investors buy and sell in their local stock markets around the globe.

Although the bulk of companies residing in the OTC are U.S. firms, many foreign companies — estimated at 30,000 — trade there as well. Some are huge names that Americans instantly recognize; some you've never heard of. Some companies specifically want their shares trading in the OTC market; others don't even realize their shares are available in America.

A couple hundred of these foreign stocks trade in the Pink Sheets as ADRs similar to those populating the New York

Stock Exchange and the Nasdaq. These tend to be the most visible, most liquid foreign shares in the OTC, although in this case "most liquid" can be a relative term since many of these stocks trade a few hundred shares a day — if they trade at all.

Unlike the ADRs on the New York exchanges, all the foreign stocks in the various OTC markets trade in an unregulated environment, where companies are not subject to the oversight of the Securities and Exchange Commission, where information is often scarce, and where brokers may not be on the up-and-up. Some companies trade in the OTC market because they don't want the obligation and cost of meeting the SEC reporting requirements mandatory of a listing on a major, American exchange. Some are just too small to make it onto a major exchange to begin with, so the OTC market remains their only option for their shares to trade in America.

Amid the lot of foreign stocks on the OTC, you'll find some very large, global names, such as Nestlé, the world's largest purveyor of food and beverages. Though the maker of chocolate bars — as well as San Pellegrino water, Nescafé instant coffee, and Purina Dog Chow, among others — is a well-known brand across America, the company is based in Vevey, Switzerland. Nestlé's shares have long been found on the Pink Sheets, rather than the more august New York Stock Exchange. Nestlé's rationale: "Why go for a more burdensome solution, when the visibility afforded by the Pink Sheets is sufficient to attract the kind of investors we would like," a Nestlé spokesman says. Nestlé reports its finances according to International Financial Reporting Standards, and adding the cost of additional GAAP reporting requirements imposed by the SEC as of 2007 just to have a traditional ADR program does nothing to benefit the company.

On the opposite end is a company like Astaldi S.p.A., one of Italy's largest construction firms, building roads and subways, airports, and bridges in various parts of the world. Though Astaldi has worked on highways in America, it's not a company likely to register in the recollection of all but a very tiny lot of Americans. Still, Astaldi's shares are available in the

United States — on the gray market, or what is often referred to as "Other OTC."

The OTC doesn't operate as does the New York Stock Exchange, where buyers and sellers come together to actually trade shares through a middleman whose purpose is to keep the markets fluid at all times by stepping in to buy or sell shares if there are no natural buyers and sellers at the moment. The OTC market instead functions like a bulletin board, where buyers and sellers essentially post their interest in trading some particular stock, hoping someone else happens along who's interested in the other side of that transaction. Think of it as essentially an electronic version of the community bulletin board you often find hanging just inside the entrance to a supermarket — a place where providers of services and seekers of products notify each other of their wares and wishes. With OTC stocks, the brokers and dealers matching buyers and sellers are under no obligation to make that match, or to even step in and ensure the market operates smoothly.

Gray-market stocks, meanwhile, are so thinly traded that you won't even find for them a bid-ask spread. (The "spread" is the standard price-quote pair that investors are accustomed to dealing with, such as, say, a quote for $69.70 — $69.75 for Apple Computer, meaning the buyer with the highest bid is willing to pay $69.70, while the seller with the lowest offer is asking $69.75.) Instead of a spread, you typically find only the price at which the last trade occurred. And given that trading in many gray-market stocks can be separated by days or even months, that price may be so stale it's near rotten. It may not even remotely reflect the worth of the shares today, as determined back in the company's home market. And it's not like when you go to buy or sell, the shares will suddenly be revalued to reflect the home-market share price; you're stuck buying or selling at whatever the price is you can negotiate here, among a very narrow pool of buyers and sellers familiar with the obscure foreign company in the first place.

You can differentiate between the Pink Sheet ADRs and all the other foreign ordinaries by their ticker symbols.

• **ADRs**: All have the letter "Y" at the end of their symbol. The ADRs for Hong Kong's Bank of East Asia, for instance, trade under the symbol "BKEAY"; British retailer Marks & Spencer is assigned "MAKSY," while Swiss drug giant Roche Holdings trades as "RHHBY." Remember: Each ADR can represent a single share of some foreign ordinary (the case with Bank of East Asia); it can represent multiple shares (each Marks & Spencer ADR corresponds with six local shares in London); or it can represent just a fraction of one share (Roche ADRs equal one-half of a share in Switzerland).

• **Ordinaries**: All carry "F" as their final letter. Australian gaming-machine maker Aristocrat Leisure trades under the symbol "ARLUF"; German retailer Metro AG, which beat back Wal-Mart's efforts in Germany, trades as "MTAGF." Because the ordinaries are literally the exact shares you'd buy in the local market in a foreign country, they always function on a 1:1 basis, so that each share you buy in the United States is the equivalent of one share overseas.

Note: Some stocks trade in the United States as both ADRs and foreign ordinaries. That can create confusion if you're not paying attention to what you're researching or trading. Again, Nestlé serves as a useful example. The company's ADRs trade in the Pink Sheets, with each ADR (symbol: NSRGY) representing one-quarter of an ordinary Swiss share. Nestlé's ordinaries, meanwhile, are also available in the OTC market (symbol: NSRGF). Here's where the confusion arises: The share price for each is dramatically different. The ADRs in early February 2007 fetched a price in the high $90s, while the ordinaries traded in the $380s — or about four times as much, since each ordinary share is the equivalent of four ADRs. If you set out to buy 100 shares of Nestlé's ADRs, expecting to spend nearly $10,000, you're in for some heart palpitations if you accidentally choose the wrong Nestlé shares and your brokerage firm tells you the cost approaches $40,000.

To find out what shares trade where, go to the website: www.pinksheets.com and choose the "symbol lookup" function. The result will show you which shares of a particular company are available in the United States—assuming the shares are available at all—and whether those shares trade on the New York Stock Exchange, the Nasdaq, the Pink Sheets, the OTC, or Other OTC.

For American investors, the foreign stocks found in the OTC market present an entirely different set of opportunities than you'll find in the ADR market. In general, ADRs represent some of the biggest companies on offer in a particular country, often global players tied to multiple economies, including the United States. By contrast, the foreign ordinaries are frequently small- and midsized companies that have limited, if any, ties to the United States, giving investors the chance to participate on a far more local level in an overseas economy.

But where you find opportunity, you also find opportunity costs. With foreign ordinaries that trade in America, those costs can outweigh the benefits. Because just as with ABC's classic *Wide World of Sports* motto, the OTC spans the world to bring you the thrill of victory . . . and the agony of defeat. While all stocks carry a certain set of common hazards—the risk that a company's products fail or that a local economy flags—foreign ordinaries bought in the United States come with some unique threats:

• **Pricing risk**: The foreign ordinaries traded in the states and the ordinary shares back in the local market would seem to be identical, since they are identical shares. However, they typically operate more like fraternal twins in that while they look alike, they don't necessarily act alike. Take Ito-Yokado, as an example, a Japanese company that merged into Seven & i Holdings, the 7-Eleven chain-store operator mentioned in Chapter 1. Before the merger, you could find unsponsored ADRs trading

fairly infrequently in the OTC market. But here's the pricing
risk you often find: Those Ito-Yokado ADRs at one point were
quoted at $35.88 a share, while the local shares were quoted in
Tokyo at the equivalent of $34.36. U.S. investors thus paid 4.4%
more to buy the shares stateside. If the same spread existed
when you sold the shares, you'd have had to clear nearly 9%
before you made the first penny of profit—and that's without
taking the brokerage commission into account.

• **Liquidity risk**: In the worst situation, liquidity risk
means you might not be able to find any buyers when you
want—or need—to sell your shares. You might not find any
sellers at your price when you're ready to buy, either, but that's a
less critical concern since the lack of sellers won't result in you
losing money. Lack of buyers for your shares, however, means
you may have to hold the stock—risking a price drop—until a
buyer emerges, or lower your asking price to encourage a buyer
into the market . . . and even then there's no guarantee you'll
get out if investors aren't interested in the stock you have for
sale. An example of the often lackluster liquidity: On Nov. 1,
2006, shares of New Zealand discount retailer The Warehouse
Group traded in Auckland for the equivalent of US$4.35. In
the United States, the foreign ordinaries were quoted at
$2.50—yet they hadn't traded in America since May 9, an indi-
cation not only that the quote was stale by half a year but that
there were few investors around to transact with even if you
cared to trade.

• **Information risk**: Because OTC stocks are not registered with the SEC, the companies aren't required to file financial reports in the states. That's not necessarily a showstopper,
since you can often find these documents online, and often in
English. However, this lack of information flow can manifest
itself as other hurdles. One example: The company you own
announces a plan to allow existing shareholders to buy a stake
in a secondary company being spun out, though not distributed
to shareholders, and to participate you must respond by a certain date. Well, companies sometimes have a very narrow window between the time the mailing goes out and the date by

which you must respond — and those dispatches don't always make it to your mailbox in time. In some instances, they don't even make it to you at all. The risk, then, is that you miss out on important corporate actions.

The market for foreign ordinaries in the United States can be a fine place to invest, particularly if you're looking to own some of the most liquid international firms that trade there, such as Nestlé. Just remember, though, that buying foreign ordinaries stateside can also subject you to a set of risks — increased risks — that, ironically, you don't face by instead investing directly overseas.

MUTUAL FUNDS, EXCHANGE-TRADED FUNDS, AND CLOSED-END FUNDS

If baseball is America's national pastime, mutual funds are surely our national investment. We Americans love them, with every other household having, on average, about $48,000 invested in a mutual fund either directly or through a 401(k) plan at work or maybe an IRA. They're easy to understand. They're convenient. The level of research necessary to pick a good one isn't nearly as detailed as with individual stocks. Little wonder mutual funds collectively held some $11 trillion of our money in mid-2007.

Exchange-traded funds, meanwhile, are gaining ground for many of the same reasons, plus they're even more convenient to trade. First introduced in 1992 with a single ETF focused on the S&P 500-stock index, ETFs have grown into a major product on Wall Street, and around the world. The Singapore Stock Exchange, for instance, trades several ETFs, including one that shadows the market in India. Here at home, ETFs held nearly $500 billion in assets in mid-2007 and traded largely on the American Stock Exchange, a relatively sleepy marketplace compared with the Nasdaq and the NYSE, but which nonetheless has all but cornered the market in ETF trading. The majority of the ETFs on the Amex focus on domestic stocks. A few dozen, though, are foreign-centric—everything from an emerging-markets ETF, to one that owns the top 50 stocks in Europe, to those aimed at singular markets such as Belgium or Malaysia, or even the European Monetary Union.

ETF DEFINED

Built like an index mutual fund, trades like a stock. That's an ETF.

ETFs own a basket of stocks that mirrors some particular index shadowing U.S. or international stocks (think S&P 500; Dow Jones Industrial Average; the EAFE Index for Asia, Australasia, and Europe; or the FTSE 100 in London). Instead of being priced once a day, after the stock market closes, as with a traditional mutual fund, ETFs trade all day long, just like shares of stock. That means the share price changes throughout the day, giving investors greater flexibility in getting into and out of an investment. You can also "short" an ETF—that is, bet on the index going down, not up. Try doing that with a mutual fund; you can't.

The big benefit with ETFs is that they tend to be more cost-effective than mutual funds since the ETFs ongoing expense ratio—the cost of running the portfolio—is generally, though not always, cheaper than with like-minded index mutual funds. ETFs also tend to be more tax efficient, meaning your tax burden is less each year.

Closed-end mutual funds are third in line, the smallest of the bunch, with the international segment holding just $57 billion or so in mid-2007. Despite their name, these funds are much more aligned with an ETF than they are a mutual fund. Sure, they pool investors' money to own a basket of stocks, which, as with most mutual funds, is picked by a portfolio manager. But closed-end funds trade like an ETF on an exchange. In fact, closed-end funds almost act like shares of company stock; just as investors push the price of, say, FedEx up and down based on perceived prospects for the package-delivery company, they likewise push the price of closed-end funds up and down based on perceived notions about the underlying fund's investments. That's different than with mutual funds, where the share price is determined solely by the value of the underlying investments. With closed-end funds, shareholders determine the value based on their view of the fund itself and where it invests — a distinction that can provide some unique investment opportunities we'll get to in a bit.

The lure of funds and ETFs is that like much of the food we buy, these investments come prepackaged to sate our needs quickly and without fussing around with the individual ingredients. Without question, they are the simplest, quickest way to play "investor," because with one decision you own a basket of stocks without mucking about with all the homework and research necessary to pick individual companies yourself.

Though international funds and ETFs are a relatively small subset of the American fund universe, they have nonetheless attracted lots of cash. Internationally minded mutual funds available in the United States at the end of 2006 held assets of nearly $1.6 trillion, about five times the level of a decade earlier.

The significant difference between ETFs and mutual funds is that mutual funds — particularly with closed-end funds — tend to be "actively managed" in that the funds hire a portfolio manager to kick the tires and look under the hood of companies to pick what that particular manager determines are the best stocks. An ETF, meanwhile, is designed to passively reflect the stocks in some index. Of course, in the "every rule has its exceptions" category, numerous mutual funds exist that passively track various international indices, while a newer breed of ETF has begun to emerge that tweaks the indexing with some decision making in an attempt to juice the returns a bit. For the most part, this is how international funds and ETFs divide up:

- **World or global**: Literally buys stocks around the world, including owning some shares in U.S. companies. If you already own U.S. stocks or mutual funds and you want your international exposure unadulterated by even more U.S. investments, then this is not the fund for your needs.
- **International or foreign**: Holds stocks of only foreign-based companies, and usually invests across numerous countries on several continents. Some will focus singularly on the industrialized world; others will focus solely on emerging markets. Many are a combination, owning both developed and emerging markets in the same basket. Along with world funds, these tend to be the most conservative international funds, since they are so broadly diversified. Most 401(k) retirement-savings plans typically offer an international or foreign fund, and you'll want to add to your portfolio a healthy-sized helping of whatever fund you have access to so that you can properly diversify your retirement account.
- **Regional**: Invests in a specific region of the world, such as Europe, Latin America, or Asia. Some carve it up even further, narrowing their focus to just Eastern Europe, or Asia excluding Japan. Riskier, in general, than international or world funds, these types of funds should play a supporting role in a portfolio — a way to overweight a particular region you find compelling for whatever reason.
- **Country**: Owns stocks in a single country. This is the most efficient way to own exposure to just one market, such as Russia or Japan, for instance. These are frequently the riskiest plays among international mutual funds because while they're diversified within a country, they aren't diversified in terms of the number of countries. Therefore, you're adding greater risk to your portfolio in the event that you own, say, a Russian fund and the Russian ruble turns to rubble, as it did in the late-1990s, devastating Russian-centric mutual funds. Still, in small quantities, they can be an excellent way to improve a portfo-

lio's returns, so long as you understand the risk and don't overdo your exposure. Oh, and technically speaking, domestic U.S. mutual funds fall into the country-fund category since the investments they own are based solely in the states.

• **Index**: Tracks a particular foreign index, the most common of which is the EAFE — the Europe, Australasian, and Far East Index. Others shadow the Financial Times Stock Exchange (the FTSE, or "Footsie") Global Equity index, which tracks roughly 7,000 stocks in 48 countries. A host of other indices track all manner of regions and countries. Overseas index funds are comparatively conservative, but they normally aren't the best way to gain global exposure, which we'll get into in a moment.

Interest in international funds and ETFs vacillates based on world events, how foreign stock and bond markets are faring, and whether the U.S. dollar is weakening or strengthening against other currencies. If U.S. investors hear that foreign stocks are rocking, or if they read in the financial press that the dollar is headed lower and that foreign investments are a good asset to own in that situation, well, then, dollars flood into international funds. When global tensions heat up or a currency crisis erupts somewhere in the world, dollars rush right back out again and back into what is perceived as one of the world's safest markets: the United States. Sometimes there's good reason for the movement. When a currency implodes or a Latin American country reneges on its debt or war erupts, shock waves ripple at blitzkrieg speed through financial markets around the world, spurring worried investors to flee small, foreign markets for the relative comfort of large, U.S. companies and U.S. Treasury notes. Their rationale: Large-company stocks tend to be safest in relation to the world's public companies, while U.S. Treasury notes are the safest bonds in the world.

In other situations, investors aren't so rational. Academic work shows time and again that mutual-fund investors often operate according to herd mentality, chasing the best of yesterday's breed. By that I mean investors read that some particular fund, industrial sector, country, region, or investment strategy posted the best returns in the last quarter or over the past year, and suddenly that's the mutual fund into which investors figure they must pump their money to share in the riches. Trouble is, by the time those funds are hot, you're way late to the party. You've missed the easy money. And though you might still pick up some gains, the greater likelihood is that you'll ride the fund into losses because hot funds-of-the-moment invariably cool as quickly as they heated up.

That said, some international-minded ETFs and funds excel — though certainly not all.

Success with ETFs and index mutual funds generally stems from the movement of overseas markets as a whole or specific countries, given that these types of investments serve to mirror some local basket of stocks. Their prices are based on the cumulative value of the investments inside that basket, and that price rises and falls at the same pace as those underlying shares. Therefore, as foreign markets move higher, so does the price of the ETF or index fund. The biggest strength of ETFs and international index funds: Low fees. The Fidelity Spartan International Index fund, a solid choice for investors who want to own the stocks in the Morgan Stanley Capital International Europe, Australasia, and Far East Index, the EAFE, charges a nearly imperceptible 10 basis points, or just 0.1% annually. That's $1 a year for each $1,000 invested. That's low. Index funds also tend to outperform actively managed funds over an extended period of time, in part because of the low fees.

A glaring weakness: No range of motion. Because these funds are designed to mimic a particular index, they operate like automatons incapable of moving outside the bounds of their tightly prescribed world. The EAFE Index serves a perfect example. Japan constitutes about a quarter of that index, and in the decade from 1989 to 1998 — a period in which Japan's economy and stock market were as dynamic as day-old sushi — the EAFE chugged in as the absolute worst performer among major indices six times, including a stretch of four consecutive years in the basement. A seventh time it was the penultimate worst performer. By owning an index fund tracking the EAFE during that period, you owned by default a big slug of one of the world's worst stock markets of the day simply because the index fund had to include Japan.

Funds run on the actively managed model could — and most did — sidestep Japan to focus on countries with more dynamic prospects at that time. By 2006, with Japan finally looking like it was pulling out of its long funk, actively managed funds began overweighting Japanese stocks again, meaning they were investing more into the country than a rote adherence to the EAFE would order.

Additionally, with many broad-based international index funds, you're typically gaining exposure to just the largest stocks in the world. You're missing out on the purest growth engines in the small- and midsized companies. Or, you're gaining the broadest exposure to the largest stock exchanges in the world, while picking up only peripheral exposure to the smallest, most rapidly growing markets.

With actively managed funds you face a different set of strengths and weakness. On the weak side of the ledger: The expense. International mutual funds are some of the most expensive funds in the business. Many — especially emerging-market mutual funds — charge internal fees of more than 2% a year, on average. Some charge closer to 3%. Such heavy fees hack away a meaningful slice of the annual returns that otherwise would accrue to your pocketbook, making these funds a pricey proposition for buy-and-hold investors. Poor stock selection is the other demon. If the portfolio manager helming your fund turns out to be a lame stock picker, your performance probably won't match what you would have earned in a simple international index fund. And, worse, you will have paid much more in annual fees for the privilege of that mediocrity.

As for the strengths . . . the best actively managed international funds are quite good at what they do — namely, digging deep into local markets to find underappreciated stocks in places where the competition among money managers is ordinarily pretty scant. That's particularly true with, again, smaller companies. Much of the empirical research has found that small-company international funds are better at beating their index than are other types of funds. That stands to reason if only because you'll find far fewer analysts poking around the smaller companies, leaving many more opportunities for portfolio managers who venture beyond the largest or most obvious investments in a local market.

HEDGED OR UNHEDGED?

A big, blinking caveat that any investor in international mutual funds must pay attention to is whether a particular mutual fund hedges its currency exposure.

Those that hedge protect against currency fluctuations, so that if the dollar gains or loses ground against the various currencies in which the fund's stocks are priced, you won't feel the impact, good or bad.

Those that don't hedge assume all the volatility that occurs as currencies fluctuate in relation to one another. We'll cover this more thoroughly in a later chapter, but when the dollar strengthens, the value of international stocks falls in dollar terms. Conversely, when the dollar weakens, international stocks gain value in dollar terms.

For investors who want to mitigate currency risk and just want exposure to foreign companies, mutual funds that hedge are the best option. You won't have to worry about what the dollar does. Investors who want the currency exposure— which, after all, provides an additional portfolio diversification benefit—should ensure the fund they're investing in does not hedge.

To determine whether a particular international mutual fund hedges its currency exposure or not, check the prospectus. Fund companies routinely specify their currency strategy. You can find the prospectus for just about any fund online these days at the website for that fund's parent company.

Finding a good fund is the trick. If you settle on an index fund, the portfolio manager is largely irrelevant since the fund is simply an amalgam of stocks encompassing some underlying index. If you choose an actively managed fund, then everything depends on the competency of the portfolio manager or team of managers. Aside from choosing one of the two international funds I have access to in my company's 401(k) plan, about the only time I've bought into an international mutual fund was in my wife's Individual Retirement Account, which she can't use to invest directly overseas anyway. To expose her to one of the best long-term investment opportunities required the use of a mutual fund — the Matthews Asian Growth & Income fund, a conservatively managed fund that mixes stocks with a healthy dollop of Asian convertible bonds, preferred stocks, and corporate debt, a world that most mutual funds don't play around in. Among mutual-fund managers, Paul Matthews is one of the best when it comes to Asia, and his team of analysts and portfolio managers is well versed in Asian investments well off the radar screen of most international mutual funds. As of the summer of 2007, the Asian Growth & Income fund was closed to new investors, though other Matthews Asia-based funds remain open.

Just as with stocks, you still have homework to do when you pick a mutual fund. If all you seek is broad exposure and returns guaranteed to match the overseas markets, you can't go wrong with an index fund or an ETF that tracks the world outside the United States or that follows the markets you're specifically interested in. As that market goes, so goes your investment, without much thought. To squeeze the most from your returns in an index fund, seek out those charging the lowest fees. After all, if two funds are both designed to shadow the same index, the only difference in their returns will be the fees they each charge. The lower the fees, the higher your returns.

If you lean toward active management, your choices are more complex. Not only do you have more actively managed funds to consider, but they each sport a different style. Some look for value, some growth; some seek income, others capital appreciation. Some run with the big stocks, others stick to small. And then there's the wide range of previously mentioned distinctions between world, international, regional, and country funds. Your best bet for researching mutual funds is at morningstar.com. There, good, basic fund research is available for free, though if you want the detailed analysis and screening tools you'll have to pony up for a subscription. One thing to remember: The financial press starting in the 1990s began bombarding investors with the idea that paying a "load" when buying a mutual fund is a raw deal. In many cases, that's true, since the load you pay — essentially the sales charge — saps your profits. However, exceptions to this rule certainly exist. If you find a portfolio manager consistently posting returns that beat the indices the fund benchmarks against, well, does it make sense to shun potentially larger profits than you'd otherwise earn in a no-load fund just because loads are supposedly bad? In short, loads are not always bad, so long as the fund you own is good.

What defines a good fund? At the end of the day, it's the consistency of the returns. If you're paying a fund manager to pick stocks, you want to see a track record of success. The fund doesn't have to lead the list of hottest performers every year, but you want to see it consistently rank among the top third in its class of peers. A fund such as the Julius Baer International Equity (A shares) serves as a good illustration. (It's closed to new investors at the moment, so this is not a recommendation.) In the one, three, five, and ten years ended in July 2007, the fund was in the top 5% of all foreign large-company funds. In any given year over roughly the past decade, the fund has never dipped below the top third. That's the kind of consistency you want to seek out in an actively managed fund. That's a fund earning its keep by routinely beating the indices in the process. All the data on returns and rankings, by the way, are available at morningstar.com's free site.

rningstar also offers a slew of research on ETFs, while
ct.com offers free research on ETFs as well as closed-
ls. Meanwhile, the American Stock Exchange, where

ETFs trade, has tools to help screen for particular types of ETFs, as well as those trading at a discount or premium to the value of the underlying stocks.

MORNINGSTAR'S STARS

According to the classic TV commercial, when brokerage firm "E.F. Hutton talks, people listen." Today, a more appropriate slogan for Main Street investors might be "When Morningstar rates, investors flock."

Once a little-known Chicago-based investment-research company, Morningstar built its reputation in the 1990s as the go-to provider for data, research, and commentary on the growing but, at the time, relatively small lot of mutual funds. It was the stars, though, that made Morningstar famous.

As a way to provide investors with a visual rating system, Morningstar began to assign stars to the funds it tracked. Five stars—good. One star—not so good. Faced with numerous mutual funds to choose from in their 401(k) plan, and thousands more outside of those plans, investors looking for an easy, uncomplicated way to decipher the crush of available data latched onto the star ratings just as they do brokerage firms' "buy," "sell," "hold" ratings for stocks. The higher the star, they figured, the more Morningstar liked a particular fund.

Yet Morningstar's stars don't actually align that way. The stars are not recommendations to buy or sell a particular mutual fund. Instead, they are symbolic representations showing which funds have produced the best and worst returns historically in a given investment style (think small-cap growth stock funds or medium-term corporate bond funds). In essence, the star ratings judge a mutual fund through the rearview mirror; they don't predict the fund's future course. Not that that's bad. Knowing that a certain European stock fund has a far better track record than another can be a very important variable when considering where to invest. You just need to understand the tool before you use it.

Within each mutual-fund category, the top 10% of funds earn a five-star rating based on performance over three distinct time periods—three, five, and ten years. Likewise, based on the same objective determinations, the bottom 10% of funds earn just one star. Funds that haven't been around at least three years aren't rated. As even Morningstar notes on its website, the stars "shouldn't be considered buy or sell signals."

Closed-end funds and ETFs have a unique investment factor: They routinely trade at either a discount or a premium to the value of the investments underlying the fund.

Remember that mutual funds are priced once a day, after the market closes, and their price—what Wall Street calls the net asset value, or NAV—reflects the cumulative value of all the stocks the fund holds, spread across all the outstanding shares of a mutual fund. So, if all the stocks held inside a fund are worth a combined $10 million, and the fund comprises 1 million shares, then each share is worth $10 ($10 million ÷ 1 million). Because ETFs and closed-end funds trade all day long on the exchange, however, their price fluctuates continually based on investors' perceptions of the fund's investment focus. The value of all the stocks in the closed-end Mexico Fund, for instance, were worth about $42 per share at the end of trading on Oct. 17, 2006. Yet that day on the New York Stock Exchange, where the Mexico Fund trades under the symbol MXF, the fund's share price bounced between $36 and $36.49, ultimately ending the day priced at $36.45, 13% lower than the NAV. That means you're buying $42 worth of value at a discount.

In the case of the Thai Fund, investors on that same October day were paying 15% more than the value of the underlying stocks—a premium.

Savvy investors pay close attention to the discount or premium because closed-end funds routinely trade within a band that sees the shares move to the high end of that band from time to time, only to shrink back to the low end for a while.

Some shares rarely trade at discounts, others rarely trade at premiums. So if you plan to own international closed-end funds, do some research at etfconnect.com, where you'll find charts depicting the relationship between the NAV and a particular fund's daily price going back to the fund's inception. Meanwhile, the Closed-End Fund Association, at www.cefa .com, provides a link to annual reports and websites of numerous closed-end funds, where you can find additional information.

U.S. BROKERAGE ACCOUNTS

This isn't so much a specific type of investment as it is an avenue for investing.

When I first started buying international stocks, discount-brokerage pioneer Charles Schwab & Co. was about the only option for accessing foreign markets from inside the United States as a small-time, individual investor. Major brokerage houses such as Merrill Lynch, Smith Barney, and others would also venture into foreign markets, but by and large they did so, and still do, only for their high-net-worth clients with hundreds of thousands, if not millions, of dollars on deposit. Schwab, however, ran a small, global-investing desk in Phoenix that catered to clients like me who wanted to buy directly overseas. I talked to the Schwab desk a couple of times in the mid-1990s, though ultimately never used the service. That desk still operates today, so Schwab remains a way for Main Street investors to buy and sell international stocks directly without opening overseas accounts.

Nowadays, however, Schwab has competition. Online brokers such as E*Trade, interactivebrokers.com, and Ever-Trade Direct Brokerage all dish up varying degrees of global accessibility. In 2007, E*Trade rolled out an online platform allowing U.S. investors to trade live in a small selection of foreign markets: Canada, the UK, France, Germany, Hong Kong, and Japan. E*Trade for a few years has been allowing investors to trade in a variety of smaller markets such as Thailand and South Africa, though not for live trading. Instead, you place your order over the phone or online during U.S. market hours and E*Trade executes the transaction for you during the other market's operational hours.

In late 2006, EverTrade, a unit of Jacksonville, Florida–based EverBank, began providing investors trading access to roughly a score of markets, from Finland to Peru. That trading, though, is limited to phone orders, not live orders online. Investors at InteractiveBrokers, meanwhile, can trade online directly in ten countries outside the United States, again generally the largest, stablest exchanges such as the UK, Japan, and Sweden. Both firms are likely to add live trading in more markets over time.

For investors wanting to own foreign stocks but transact only within U.S. borders, these accounts are the best option. You have a fairly broad range of established markets to trade in, representing the vast bulk of the world's most liquid stocks. As such, you can buy and sell shares unavailable anywhere in American markets. You can trade during local market hours, if you wish, or you can place your order during U.S. market hours to be executed while you're likely asleep. You won't have any currency conversions to muck about with in transferring money into your account; all the necessary conversions are handled by the firm during the transaction, and often at so-called interbank rates, the institutional pricing that foundations, pension funds, and other professional investors pay. And if you do want the accounts denominated in a foreign currency, they can be, so long as your preferred scrip is one of the various, major foreign currencies — yen, pounds, euros, and the like. Brokerage costs, as well, can be pretty competitive: At InteractiveBrokers, for instance, Canadian shares cost just a penny apiece to trade, while the firm charges a low fee (equivalent to about $12 in 2007) to trade up to £50,000 in the UK.

Still, for all the benefits of these U.S.-based brokerage accounts, they have their shortcomings — namely, added costs and limited market reach.

If your interest in global investing extends beyond London, Tokyo, Paris, and other major markets, the U.S. accounts are sure to feel almost xenophobic in their confinement. None provide broad entry into developing markets, and where they do venture into secondary markets you have no direct access, resigned instead to placing an order in the United States and either accepting shares bought on the gray market here in the states (remember, that's risky) or waiting for the trade to be executed overseas when that market is open.

Then there's the issue of price. U.S. firms, to compensate local dealers and custodians whom they must work with overseas, typically mark up the price of the stocks you want to buy or sell. They do this by widening the "spread," that gap separating a stock's bid and ask prices. Schwab, for instance, adds about 1% to the stock quote, on average, both coming and going, though that can sometimes go higher. Prices for shares traded in South Korea, for example, can be as much as 3% different. In effect, this means you face an immediate hurdle of between 2% and 6% that you must beat before you tally any profit. Maybe that doesn't seem like much, but realize that in an average year, 6% to 8% is a fairly decent return. You're paying the equivalent of nearly one year's return in some cases just to trade. That's expensive.

You must also be aware of minimum trade sizes. Schwab requires that you pony up at least $5,000 per trade, sometimes more depending on the market. Stocks in some countries, notably Singapore and Hong Kong, generally trade in so-called board lots. So, for instance, if you wanted to buy shares in DBS Group Holdings, Singapore's largest bank, you needed a minimum investment of roughly $12,000 to trade the shares through Schwab in late 2006, when 1,000 shares of the banking company cost about 19,200 Singapore dollars. Of course, Schwab and the other brokers have no say in that and you'll face the same minimum trading directly in Singapore or Hong Kong or wherever. You just need to be aware of this in an American brokerage account since it's not a factor when trading U.S. stocks.

Liquidity is another potential problem. Penny stocks — those shares that trade for less then $5, often less than a buck— have a bad reputation in the states, and for good reason, given that they're frequently the playground of some scurrilous thieves promoting some of the vilest stocks imaginable. But in many foreign markets, particularly in Asia, the UK, and Ireland, stocks are typically priced at just a couple of dollars or less per share. It's the norm. They're not sketchy companies, far from it. In many cases they're blue chips in their local market. But instead of issuing tens of millions or hundreds of millions of shares, as do U.S. firms, they issue billions of shares, which keeps the stock price at low levels relative to what American investors are accustomed to. Here's the problem, though, in trading low-priced foreign stocks in the United States: You could have trouble buying or selling the amount of shares you want to trade.

Consider Thai Union Group, the Thailand-based food company that owns the Chicken of the Sea brand, one of the leading brands of tuna on American grocery shelves. At about 23 Thai baht as I write this, Thai Union's shares fetch the equivalent of roughly 61 cents. Buy those shares through a Thai broker trading for you directly in Thailand and you'll have no problem investing, say, $10,000 in the company. Aim that same sum at the Thai Union stock trading over-the-counter in the United States, and you could have some real trouble accumulating the roughly 16,400 shares necessary to fill your order. While that much stock is readily available on the Bangkok Stock Exchange, Thai Union's home market, it's not readily available in the United States. In fact, in late September 2006, for example, pinksheets.com reported that the last recorded trade on the OTC in Thai Union stock was May 4, nearly five months earlier; volume was nowhere near 16,400 shares. That's the picture-perfect definition of a liquidity problem, and it's widespread if you don't have direct access to a particular country and instead trade foreign shares available in the United States through a U.S. broker. Worse, while getting into the stock can be rough enough, getting out quickly if you need to can be impossible since there are so few natural buyers of Thai Union stock in the U.S. market. You could be stuck holding the shares for a long while, or you might have to accept a steep haircut in the price at which a buyer is willing to step in and take the shares off your hands.

You may also face some additional fees, such as the "monthly activity fee minimums" at InteractiveBrokers. Because the firm is built around active traders, InteractiveBrokers requires a minimum amount of monthly activity that generates commissions. Buy-and-hold investors are welcome, but just be prepared to pay $10 a month, $120 a year, to keep your account open.

Finally, with U.S. brokers you're not likely to have access to investment research, if that's important to you. The firms do not employ research analysts and generally do not offer investment advice on foreign stocks. They can dig up some news and other bits of information off the various news services they subscribe to, but it's news you can find yourself online. The brokers won't be offering detailed buy, sell, hold recommendations for specific stocks, industries, or countries.

GLOBAL INVESTING WITHOUT THE CURRENCY RISK . . . SORT OF

Perhaps the most notable risk you take overseas, outside of a company imploding, is that the currency moves unfavorably against the U.S. dollar. As you'll see in a later chapter, that can wipe out your profits, even when your stock is up, or it can magnify your losses when the shares are down. But there is a way to mitigate some of that risk, if you choose to.

Enter InteractiveBrokers' Universal Account.

Say you deposit $10,000 into your account and you want to buy shares in BIC Group, a world leader in lighters and razors and pens, a brand stocked in millions of American medicine cabinets, school knapsacks, and office drawers. Only it's French, and the shares trade in euros since the stock is listed in Paris, *not in the states. For the sake of mathematical ease, let's assume for a moment that the euro and the dollar are equal, so $1 is the same as €1.*

Into the Universal Account you deposit your U.S. dollars to buy $10,000 of BIC. InteractiveBrokers then lends you €10,000 to complete the trade, using your dollars as collateral.

Assume BIC's stock, priced near €50 in the fall of 2006, goes precisely nowhere during the time you own it, yet the dollar soars in comparison to the euro. Now $1 buys you €2, basically meaning the value of the dollar has doubled. Although the €10,000 stake in BIC is still worth €10,000, your original $10,000 investment is worth only $5,000 now because the dollar moved so sharply against your foreign-denominated stock. So, if you owned those BIC shares in a European brokerage account and had converted your dollars to euros to buy them, well, you'd be looking at a big loss right about now because, basically, the €10,000 will buy only half as many dollars as previously.

Yet because you bought BIC in your Universal Account, you're out nothing. Remember: You borrowed the necessary euros to buy BIC; you didn't convert your dollars. The shares are still worth €10,000, so in selling the shares you have the cash to replace the borrowed funds—and you still have your $10,000 in the United States. The entire exercise has essentially been a zero-sum game for you. You will pay interest on the borrowed funds, but you'll also earn interest on the $10,000 on deposit.

Of course, nothing is without risk on Wall Street. If BIC goes nowhere yet the dollar tumbles against the euro (meaning a weaker dollar), so that €10,000 is now worth $20,000, well, just as you saw no loss when the dollar rallied, you will likewise see no gain when the dollar flags. In this instance, foreign currency exposure would have doubled your money, yet you still have just the $10,000 waiting for you in your U.S. account.

InteractiveBrokers' Universal Account doesn't mean you are entirely absent currency exposure. As foreign-stock prices ebb and flow, and as currencies fluctuate, the value of your foreign holdings moves around while your dollar account remains static. Here's a quick example assuming BIC gains 25%, to €62.50, and the dollar loses 10% against the euro:

Beginning Value	Ending Value
200 shares x €50 = €10,000	200 shares x €62.50 = €12,500
$1 = €1 ($10,000 = €10,000)	$1 = €0.90 ($10,000 = €9,000)
Total invested = $10,000	Total repatriated = $13,889

You sell those BIC shares for €12,500, but because the dollar is weaker now, you're repatriating not $12,500 but $13,889 (€12,500 ÷ 0.9). Your account didn't gain 25% . . . it gained almost 39%, boosted by the way the U.S. dollar moved in relation to the euro.

We'll cover more on the impact of currency movements in a later chapter. But that's how you can use an InteractiveBrokers account to either mitigate some of the currency exposure you face overseas or accept full exposure—whatever fits your strategy.

CHAPTER 3

OYSTERS ABROAD

Setting Up Accounts and Trading Stocks (Almost) Everywhere

The e-mail was short.

Good day. I'm a U.S. investor looking to open a brokerage account that will allow me to trade stocks on the New Zealand and Australian stock exchanges. I'd like to know if it's possible for a U.S.-based investor to open an account at Ord Minnett? If so, please let me know what documents you require, and the minimum amount to fund the account.

That was the electronic message I dispatched in the fall of 1995 to Ord Minnett Securities, a now-defunct New Zealand brokerage firm I'd found through an Internet search of brokerage houses in the southern Pacific. Ord Minnett had an online presence advertising its existence and the services it offered investors. The firm did not offer online trading, which at that point was still a fairly novel utility outside the United States. Ord Minnett was the sixth or seventh firm I'd contacted in Australia and New Zealand that fall. All the others had responded with courteous regrets, several telling me — incorrectly — that the U.S. Securities and Exchange Commission wouldn't allow them to accept American investors, though none ever provided a legitimate reason when I asked.

Ord Minnett's reply arrived a few days after I sent the e-mail, landing in my in-box sometime in the wee hours of my morning. Ted the Broker had sent a detailed, cordial note informing me that he would be glad to help with opening an account. All I needed to do was reply with various details, Ted the Broker wrote, and fax to New Zealand a copy of my passport so that the firm could verify my identity. With that, Ted the Broker would complete the necessary documents for me, saving us both the hassles of all the back-and-forth-across-the-world paperwork. Dangerous as it all sounds now, in a world rife with online larceny of one form or another, identity theft wasn't such a worry then as it is today. Moreover, brokerage firms today aren't seeking personal details over e-mail but are typically either making applications available online that you print out and mail in, or relying on secured networks that allow you to complete the application electronically, so you won't have to ship your personal information in a manner that makes it susceptible to low-life creatures prowling for victims online.

After all the appropriate papers were signed and faxed, Ted the Broker finally wrote, "I will inform you when the accounts are open, and send you instructions for wiring your funds."

Before Christmas arrived that year, I owned shares of companies I'd never heard of until a few months earlier, in a country I'd never before visited — and still hadn't as of 2007 — through a brokerage firm I didn't know existed, with the help of man I'd never met nor even spoken with on the phone.

The brief summation, to be sure, bypasses some significant details that I will come back to. But I just want to emphasize the main point: Namely, that's how easy it can be to buy stocks overseas — you find a brokerage firm; you make contact; you open an account; you wire your money. You're golden.

And remember: That was 1995. Today global investing is considerably easier, what with high-speed Internet connections that make light work of locating overseas brokers and completing applications online, not to mention the ease of research, downloading a company's glossy reports and executive speeches, and trading in real time instead of faxing orders or dispatching e-mails during your working hours for a broker to act on during his working hours, which you only find out about a day or so later.

This chapter, then, is all about the mechanics you need to know for locating and approaching foreign brokerage firms, opening and funding brokerage accounts, linking bank accounts where necessary (almost always a necessity), and researching companies. We'll also touch on some factors you need to keep in mind, such as the ways in which financial language can differ overseas and the tax issues you'll face at home and abroad.

We'll start with the most important step: finding a local broker.

WHERE DO YOU WANT TO GO TODAY?

Asia.

That was my destination when I first decided to invest overseas directly.

I wanted to own companies from around the Asian side of the Pacific Rim that were likely to benefit from the growth of the consumer class emerging in countries ranging from India to China to the whole of Southeast Asia. Companies that were not readily available, if at all, in the U.S. stock market. Stock exchanges in Australia, New Zealand, Singapore, and Hong Kong all stood out for one overriding reason: English. Communicating with a brokerage firm would be substantially easier in a common tongue, and given that this was my first financial venture abroad, I was all about the ease of the process.

Ultimately, New Zealand was my choice by default. No brokers in Singapore at that time were willing to work with me (not the case today, by the way), nor were any in Australia. Ord Minnet was the only firm to welcome me. In that context, New Zealand seemed an absolutely wonderful place to open my first foreign brokerage account.

Still, I did have reasons for wanting to be in New Zealand to begin with. Even before my brokerage-firm search had been narrowed for me, I'd found in my research a few consumer-oriented companies there that were doing business in Asia and that I wanted to own. The New Zealand account, I knew from reading through Ord Minnett's menu of services, offered access to the Australian Stock Exchange as well, essentially a two-for-one ticket.

So, for me, New Zealand it would be.

Thus, the first question you have to ask yourself as a global investor is: "Where do I want to invest?"

From that answer flow all the steps you'll need to take to put your cash to work overseas. But instead of telling you what those steps are, let's work through a real-life example so that you can see the process in action and apply it to your specific needs. And where we're headed is . . . Vietnam.

Yes, Vietnam is a Communist country. Yes, the very word "Vietnam" conjures sour memories for many Americans, despite the decades since that conflict ended. So there are certainly some challenges to overcome. Still, Vietnam is awakening as an economy and deepening its ties to the pan-Asian and global economies. Though undeniably poor, the country has been clocking some of the fastest growth in Asia, and in 2006 the lawmaking National Assembly named as president and prime minister two business-oriented reformers — a corruption fighter as president and a prime minister who built a record of fostering economic growth as deputy prime minister. Meanwhile, the Walt Disney Co. has targeted Vietnam as part of its emerging-market growth strategy, and computer-chip behemoth Intel in 2006 announced plans to build a $300 million assembly plant in Ho Chi Minh City. All of this I know, by the way, simply from reading and forming opinions based on the preponderance of facts accumulated through the trove of research found online. The opinion may ultimately prove wrong or right, but it's not like you need an advanced degree in economics or some inside dope to see that Vietnam is pushing to boost its economy, join the world stage, and improve the lives of its citizens. Taken to the next step, that will eventually benefit the publicly traded Vietnamese companies looking to profit from the rise of industry and consumers. Ultimately, this is just basic research and analysis.

What you have in Vietnam is the emergence of a new Asian tiger. When Vietnam will really break out, who knows? Again, prognosticating economies is best left to the prognosticators—who may or may not be right, as well. Success as an investor doesn't mean you enter a country or buy into a company just as the curve ramps up. No one is lucky enough to do that consistently. Success generally requires patience. It means you're often early to the party, sitting around while the host pretties up the place. That's likely to be the case with Vietnam, as the government struggles with balancing capitalism and communism, as the country deals with rampant corruption, and as the locals grow into a new way of thinking and living. Bumps are bound to jostle the economy along the way, upset the stock market, and scare investors. Moreover, Vietnam will never be China; the population of vaguely 84 million is 15 times smaller than that of China and not large enough to generate the magnitude of excitement investors envision when they think about 1.3 billion potential Chinese consumers.

Then again, Vietnam doesn't have to be China to be a great destination for investors. Vietnam has plenty of long-term opportunities just growing into its own as a vibrant Asian economy. Banking, for instance, will certainly benefit, as it almost always does in emerging economies. So too will the typical infrastructure investments such as heavy construction, telecommunications, and utilities.

But can you invest in a place like Vietnam?

Let's go find out . . .

Type "Vietnam brokerage firms" into any Internet search engine. Using Google, the first link that pops up— chinese-school.netfirms.com—opens to the "Vietnamese Brokerage Firms List." Scanning the list, you'll see that the first firm that offers a Web address is Saigon Securities Incorporated. It can't be that easy, can it? Your first effort at unearthing a foreign broker—in one of the most underdeveloped Asian economies — and it's as simple as one Google search?

Well, not exactly.

But it's not much harder.

The website address listed is a dead link. But who gives up after one failed attempt? Google the name "Saigon Securities Incorporated" and the company's correct home page shows up atop the list. From there it's a game of hide-and-seek. The Saigon Securities home page is in Vietnamese, not terribly useful if you don't speak the language. Only a few countries in the world actually operate in English. Luckily for American investors, much of the finance world does. Many public companies and brokerage firms in foreign lands often operate shadow sites in English, and Saigon Securities is one of them. Typically, you'll find a small British Union Jack somewhere on the page, or maybe the letters ENG. Those indicate the path to the English pages. On Saigon Securities' home page the only two English words — "Select Language" — mark your target.

Inside the English site, way down at the bottom of the page, is the most important link: "Contact Us." Spend all the time you need playing around on a brokerage firm's website to get a feel for the services a firm offers, maybe poke around in whatever country or company research is available, but the "Contact Us" link is your ultimate destination. This is the communications link needed to determine whether you're a welcome investor. Saigon Securities offers electronic access to two branches—one in Ho Chi Minh City, one in Hanoi. I picked Hanoi, if only because I'd like to one day visit what I hear is a beautifully quaint, quiet northern Vietnamese city. And if I do, maybe I'd like to stop in and check on my account, if I ultimately decide to open one.

The e-mail I dispatched was largely identical to the one sent to Ord Minnett in New Zealand 11 years earlier:

Good day. I am a U.S. investor looking to own stocks in Vietnam, and I would like to know if Saigon Securities will accept the account of a U.S.-based investor. I am

particularly interested in online trading opportunities,
if they exist. If this is possible, please let me know.
Regards.

A few days later I had my reply:

Dear Mr. Opdyke, We are currently building online
trading system. You are welcome to have trading
account at Saigon Securities Inc. (SSI). At the moment,
SSI holds over 60% of foreign investors' accounts in
Vietnam. Please contact me for any further clarifi-
cation.

So, there it is. American investors can open an account
and trade stocks directly in Vietnam, of all places. As of 2007,
I'd yet to do so myself. The Vietnamese market as I write this is
expensive by my standards, and I'm waiting to see how the
online access works once it's operational. If it provides an
English option, I'll pursue an online account at some point,
since immediate access to your cash balance, stock holdings,
and instantaneous trading is the way to go in an electronic age.
Still, if online access is in Vietnamese only, then I'll just establish an account in which I e-mail my orders to a broker, since,
personally, I want access to an economy with as much promise
as Vietnam holds, albeit at much lower prices.

In all honesty, locating a local broker willing to work with
foreign investors doesn't always pan out, so your first attempt
may be shot down. Though far more brokers are far more willing to work with American investors these days, some still
don't or won't. A London firm sent me a message in early 2006
reporting that it didn't work as a private-client stockbroker for
foreigners and thus could not meet my needs. Another insisted
that its back-office systems would not allow it to comply with
SEC regulations — which don't exist, by the way — for handling
an account for a U.S. citizen.

No worries. Just keep e-mailing the local brokers you find
through Internet searches. There's always more than one in

each country. In fact, a week or so after the London brokerage firm dispatched its regrets, StockTrade, an online broker based in Edinburgh, Scotland, sent an e-mail saying it would be happy to work with an American. The note included the firm's commission schedule and a handy link to the application process.

A shortcut that works well in many markets: Search for the local stock exchange.

Type into any search engine "Budapest stock exchange" or "London stock exchange," or, if you've no clue where the exchange is located, replace the city with the country's name, since some countries — such as China, with its Shenzhen and Shanghai markets — have multiple exchanges, while others, such as Colombia's Bolsa de Valores de Colombia, aren't named for the capital city. Most exchange websites, though not all, have a link to the firms that make up their membership — the financial firms licensed to conduct business at the exchange. This list, under either a "Membership" or "Brokers" link, will include banks and even insurance companies from time to time, but you'll also find the names of the local brokerage firms and, typically, their Web address. That doesn't mean you'll capture all the local brokers that way, particularly the online-only firms, since the exchange members are often larger, bricks-and-mortar establishments. But it's a useful backup plan if you're having trouble finding brokerage firms in some country.

And if you still can't find a broker in a particular market willing to work with you, then think regionally.

On occasion, you will stumble upon the matryoshka dolls of the brokerage world — firms where, like the Russian nesting-dolls toy, what you see hides so much more. Take, for instance, Boom Securities in Hong Kong. The firm runs boom.com, a website that provides online access to trading in its home market — and then some. Aside from Hong Kong, boom.com provides online trading — in English — on 11 additional Asian exchanges stretching from the Sea of Japan up north to the Tasman Sea way down south: Australia, China (Shenzhen and Shanghai . . . one of the few accounts that offer this access), Indonesia, Japan, Malaysia, the Philippines, Singapore, South Korea, Taiwan, and Thailand. You don't need to convert currencies when trading between countries, and you can denominate the account in U.S. dollars, if you wish; or Hong Kong, Singapore, or Aussie dollars; or yen. The beauty of such breadth: In one account you've covered every major developed market in Asia except New Zealand, and all the key developing markets except Vietnam and India (and you already know New Zealand and Vietnam are available, though India is more problematic).

Finding one of these matryoshka firms is the electronic equivalent of unexpectedly finding a $100 bill in your jeans — you didn't know it existed and you weren't looking for it, but you know it's going to come in really handy.

Similar matryoshka-doll firms pop up elsewhere around the globe. Through Kim Eng Securities in Singapore you can trade the local market as well as Hong Kong and Malaysia. Directbroking.co.nz provides entry into New Zealand and Australia. From Budapest, Concorde Securities will trade for you across a vast stretch of Central Europe: Hungary, Poland, the Czech Republic, Slovakia, Romania, Croatia, and Estonia. Concorde's online account in 2007 was only available for Hungarian trading, but the firm's brokers operate well in English and you can phone, fax, or e-mail buy and sell orders for all the markets. On Gibraltar, a British peninsular colony on the southern tip of Spain, investorseurope.com lets you trade a huge swath of the world, buying and selling in every Western European and Scandinavian market; some of the emerging Central and Eastern European markets, including Russia and Latvia; and a few of Asia's larger exchanges, such as Australia and Hong Kong.

U.S. investors have the ability to trade stocks in the countries on the next page. Trading is available either directly through local brokerage firms in the country or through a regional brokerage firm that provdes multicountry access.

NORTH AMERICA

United States

Canada

Mexico

AUSTRALASIA

Hong Kong

Singapore

Japan

Thailand

Indonesia

Taiwan

South Korea

Malaysia

China

Philippines

Australia

New Zealand

Vietnam

EUROPE

United Kingdom

France

Germany

Austria

Italy

Spain

Netherlands

Luxembourg

Switzerland

Belgium

Ireland

Sweden

Finland

Norway
Denmark
Portugal
Greece
Russia
Ukraine
Kazakhstan
Kyrgyzstan
Tadjikistan
Estonia
Latvia
Lithuania
Poland
Turkey
Hungary
Romania
Croatia
Czech Republic
Slovakia

AFRICA/MIDDLE EAST

Egypt
Morocco
Tunisia
Sudan
South Africa
Namibia
Botswana
Lebanon
Oman
Jordan
Kuwait
Qatar
Bahrain
United Arab Emirates

SOUTH AMERICA/LATIN AMERICA

Brazil

Peru

Aside from sharply shrinking the number of accounts you need in order to trade the world, matryoshka firms can come in handy for one key reason: At the moment you open a boom.com account, for instance, your only interest in Asia might be Hong Kong; yet later you come across news items in your research that stoke your interest in South Korean or Malaysian stocks. Far easier it is to have an account already in place through which you can buy South Korean or Malaysian shares instead of having to go about the process — again — of finding a local broker and opening an account. With a matryoshka firm, you're good to go whenever the need strikes.

Through the years, I have continued to expand the number of countries in which I operate accounts, largely because so many are now open that previously shunned Americans. I also routinely contact brokerage firms in countries where I do not have accounts but might want to one day, looking for those that will cater to a U.S. investor. And when I'm looking to invest in a specific country I cannot currently access through my accounts, I go hunting specifically for matryoshka firms in that region, since I'd rather have access to multiple markets where possible.

Even today, not all brokers want to muck about with foreign accounts because their back-office systems and procedures aren't necessarily conducive to transoceanic clients. Other firms don't mind Americans in theory but aren't willing to handle relatively small accounts, so they require large balances, sometimes on the order of $100,000. Of those that offer online trading, their sites often aren't in English, which isn't a problem if you speak the language but can be a significant hindrance if you don't. Below is a partial list of brokerage firms that will work with Americans, and some of the markets in which they operate. It's not a complete list by any stretch, and the list changes on occasion as brokerage firms close or merge and others open. This roster will, however, give you an idea of firms you might contact to meet your interest in a particular market.

A sampling of overseas and domestic brokerage firms that offer access to U.S. investors—either through online trading or e-mail/phone calls—and some of the markets in which you can trade:

FIRM (WEBSITE)	HOME MARKET	MARKETS AVAILABLE
Boom Securities (www.boom.com)	Hong Kong	Hong Kong, Japan, Australia, Thailand, South Korea, Taiwan, China, Singapore, Philippines, Malaysia, Indonesia
Kim Eng Securities (www.ketrade.com.sg)	Singapore	Singapore, Malaysia, Hong Kong
Direct Broking (www.directbroking.co.nz)	New Zealand	New Zealand, Australia
InvestorsEurope (www.investorseurope.com)	Gibraltar	Throughout Western Europe, Scandinavia, and the Baltic trio, as well as Russia, Greece, and Poland, across to Australia and Hong Kong
Concorde Securities (www.concordesecurities.hu)	Hungary	Hungary, Poland, Romania, Croatia, Czech Republic, Slovakia, Estonia
Saigon Securities Inc. (ssi.com.vn)	Vietnam	Vietnam
StockTrade (stocktrade.co.uk)	United Kingdom	United Kingdom

ArabFinance.com (www.arabfinance.com)	Egypt	Egypt, though other Middle Eastern exchanges are expected to be added
BoE Securities (www.boe.co.za)	South Africa	South Africa, Namibia
Stockbrokers Botswana (www.stockbrokers-botswana.com)	Botswana	Botswana
Interactive Brokers (www.interactivebrokers .com)	USA	Roughly a dozen markets, generally the largest in Western Europe and Asia
Schahin Securities (www.schahinsecurities .com.br)	Brazil	Brazil
Essham Securities (www.esshamsecurities .com)	United Arab Emirates	Dubai, Abu Dhabi
Actinver (www.bursamex .com.mx)	Mexico	Mexico
EFG-Hermes (www.hermesonline .com)	Egypt	Online: Egypt and United Arab Emirates; offline: Morocco, Tunisia, Sudan, Jordan, Lebanon, Kuwait, Qatar, Bahrain, Oman
EverTrade Direct Brokerage (www.everbank.com)	USA	More than a score of markets stretching from Canada to Finland, Luxembourg to Mexico, Peru to the Philippines to South Africa
E*Trade (www.etrade.com)	USA	Canada, France, Germany, Hong Kong, Japan, United Kingdom

Ktrade (www.ktrade.ro)	Romania	Romania
Vanguard (www.vanguard.ro)	Romania	Romania, Bulgaria, Austria; Croatia and Ukraine to be added
Visor Capital (www.visocap.com)	Kazakhstan	Kazakhstan, Kyrgyzstan, Tadjikistan

You'll see from the list that several firms overlap each other in their market coverage. From that you might think: Why have two or three accounts when one will open doors in multiple markets? The answer: Costs.

Matryoshka firms sometimes charge extra fees for holding securities in other markets. Kim Eng, a Singapore brokerage firm, charges a few dollars every quarter as a custodial fee for securities purchased in Hong Kong, for instance. Yet you avoid those fees by holding the same Hong Kong shares at Hong Kong's boom.com. Operating out of multiple accounts, then, can make some sense financially.

Still, the matryoshka firms are the most efficient means of gaining broad access to global markets, and they are particularly useful when they provide English-language trading in markets that are all but impossible to trade in otherwise. Not to pick on boom.com again, but along with all those other Asian markets, the firm lets you trade directly on the Shenzhen and Shanghai exchanges, access you won't find in many other places. If you're a China bull who wants broader access to the Middle Kingdom than provided by the ADRs or China funds available in the United States, then Boom is beneficial.

CSN, CDA, AND FIN . . . ALL AROUND THE WORLD YOU'RE JUST ANOTHER NUMBER

In the United States, opening a brokerage account requires only that you, well, open a brokerage account. Overseas, that's not always so.

When you buy stock through a U.S. broker, and assuming you don't request that the actual shares be placed in your name and delivered to you, the shares are held in "street name." That just means the brokerage firm aggregates all the shares of some particular company its clients own and keeps those shares in the brokerage firm's name—what's known as street name. Internal, electronic records detail which clients own how many shares of that company.

By contrast, many countries require that you register your shares in some central location, usually a central depository. In Croatia, for instance, your brokerage account must be tied to the Central Depository Agency, where ownership information is recorded electronically for all Croatian securities. Accounts in Singapore are likewise linked to that nation's Central Depository, and Singaporean brokerage firms customarily offer a "nominee service" to foreign investors. This is similar to the street-name concept in the United States, the difference being that you must apply for a depository agency subaccount so that your Singaporean shares can be kept safely overseas. To trade in New Zealand you need two numbers: a Common Shareholder Number (CSN) and a Faster Identification Number (FIN). The shares you buy in New Zealand are held in your name by the registries. These registries, not the brokerage firm, communicate with you directly regarding dividend announcements, financial results, and various corporate actions. You need the CSN so that the registries know who you are. Separately, the FIN operates much like an ATM personal identification number; you need it when you sell your shares.

Obtaining the additional numbers and registering in the various places you must register is not terribly difficult or time consuming, and you generally don't even need to know this requirement must be met. Brokerage firms universally will inform you of this need when you open your account and, in most cases, will do the legwork for you. Just ask up front about the necessity of these additional registration requirements if you want to be sure your account is set up properly.

DIY OR TLC?

What type of account do you want?

As I mentioned earlier, when I funded my first overseas account in New Zealand in 1995, I had one choice: broker-managed. No online-trading options existed. The only problem that ever created, if you call it a problem, was a broker questioning my stock selection when the stocks I wanted to buy were not on his firm's "buy" list. I politely shooed him away and continued with my plan.

Today online trading proliferates. Every account I own functions electronically, even that New Zealand account. Still, not all foreign firms offer online trading—or at least not in English—and not all investors want it. So, you have to decide what type of account you desire, then balance that against what's available.

For do-it-yourself investors, look for an online trading link, sometimes called a "direct" link, on the foreign-firm websites you visit. Even then, however, you might still be forced into a broker-managed account if the online version is available only in a local tongue that you do not speak. If that's the case, ask if you can pay a reduced commission for your trades, particularly if you will not be seeking stock-selection advice and won't be requiring much effort from the broker aside from placing an order every now and then. Many firms will offer discounted rates. Some will not.

For folks in need of a little hand-holding when trading overseas, almost every firm will provide you with a broker who can proffer advice and dispense research. You will, however, generally pay more in commissions to cover those costs. How much more depends entirely on the firm you choose, the size of your account or your trading volume, and where in the world you're buying and selling. If the firm's website doesn't list the commission breakdown—and not all do—just ask for it in your correspondence.

WIRED

There is something unsettling when you wire cash around the world. No matter how many times I do it, I always leave my local bank wondering whether my money will arrive at the intended destination or whether a bank teller might mistakenly transpose some account number or routing number and send my money to a village bank in some lawless country from which I will never be able to retrieve my dollars. Certainly that's a melodramatic take on reality, since a bungled wire transfer can be rectified fairly easily. Still, you can't help but feel that way at times.

To date, my money has never misfired.

Unless you plan to visit every country where you want to open an account—and unless you plan to carry a huge wad of cash with you—wiring money from your U.S. bank account is the safest, most efficient, most convenient way to fund a foreign brokerage account. Once your overseas brokerage account is open, ask your brokerage firm to send you wire-transfer instructions; some automatically include these details when they welcome you aboard as a client. Just take those instructions to your local bank and request the money be sent—that's as difficult as the process gets. You're likely to pay a few dollars as a wiring fee, typically nothing more than about $40, though depending on the type of bank account you have and the relationship with your banker, the transaction may cost you nothing.

The only real decision you'll need to make is what currency you want your foreign brokerage account denominated in, since many firms often give you a choice among the local scrip and a few of the world's major currencies. Where you invest will generally determine what denominations are available, assuming you don't want your account based on the local money. In Asia, options usually revolve around the yen and the U.S., Hong Kong, Singapore, and Australian dollars. In Europe, it's commonly the British pound, the U.S. dollar, or the euro, or sometimes the Swiss franc.

MONEY IN THE BANK

I received my first foreign dividend check in the summer of 1996 — $90, from what was then Fisher & Paykel Industries in New Zealand. The key words there are "in New Zealand." The check, logically enough, was denominated in New Zealand dollars. To the teller at what was then a NationsBank branch in Dallas, Texas, that check could just as well have been denominated in Persian darics from the 6th century BC. She refused to accept it. I reminded her that this very same bank branch just several months prior had wired my money to New Zealand, and thus the bank obviously knew how to handle foreign-currency transactions. She wouldn't budge. "Not going to happen" was her exact quote. The bank, she concluded, didn't have the systems in place to provide currency conversions inside a retail checking account.

I e-mailed Ted the Broker with my dilemma. He replied a day later that Ord Minnett couldn't accept the check for deposit into my brokerage account, either, because the document was marked "Do Not Cross," a notation meaning I could not simply sign the check over to the brokerage firm. In simple terms, I had to deposit this check into an account that was both in my name and denominated in New Zealand dollars — essentially, a New Zealand bank account.

I did not have a New Zealand bank account.

When I opened my Ord Minnett account, I was a relative oddity for the firm. "We don't get many Americans wanting to invest their money down here," Ted once e-mailed me. "Most of your mates don't even know what New Zealand is, much less where we are." As such, he didn't think to warn me that I would need a bank account as well. But a New Zealand bank account would be the only solution to the problem, he informed. And over the next few days he helped me establish with the Bank of New Zealand a "call account" linked to my brokerage account. With that call account — essentially a basic savings account — I was able to deposit that first check and then arrange to have all future dividends directed there.

Just as you'll sometimes need to tie your brokerage account to a central depository or registry, you'll also sometimes find in parts of the financial world a need to tie a local bank account to your local brokerage account. Otherwise, your dividend checks will flow directly to your American mailbox, and the likelihood is great that your bank teller will laugh at your attempt to deposit or cash a check denominated in, say, Turkish lira. As well, unless you have a bank account, the proceeds from your stock sales may sit idle in your brokerage account, earning nothing while the funds are not invested.

This need for a local bank isn't universal. With many brokers your dividends land in your brokerage account and earn competitive, local interest rates, similar to the process in the states. Just be sure to ask your foreign firm how dividends are handled: Are they sent directly to you in the United States, or can they be directly routed into your brokerage account? If not, ask if you can arrange a call account or some other bank account tied to your brokerage account.

In some cases, if you own investments in Country B through a brokerage firm in Country A, you will have to set up a bank account tied to the shareholder registry in Country B, where the company you own is based. For instance, for years I've owned shares of Aristocrat Leisure Ltd., a major player in the business of building the gaming machines populating casinos from Las Vegas to Macao and the pachinko parlors popular throughout Japan. At the time I bought the shares, Aristocrat was not paying dividends. That changed a few years later, and one day I found in my mailbox a dividend check from Australia. Again, the bank I was dealing with at that time, Bank of New York, would not accept a check issued in a foreign denomination, though I expected as much.

I had changed brokers in New Zealand by this time, and my new firm, just as with the Bank of New York, would not accept a check denominated in Aussie dollars that, again, was marked "Do Not Cross." I returned the check to the Australian share registry and told them of my dilemma and asked that the money be directly deposited into my New Zealand brokerage account.

Not going to happen, I was essentially told. The registry could not directly deposit across national borders. In a series of e-mail exchanges, the share registry told me that my only option was to open a bank account in Australia, and then the registry company could arrange to have all dividends deposited there directly. Thus it is that I came to own a bank account in Sydney at the George Street branch of Australia and New Zealand Bank—a branch into which I have never set foot.

If I ever hope to see that money, though, that shortcoming will have to change.

While ANZ Bank makes easy work of opening a bank account from thousands of miles away, the bank makes withdrawing those funds measurably more difficult. To reclaim your cash, you must eventually show up in person at the bank branch in Australia to provide proof of your existence. It's not like I'm lamenting a trip to Australia, a country I've wanted to visit for years. It's just that as an investor with international aspirations, you need to know that in some places the process can be much more difficult than it need be.

SPEAKING OF DIVIDENDS

In some instances, you may not want to receive the dividends as cash but would rather have that cash reinvested in the same company's stock. That, too, is possible—though not universally—if you contact the broker or share registry to make necessary arrangements. For instance, I am a long-term bull on Bank of East Asia. Aside from being the largest independent bank in Hong Kong, BEA is expanding its network of retail banking in China and has branched into wealth management for local Chinese citizens. China's government in 2006 launched a program to let mainland Chinese invest some of their savings overseas through select foreign banks—a sweeping change for China, given the government's traditional intolerance for allowing the renminbi to leave the country in any real amount. BEA was one of the first to receive the necessary license and should benefit as local residents look to diversify their savings into investments priced in Hong Kong and U.S. dollars and euros.

Instead of having to find a way to put to work the dividends BEA pays me, I'd just as soon put that money back into a company I have some confidence in over the long haul. I sent a brief e-mail to my brokerage firm's help desk asking if I could leave standing orders for all my BEA dividends to flow back into BEA stock, and the firm arranged it without fuss.

On occasion, however, your standing orders to have dividends directly deposited to a bank account or reinvested in company stock will misfire. I once received a fairly healthy special dividend from Lion Nathan, an Australian brewer that I bought when it was originally based in New Zealand. For years the dividends flowed routinely into my Bank of New Zealand call account. But for unknown reasons, the registry company mailed that check to me in the states — and getting those funds into my New Zealand bank account took more than a month.

Returning the check to the share registry, I explained in a letter their mistake and requested that the funds be credited, as usual, to my call account. I also sent an e-mail to the registry to let it know the check was back in the mail, and why. (Always send an e-mail when you put a check in the mail or when you wire funds. You want to alert the firm that your money is on the way so that the appropriate folks know to be on the lookout for the cash and where this money should go when it arrives.)

Something, I knew, was amiss, however, when three weeks after mailing the check to New Zealand the special dividend had not yet dropped into my call account, which I monitor online on occasion or when I've sent money to be deposited. Historically, two weeks has been plenty of time for dividend checks and other correspondence to reach one of the world's southernmost brokerage firms. But I had a ten-day business trip to Asia commencing and I figured I'd give the check that much more time to clear. I continued to track my call account online every few days from Japan and China; the cash never showed up. Finally, I e-mailed both the registry and the brokerage firm to alert them to the problem. Both immediately began their detective work, and within one day the registry informed me that the money had indeed been wired to the brokerage firm. In turn, the brokerage firm said it had found an unallocated wire equal to the missing amount. The firm credited it to my account, with interest going back to the day the wire arrived. The problem: In wiring that special dividend into my call account, the registry failed to include my account number on the transfer.

Don't read that example — or the one about managing foreign dividend checks, or needing to unexpectedly open an Australian bank account, or having to travel thousands of miles to reclaim my money from Australia one day, or having to list your stocks with registries and central depositories — as horror stories. They're not nearly as significant as they appear. I'm shining an unnaturally bright light on them to provide a fair assessment of the kinds of issues you will occasionally confront when you dare to be an international investor in the truest sense of the term. Yes, each matter requires a bit of legwork, but in the course of a dozen years investing overseas, I'll bet that cumulatively I've devoted less than a week to sorting out problems — and the returns I have accumulated have made those efforts worth the time.

THE LOCAL BAZAAR

Though this book is focused exclusively on stocks, stocks are not the only opportunities you have when you open a foreign brokerage account. Government and corporate bonds, mutual funds, certificates of deposit, local stock options, and even local initial public offerings (IPOs) are frequently — though not always — available. If you want, you can even "short" local stocks, meaning you can bet on a stock's decline by selling shares in companies you own and repurchasing them later at, you hope, a lower price, pocketing the difference as profit—essentially a sell-high, buy-low strategy.

This wide variety of offerings has several advantages. In the early part of the 21st century, as U.S. interest rates plunged to historical lows and bank savings accounts, short-term CDs, and money market funds were yielding less than 1%, you could park your dollars in other parts of the world and pocket far meatier returns. A simple savings account in New Zealand at that time paid between 5% and 6%. Kiwi corporate bonds were up near 8%, while similar bonds at home were closer to 4%. Those cash and bond opportunities are an excellent way to directly own currency without taking on the earnings risk inherent in a stock, or the volatility inherent in trading currencies. Of course, you will be taking on currency risk, but presumably you're investing overseas because you want that exposure to foreign currencies as a hedge against the U.S. dollar.

In the United States, while you can put your money into some pretty good foreign mutual funds, not all will dip as deeply into the local market as do the local mutual funds that know their backyard better. Plus, you'll find a much wider breadth of options among the local funds, such as currency funds, which are not common in the United States.

As a U.S. investor, the only foreign IPOs that come across your radar screen are the big-company ADR listings that make a splash on the New York Stock Exchange. Generally, though, as a small-time investor you likely won't be able to horn in on that action; all the pension funds and mutual funds and hedge funds ordinarily grab the shares first because of their ties to the investment banks that underwrite the IPOs. Overseas, though, you often can buy into many of the IPOs. Some of the bigger ones can still be impossible for individual investors because of the huge demand among the local mutual funds and hedge funds. Still, if you're an investor who likes to invest in the IPO market, an overseas brokerage account will give you access to smaller and medium-sized companies that never show up in the states.

You will, however, stumble upon certain markets occasionally where you're locked out of certain investments for various reasons. Hong Kong, for instance, won't allow U.S. clients to buy into local IPOs. Other brokerage firms don't make a market in mutual funds, and so if that's what you want to own, you're out of luck.

Once you find a brokerage firm willing to work with you, ask for a list of investments you can buy in your account, or troll the website, where firms routinely detail the services and products they offer.

RED TAPE

For the record, neither the U.S. Internal Revenue Service nor the Securities and Exchange Commission cares what you do with your money. Really. They do not care.

So long as you pay any appropriate taxes and fill out the appropriate paperwork when necessary, U.S. government agencies by and large couldn't care less if you send your money to Brazil or Botswana.

That, however, contradicts what you will sometimes hear from foreign brokers.

Some firms insist that they cannot do business with Americans because SEC rules or IRS tax laws prevent them from allowing a U.S. investor to open an account overseas. Don't believe it. It is simply not true.

The IRS imposes no regulations on foreign brokerage firms that do not advertise or solicit business from U.S. investors. Instead, the regulations are imposed on U.S. investors who themselves go in search of brokerage firms and banks overseas. During each tax season, you must report any foreign profits, interest, and dividends on your tax return, as well as fill out and mail to the Treasury Department a simple document — Form TD90-22 — detailing what accounts you own and where, when valued at more than $10,000 in aggregate.

In other words: If you seek out foreign bank or brokerage

accounts yourself, if you report the existence of those accounts to the Treasury Department each year (assuming that's necessary based on the size of the accounts), and so long as you report the dividends and capital gains you earn and then pay the appropriate U.S. taxes, *neither the SEC nor the IRS gives a flying flip about where in the world you send your money.*

Of course, that doesn't mean you'll be able to convince a recalcitrant foreign brokerage firm that it's dead wrong and that it should, therefore, open its doors to your money. That hasn't yet worked for me — I generally get back curt replies of the "tough luck, Yank" variety, particularly from Western European firms — so good luck trying. Still, you at least know what the truth is when you hear the misinformation.

For most investors, the red tape you'll most often confront centers on taxes, both at home and abroad. As I mentioned above, you will owe Uncle Sam taxes on all dividends, interest, and capital gains you book in a given year; if you have capital losses, you can write those off up to the annual limit the IRS allows and then carry forward into the future tax years any remaining losses, just as with capital losses you amass in U.S. stocks.

Some countries don't tax foreigners because they want to provide an incentive for direct foreign investment. In other instances, companies cover all or a significant portion of the tax paid by adding in a special dividend (see "Supplementary Dividend" below). In most countries, however, you will pay taxes there, too, though you won't have to fill out tax returns. Generally, those countries pull the taxes out of the income stream. So, for instance, if you receive $100 in dividends from some investment in a country that imposes a tax of 20% on dividends, well, you'll see a dividend payment land in your account for $80. That $20 tax you paid you'll report on your U.S. tax return.

Be aware that the United States and a variety of countries participate in a treaty under which the tax on foreign investors is reduced by a certain amount. Switzerland, for example, takes 35% of all dividend payments as a tax, but under the treaty that shrinks to 15%. This reduction doesn't happen automatically; you must fill out the necessary paperwork and show the appropriate documents to prove that you're a U.S. investor who owns the local shares. That typically requires no more effort that reminding the brokerage firm to include with your account application whatever paperwork is necessary.

The real challenge that can arise is gathering all the information on capital gains, dividends, and interest accumulated during the year that you'll need to report on your U.S. tax return. Most countries don't operate on a U.S. timetable, meaning they're not in the business of providing tax data to you in time for an April 15 tax-filing deadline. That's not much of a problem, though. During the year you will receive in the mail or by way of periodic e-mails a record of trade-settlement receipts when you buy and sell shares, as well as a report when dividends are paid. Banks and brokerage firms will also dispatch to you monthly or quarterly account statements that likewise detail dividends received and interest earned. Stashing those reports in a file folder when they arrive doesn't require much effort. Then, you just pull them out at tax time and you're pretty much good to go.

You may need to contact the brokerage firm in late January or February and request that it e-mail you a copy of December's activity, just to be sure you have the full year's data, since the final month's information may not make it to you as quickly as you'd like. But requesting that information has never caused me trouble. During a cross-country move one year, I lost several months of bank account and dividend statements from one of my foreign accounts. I e-mailed the bank and the brokerage firm, and within a few days each replied with a history for the year— and a courteous letter thanking me for being a customer.

LINGUA FRANCA

Just about anywhere you go overseas, it helps to understand certain words in the local language. Maybe that means knowing that "hola" is hello in Spain or that "the lift" is an elevator at your British hotel.

Investing is no different. There are certain words and operational realities that are idiosyncratic to certain markets and regions. You'll likely figure them out along the way once you're interacting in some particular stock market for a while, but you might as well know about them now so that you can shorten the learning curve.

Shareholder reports: One of the more dramatic differences in owning foreign stocks is that you will not generally receive financial reports on a quarterly basis, as you do with U.S. stocks. The rest of the world, by and large, is not so focused on such a short window of operations. Instead of providing a look at the finances every three months, many foreign companies report their numbers semiannually. As such, you will receive half-yearly and annual reports. Not unlike the quarterly and annual reports distributed by U.S. companies, the half-yearly reports will typically be small pamphlets, while the annual reports will be a thick, glossy recount of the past year. It's not a given, though, that those reports will arrive in your mailbox. I have yet to receive an annual or half-yearly report, as they're called, from any holdings in Asia (though I do download them from the company websites). You will sometimes have to inform the company, its shareholder registry, or your brokerage firm that you want to receive the reports.

Board lots: In the United States you can call a broker right now and buy just a single share of Microsoft if you wish. That's not so in some countries. In markets such as Singapore, Malaysia, Hong Kong, and elsewhere, you must trade a certain number of shares, generally called a "board lot." The board lot in, for instance, Hong Kong–listed China Gas Holdings, a supplier of natural-gas services in China, is 200 shares, meaning you'll buy the stock in multiples of 200 shares. Some board lots are 50 shares, some are 3,000 shares. Some are one share.

You'll stumble upon this when you place an order to buy shares in some country and the broker or your online firm replies with a note — or a pop-up box on your computer when you place the order—that your order could not be filled. In most cases the reason is because you did not adhere to board-lot requirements. You'll generally find board lots spelled out for each company on each exchange's website.

Gearing: All companies provide an analysis of how much long-term debt they have on their balance sheets as a percentage of shareholder equity. U.S. investors know it as the "debt-to-equity ratio." In many parts of Asia and the southern Pacific, however, "gearing" is the word you will come across instead in company reports and, often, in management's analysis of how things are going. The calculation: long-term debt divided by shareholder equity, both of which are found on a company's balance sheet.

Dividends: Nothing confusing linguistically about dividends. Nevertheless, while an increasing number of U.S. companies started paying dividends after a variety of corporate earnings scandals in the early part of this century, companies in many foreign markets are much more likely to pay you a dividend to begin with, and the yield is frequently higher than in the American market. For income-oriented investors, then, looking for yield outside the U.S. can be a way to increase cash flow, since it's possible to find well-established foreign firms paying dividends that equate to yields of 7% or more, substantially above the typical U.S. stock. Certainly, though, you must take into account currency fluctuations.

There are two schools of thought on the value of this. One argument holds that it's better for companies to keep that money and put it to use in growing the business. The counterargument holds that investors are better served receiving dividends as their share of the annual earnings stream. There's merit in both arguments. Personally, I'd rather receive the dividend. In a world where accounting rules do not necessarily reflect financial reality because of all the arcane and bizarre ways companies are required to reflect income and expenses, dividends are about the only financial item that can't be jacked around. A check in your mailbox or a direct deposit to your brokerage account is real money and proof that some level of real earnings do exist.

Scrip Dividend: You likely know this as a "dividend reinvestment program" with stateside stocks — a program in which you choose to accept all or a part of your dividend in the form of additional shares of the company. The same scheme is available globally as a "scrip dividend," though not every company will offer the arrangement. In some instances, companies will provide the additional shares at a discount of 5% or maybe even 10%. But even where scrip dividends are an option, they may not be an option for foreign investors, so don't be surprised if you're rebuffed by some companies.

Supplementary Dividend: Most U.S. investors won't be familiar with this — an extra dividend paid alongside the regular dividend to help cover the cost of the taxes. Supplementary dividends are generally paid to nonresident shareholders, i.e., foreign investors. In New Zealand, for instance, Macquarie Goodman, a property development and management firm, paid a dividend of 2.1 cents per share in September 2006. New Zealand's tax authority, Inland Revenue, wants a piece of that income and imposed a 15% nonresident withholding tax. To compensate foreign investors for the taxes paid to New Zealand, Macquarie Goodman also paid a supplementary dividend of 0.1612 cent to wholly or partly offset the tax bite.

It works like this: Assume you own 5,000 shares of Macquarie Goodman. The firm pays you that dividend of 2.1 cents per share, or $105, and then tacks on that additional 0.1612 cent per share, or $8.06. The gross dividend, then, is $113.06. Inland Revenue then taxes the amount at 15%, or $16.96. Your net distribution is $96.10. Without the supplementary dividend, you would have received $89.25.

Franking/Imputation Credits: You'll see this a lot coming out of Australia and New Zealand. Essentially, this is a mechanism to avoid double taxation. In the United States, a company is taxed on its profits and then the portion of those profits distributed to shareholders as dividends is taxed again at the shareholder level. Thus, the same dollar is taxed twice. Australia addresses that with franking or imputation credits. When an Aussie firm pays a dividend, stockholders also receive a franking credit equal to the amount of taxes the company has already paid on the money. In effect, each dividend comes with a tax credit attached so that corporate profits aren't taxed twice (maybe U.S. lawmakers can learn something from Down Under?). Credits can either be fully franked, partially franked, or unfranked. Fully franked means the entire dividend carries a credit. Partially franked means, as you would expect, that only a portion of the dividend carries the credit. Unfranked is self-explanatory.

This won't help you much in the United States, since the IRS taxes dividend income regardless of country of origin. But you should at least be familiar with the term since you are certain to wonder about it the first time you see the term on a dividend statement.

Stock Price: I mentioned this earlier, but it's worth repeating here—what's "normal" among stock prices varies from country to country. You'll find lots of stocks in New Zealand, for instance, priced at just a few local dollars per share. The same goes for many countries in Southeast Asia as well as the UK and Australia. That's the investment-culture norm for those markets, so don't read into it that the companies are speculative penny stocks, which is what they'd be seen as at those price levels in the states.

Conversely, prices in other counties are huge in local currency terms. South Korea's Daegu Bank, for instance, was priced at more than 15,000 Korean won in the fall of 2006. In Austria, Germany, and Switzerland, you'll come across numerous stocks priced into the hundreds of euros and francs per share. In Bulgaria, stocks often trade in thousands, and even tens of thousands, of lev, the local currency.

In either case—high price or low—the real measures of value remain the same: price-to-earnings, price-to-sales, price-to-cash flow, price-to-book value. All things equal, two stocks both trading at a price/earnings ratio of 12 have the same value to investors, regardless of whether their nominal prices are 2 Australian dollars or 20,000 Japanese yen.

Stock symbols: As an investor, you likely know Microsoft by its New York Stock Exchange symbol, "MSFT." You might know Anheuser-Busch, the big brewer of Budweiser beer, as "BUD." Overseas, symbols aren't always so easy to remember . . . largely because some markets aren't using letters but numbers. Hong Kong's global trading and retailing giant Li & Fung Group, for instance, is known locally on the Stock Exchange of Hong Kong as "0494." In Tokyo, Toyota Motor Corp. (traded in New York under the relatively obvious symbol TM) is listed under the significantly less obvious symbol "7203."

Most markets use letters, not numbers. But just be aware that several don't. In fact, some, among them Singapore, use both. DBS Group, one of Asia's largest banking concerns, trades on the Singapore exchange as "D05." Jardine Cycle & Carriage, a leading distributor and dealer of autos, trades under the perplexing symbol "C07."

Accounting Rules: Essentially there are two major standards by which the world's companies report their financial results to investors. Some companies, including most of those in the United States and some foreign firms, rely on Generally Accepted Accounting Principles, or GAAP. Much of the rest of the world, particularly the European Union, Japan, and, increasingly, South America, use International Financial Reporting Standards, or IFRS.

The two sets of rules differ in various ways, but unless you are an accountant, those differences are largely arcane. What you need to know as an individual investor is that IFRS and GAAP are basically interchangeable in terms of credibility.

The European Parliament mandates that public companies in the European Union use IFRS, all the major accounting firms have accountants on staff schooled in IFRS, and the SEC is moving toward accepting IFRS-based financial reports instead of requiring that U.S.-listed foreign firms reconcile their accounts to meet GAAP standards.

In short, if a company you're researching reports its results according to IFRS, don't worry that the accounting is somehow inferior to U.S. standards or that the numbers are sketchy. Some of the world's biggest companies use IFRS. Moreover, talk to accountants and portfolio managers around the world and they'll tell you that both accounting principles have their strengths and shortcomings, and both are moving progressively toward each other. As long as a company uses a reputable accounting firm and either GAAP or IFRS rules, you can generally have faith in the numbers. You'll know which firm is auditing a company because the annual report will almost always include an auditor's letter. The big global accounting firms to look for include names such as Pricewater-houseCoopers, Deloitte Touche, Grant Thornton, KPMG, Ernst & Young, and BDO. There are others; you just need to do a smidgeon of research online to find out if the firm auditing the company you're researching is reputable.

Don't misinterpret those words. None of that is to imply that overseas accounting presents no worries. As investors in even industrialized countries have seen (Enron in the United States; Parmalat in Italy; Royal Ahold in the Netherlands), corporate chieftains are quite adept at doctoring the accounts to make their businesses look more attractive or, in the worst cases, to steal from shareholders. Particularly in frontier markets you must be vigilant about the accounting. Companies in freshly emerging countries operate in environments often protected by government regulations, with loose standards, even looser regulatory agencies, and audited by local firms that don't apply rules as rigorously as do the respected international firms. In other instances, foreign companies are public only in name. Though they're listed on an exchange, they're controlled by the founding family, and those families still run the company like it's their personal financial fiefdom, in the process trampling all over shareholder rights simply because they can. And in some countries, you'll find former state-owned industries now listed on stock exchanges yet still run by the previous managers who still think like state bureaucrats and who have no compunction jimmying with the numbers to keep their jobs secure.

So, yes, there's always that possibility that some company you own overseas fabricates its numbers, that the fabrication comes to light, and that dismayed investors pummel the stock. Truthfully, though, that's a risk you face in the U.S. stock market as well.

Look, if the people paid large dollars to weed through a company's finances can't unearth the illicit dealings of a corrupt management team, then the average investor isn't likely to either. Regardless of what emerging market or developed country you invest in, the best you can do at some point is believe in the auditors and have some faith in the fact that most executives are honest and spend their days trying to make a bigger, better company. Otherwise, there's no reason to invest in any company at all—even in the states.

FOREIGN FINANCIAL REPORTS: DOLLARS AND SENSE

Pay close attention to the currency a company uses in its financial reports. Particularly in developing markets you'll find that the finances aren't necessarily reported in the local currency. With English-based reports, companies will sometimes use the U.S. dollar as the base currency. In Singapore and Hong Kong you'll sometimes come across companies that report in Chinese renminbi.

The problem arises because the stock is generally priced in local bills. And when the finances are in one currency and the stock price in another, well, you can see how that might just foil your research, particularly when calculating P/E ratios and such.

You might come across a Singaporean company you like, for instance, and find that its stock is trading at, say, three Singapore dollars (S$3) per share. You read through the company's annual report and see that it earned 30 cents a share last year. Based on that, the stock might seem fairly cheap at just 10 times earnings. But if that 30 cents is actually in renminbi, your calculations are way off. Thirty renminbi was the equivalent of just six Singaporean cents at the end of 2006.

Suddenly that stock that seemed relatively cheap at 10 times earnings is substantially more dear at 50 times earnings. So pay attention to the currency a company is using to reports its financial results.

CHAPTER 4

GETTING AROUND

The Art (and Science) of Picking Great Stocks Outside America

The science of investing overseas resides in opening the necessary accounts, and that's all a matter of logistics. The art lies in picking the companies you want to own.

If I mention such names as General Electric, Pepsi, McDonald's, IBM, Ford, Pfizer, and Continental Airlines, I'll bet every American reading those names will instantly know those companies or at least have some familiarity with what they do. You grow up hearing the names, shopping the stores, eating at the restaurants, using the products, and buying the services of American companies, so you instinctively understand their business to a certain degree when you're an investor. Familiarity breeds comfort and gives you a base of historical knowledge when you're looking for investments in the states. Want to own drug stocks because all those graying baby boomers will be popping pills to stay active, healthy, and amorous late into life? You reflexively know to look at pharmaceutical companies such as Pfizer, Merck, Bristol-Myers Squibb, and Johnson & Johnson, among others.

But if I mention Alliance Boots plc, Türk Hava Yollari, or MTN, you probably won't recognize that Boots is a leading drugstore chain in Britain; that Türk Hava Yollari, better known to the English-speaking world as Turkish Airlines, is one of the fastest-growing airlines in Europe and serves one of the most heavily touristed countries on Earth; and that MTN is South Africa's leading mobile-phone company and a major player in some of the world's most rapidly expanding markets for cell phones, namely, Africa and the Middle East.

American investors don't recognize the names of most foreign companies or a firm's line of business for obvious reasons — we don't interact with foreign economies on a daily basis and, as such, don't see the MTN ads all over Johannesburg and Cape Town. What seems exotic and unfamiliar leads to a certain sense of trepidation, which is understandable, though in the end limits your profit potential. Moreover, investors might wonder why some particular foreign company has strong growth prospects in its market when in the United States the same industry is flea-bitten, nonexistent, or disintegrating.

Ever heard of China Sky Chemical Fibre Co.? There's not much reason anyone outside the nylon-fiber market ever would. The company, based in China's coastal Fujian province and traded on the Singapore Stock Exchange, is a key player in the high end of the nylon-yarn market in mainland China. Textile companies are long-suffering in America, where the industry has been in decline for decades along the Atlantic seaboard. Not so in Asia, where much of the world's clothing is made. World demand fuels Chinese textile growth in particular. China, as of 2006, had more than 100 companies working in the nylon and polyester business in some fashion. China Sky is the largest of the bunch, with about 6% of the market.

Trivial information to many; a potential investment idea to others who see that along with supplying the world, China Sky must also supply internal demand since, as with beer, synthetic-fiber consumption increases alongside personal wealth.

Picking individual stocks to own, whether China Sky or MTN, is the most significant skill any investor buying individual stocks develops — doubly so for global investors who are generally unfamiliar with local companies and thus must come to their investment decisions through research conducted from thousands of miles away. Despite the widespread misconception that picking stocks requires an MBA from the Wharton School or personal lessons from Warren Buffett, the fact is that although the process certainly requires some time and an open mind, finding good companies to own is not quantum physics. Ideas pop up all over the place, if you're open to them. From there, you simply have to learn how to research a company, its business, its industry, and its trading history to get a feel for its current operations, its future prospects, and whether the stock's price at the moment is worthy of your money. That isn't as difficult as it might sound, even for stocks trading on the other side of the world.

Many books have been written on how to value stocks, so instead of rehashing that, we're going to look at the first steps in the process of finding the data and information you'll need for your analysis. In short: Research. Our goal: To ultimately build a well-rounded view of a company, its industry, and the country in which it's located.

INVEST IN WHAT YOU UNDERSTAND

A simple rule, but a wise one: Just because you're investing in an exotic locale doesn't mean you must go exotic with your foreign investments. Stick to the companies you can understand.

Aside from some accounting differences and the use of strangely colored money, business is business the world over. Companies start up to sell goods and services to consumers and businesses for the sole purpose of making a profit. But not all companies are in industries that are easily accessible to the investor mind. If you read a company's reports and its "About Us" link on its website and you can't understand the business model, then there's no reason to put your money there, regardless of how hot the stock or the industrial sector might be. That's not to imply a company is shady. It's just that if you don't see why investors are rushing in, you'll never see why they're rushing out.

Not understanding a company's line of work is OK. I don't begin to understand some of the bleeding-edge technology industries, such as companies building all those nanotechnology products these days. So I avoid them, even though that means I forsake some potentially huge returns—though I also miss out on some potentially gargantuan blowups.

Beer I understand. Washing machines and medical devices and hotels and banks and water companies and slot-machine makers and restaurants and mobile-phone firms. Those businesses are self-explanatory. You can see where the demand is. You know the market exists. And, frequently, lots of data and research are available online that will help you determine how the market is growing or contracting in a particular country or region.

So, simplicity aside, know your own limits. Don't invest just to own a hot stock in a hot country. Buy what you know.

The launching pad for all your research is the company itself. Rare it is these days to find a publicly traded company that does not operate a website replete with current and historical financial data. Rare, but not extinct. You will on occasion find companies that don't, particularly in emerging Eastern and Central European nations.

For instance, Croatia. That Adriatic country is rushing toward inclusion in the European Union and is emerging from the dark shadows of a violent civil war that cleaved apart the former Yugoslavia, leaving a handful of independent nations. Croatia is emerging not only as a viable economy but also as a fairly unspoiled tourist destination—a perfect confluence of events for investors who want to own some of the Croatian tourism stocks. Yet there's an unavoidable roadblock: While you can easily find major Croatian tourism companies through a simple Google search (Hoteli Croatia d.d. and Atlas Travel both pop up when you plug in "Croatia hotel companies"), the websites as of late 2007 did not offer investors any financial resources. That's of no help.

Your only option: Send the company an e-mail through the online "Contact Us" link. Ask first if the company produces its financial reports in English and, if so, request that copies of the last five years of reports be mailed to you. I've never yet met a company to decline this request, though I imagine there will be a first. Certainly, this is substantially more time-consuming than instantaneous access to electronic reports. But sometimes your only option is, well, your only option. Never let a small hurdle keep you from potential profits.

Thankfully, you will more often come across companies that provide online a great deal of information about their finances and operations. But how do you narrow your search to a particular company to begin with, especially when there are roughly 50,000 public companies in the world and you don't have a clue which ones do or don't exist in a certain market?

The short answer: Reading. A lot. Anything and every-thing that captures your attention.

Valuable sources exist all over the place — and in random places — for finding public companies in foreign markets, or for stoking ideas that lead you to specific industries in particu-lar regions of the world. Three key sources:

- *The Economist* (weekly newsmagazine)
- *Financial Times* (daily newspaper)
- *The Wall Street Journal* (daily newspaper)

The first two are British publications. *The Economist* is widely available on newsstands or through a subscription, and it's one of the very best magazines in the world for news of the world — political, cultural, social, and business. The *Financial Times* is available in larger metro markets, though it's also avail-able by subscription in nonmajor markets. *The Wall Street Jour-nal,* meanwhile, is widely available. The latter two specialize in financial reporting and devote a great deal of space to foreign business news. There's not a week that goes by when I don't clip from these publications anywhere from one to a dozen items that I want to explore further—sometimes even the smallest blurb or, possibly, an advertisement.

These aren't always stories about a specific company; sometimes they're stories about an industry trend or the happenings in some country. In no particular order, the following are the headlines from a random sampling of stories pulled from my file, and the rationale for clipping each in the first place:

• "Bank deal points the way for Europe." *Financial Times.* Two things about banks: 1) They can be a great way to play an expanding economy, since they are one of the first industries to respond to improving economic conditions; and 2) if you can buy their stocks at a cheap enough price, you'll often be paid a dividend well in excess of the local market average, meaning you'll be paid handsomely to simply hold the stock and wait for the improving economy to arrive. This particular story used a European bank merger to discuss other banks in Europe that stand out as targets that could get snapped up in other mergers. That's a list of potential investments to begin researching right there, not because they're takeover targets but because they're likely well-run banks or they're located in growing markets in which larger banks want to gain a foothold—why else would another bank want them? I happened to be especially interested at the time in Turkey, and this story mentioned two Turkish banks on my list of stocks to research: Akbank and Işbank (pronounced Ahk-bank and Ish-bank). This clip provided context for banking issues afoot in Europe, as well as a source of bank ideas I was unfamiliar with.

• "Emerging Giants." *Business Week.* A story on multinational companies based outside the United States that are making their presence known well outside their home countries. The list includes 25 multinationals from places such as China, Brazil, Russia, India, and Egypt. Along with companies to at least poke into are factoids like this: "Of the 1.2 billion new cellular-phone subscribers worldwide by 2010 . . . 86% will be in developing nations." *That* is a wonderful piece of data to highlight, circle, and put big stars next to. That's the kind of information that sends me to the Internet searching for mobile-phone firms in places like Africa, the Middle East, parts of Asia, and Latin America.

- "Out of Africa." *The Economist.* Though this story is about the Johannesburg Stock Exchange becoming a publicly traded company on its own market, the story mentions that the Jo'berg exchange is seeking to harmonize listing requirements with other exchanges in the region. Despite the fact that that effort had gone nowhere as of 2007, some countries, the report noted, were showing some interest in the prospect of a pan-African exchange. That means a South African brokerage account at some point could provide a way *into* Africa on a broad scale — multicountry access to public companies across a broad swatch of southern Africa, one of those matryoshka-doll firms. For a global investor with potential interest in some of the stabler, more viable African economies, that bit of knowledge is useful.

- "For South Korea, 'Emerging' Label Can Be a Burden." *The Wall Street Journal.* South Korea is a paradox: The Asian nation is one of the dozen largest economies in the world and has one of the world's largest stock markets. Yet South Korea remains lumped in among emerging-market countries. A big part of the reason is North Korea and the tendencies of that global pariah to rattle cages with nuclear-weapons tests. That creates risks south of the 38th parallel that separates the two countries. Investors cannot quantify the likelihood that a rogue state will or won't act out against its neighbor, creating an unknowable risk factor — and investors hate unknowable factors. Because South Korea is part of the emerging markets, index makers include it in their emerging-market indices, which in turn means mutual funds include South Korea in their emerging-market mutual funds. Conversely, the country doesn't make an appearance in the index funds for developed markets that it so clearly is a part of. As this story noted, if

South Korea is ever reassigned to the developed market, "it would trigger a wave of stock buying," as managers of developed-market index funds rush to shift some of their trillions of dollars into South Korean stocks. Keeping with the theme that arriving early to a party is often the most profitable strategy in stocks, this is the kind of information that should prompt you to take a look at South Korea, which brokerage firms will allow you to invest on the Seoul Stock Exchange, and what companies are doing well in that market. (This is a case where owning South Korea as a whole through an ETF in the United States would likely be just as beneficial, since if South Korea does get pushed into the developed-market category, the entire South Korean stock market is likely to be revalued higher.)

• "We are changing the skies." *The Economist.* This wasn't an article; it was an advertisement—for Turkish Airlines. The world's airlines operate in one of the most bloodthirsty, cash-hungry industries imaginable, one where competitors jockey to undercut one another's ticket prices on a whim, where customers expect airfares as cheap as a bus ticket but in-flight service as elegant as a Michelin-rated restaurant, and where the cost of equipment necessary to provide the service—the planes—can top $200 million or more. Still, until humans can teleport themselves from Point A to Point L, this industry isn't going away. In fact, it's expanding, particularly outside the United States, where increasing personal wealth leads to increasing numbers of passengers in the air. This particular ad notes that Turkish Airlines is "Europe's fastest-growing airline." Not enough to hang an investment on, certainly, but just enough to at least spur you to examine the company to figure out if there's an investment opportunity or not.

I don't invest in every idea I come across. No investor does—or should. Nevertheless, clipping items of interest and taking the time to do even a modicum of initial research builds a certain investment fluency, a body of knowledge that will serve you well over time.

Sometimes the items I clip do prompt me to act. That Turkish Airlines ad, for instance, ultimately led me to examine the rise of no-frills air carriers taking flight around the world, particularly in Central Europe and Southeast Asia, and more often than not invoking the Southwest Airlines model. That's how I came to own a small stake in Air Asia, a rapidly growing low-cost carrier flying passengers for peanuts all over Asia from its base in Kuala Lumpur, Malaysia. Likewise, an article I once found at an online Asian news site while researching Chinese travel habits reported a dramatic rise in the number of Chinese passport holders, noting that, outside of the Japanese, the Chinese were now responsible for the largest number of border crossings in Asia. Hmmmmm . . . You have to figure that if 1.3 billion Chinese are now beginning to travel in large numbers, the travel-services industry is certain to feel the impacts. That should be especially true throughout Asia, because the Chinese, just as Americans do, tend to stick close to home when they first venture into vacationing. Nearby for the Chinese obviously means the rest of Asia.

And what services do travelers the world over most need? Places to eat. Cars to rent. Casinos to gamble in. Amusement parks to play in. Airplanes to fly in. Malls to shop in. And, of course, hotels to sleep in. Because no matter where you land or how you arrive or what you do during the day, you need someplace to lay your head at some point. That bit of simple-minded reasoning led me to research Asian hotel chains through a variety of online searches.

Until that time, I'd never heard of Shangri-La outside of its mention in James Hilton's *Lost Horizon* and its generic use as an earthly utopia. Over a couple of weeks of research, however, I built a profile of Shangri-La Asia Ltd., a Hong Kong hotelier I found by typing into Google "Asia top hotel chains" (I figure if I'm looking for an Asian hotel company, it might as well be one of the best). Shangri-La Asia was one of the first links to pop up. And it turned out the company is a highly regarded brand name in the region. The company's two brands — the Shangri-La and Traders hotel chains — stretch across mainland China, throughout the rest of the Far East, and into India, the Middle East, and now North America and Europe. Those brands are well known by Chinese consumers, which will serve Shangri-La Asia well as increasing numbers of Chinese travelers on vacation or business trips look for a trusted brand to shelter them for the night. Shangri-La, moreover, has plans afoot to add roughly 20 or so new hotels across China, in secondary and tertiary markets, catering to local and foreign business travelers who are increasingly venturing into the quickly growing interior of China.

The company's financials looked healthy and stable, and Shangri-La's stock was depressed at the time, according to historical price charts found on the Hong Kong Stock Exchange website.

That research led me to scribble these notes onto a Shangri-La annual report printed off the company's investor relations website:

> *Asia travel market boom. China leading source of consumer travelers. Biz travelers next as Chinese biz expands from locally to regionally focused. Trend is long-term. Big risk: Another bird-flu scare, though will be short-term anomaly. Additional hotels in China will strengthen brand among Chinese tourists. Good financials. Stock cheap. Decent dividend about 2%.*

Now, to Wall Street's professional analysts, that type of research is simplistic. They tear apart a hotel company's finances to determine revenues per available room, something the analytical community calls RevPAR, among other items. They want to know the average daily room rate a hotel chain is generating. That's fine; analysts are paid to figure out pricing trends to build the revenue-forecasting models their clients want to see. But you don't need to calculate RevPAR to know that Asia is a booming region of the world and that swarms and oodles and platoons of Chinese travelers spending money on vacations and business trips will benefit a hotel company.

That's not RevPAR, that's CommSen, as in "common sense." I would fully expect Shangri-La to hit any number of bumps along the way, just as every company does at some point. But unless management destroys the company (and Enron proved no one can predict that), this Hong Kong hotel company seems well positioned to benefit over the long haul from consumer growth in Asia and China.

So, through a Singapore brokerage account I'd opened earlier, partly to gain access to Hong Kong, which this account provided, I ultimately bought shares of Shangri-La Asia.

They've since tripled. I still own them.

Oh, and you might be wondering: Why would anyone even think to be online searching out Chinese travel habits? Because for the last several years the American press has been awash with stories of China's stunning growth and commentary on China rapidly becoming one of the world's largest economies. As an investor with a global bent, that incessant drumbeat is certain to have you thinking about ways to profit. It's not much of a leap to tie together a growing economy and increasing personal wealth with greater demands to spend that wealth on leisure activities such as travel. It's all just a matter of starting with one fact and then thinking: What is the result of that fact? What is the next, logical step in the process?

Finding the information to link all of that with Shangri-La and then to build out a profile of the company wasn't hard. Likewise, it required no inside connections to the company or the hotel industry. In this case, everything was available online. So let's look at where you find the kind of data needed to build a useful profile of a company, industry, or country. I've already mentioned *The Economist, Financial Times,* and *The Wall Street Journal.* Other sources include the following.

Corporate websites: I mentioned Işbank several pages back. The Turkish bank serves as a good example of the kinds of company-specific financial data widely available online. Işbank posts on its English-language site annual and quarterly reports going back several years, and an archive of the presentations that company executives have made to institutional investors.

Company websites should be one of the primary places you visit when doing your homework. They're generally chockablock with all sorts of information giving you a broad, basic understanding of the lines of business a company is involved in. Companies almost universally post their latest news on their home page and provide a "Contact Us" link that you can use to request information you might not be able to find online, such as prior years' financial reports.

Along with financial data, companies post an abundance of details about the products and services they offer and about the markets in which they operate. You'll often find stock-related information such as the ticker symbol, the exchange on which the shares trade, and, sometimes, a list of analysts and the firms producing research on the company. That list of analysts or brokerage-firm names can come in handy: Plug the company name and the analyst's or brokerage firm's name into a search engine and sometimes you'll locate recent research reports that have been posted elsewhere and that you otherwise might not have access to.

Many companies let you sign up to receive corporate e-mails announcing new products, the latest financial results, and other news. This is the best way to keep tabs on what's happening inside the companies you own, or the ones you're interested in following while you research the stock or the industry.

Stock exchanges: Just about every stock exchange you might be interested in will have an online presence. That doesn't mean you will always find what you're looking for, though. Exchanges are hit and miss with the quantity and quality of data they dish up. Many contain a trove of corporate and stock-specific information. Hong Kong's stock exchange, for instance, publishes online every day the news announcements Hong Kong–listed companies release. A search function, meanwhile, lets you access a company's corporate news releases over the past year.

At the London Stock Exchange you can buy a company profile for £10 (roughly $20 in 2007) that provides a smorgasbord of research goodies for the serious global investor: five years of fundamental data, updated daily; five years of balance-sheet and income statements (though you can often find that for free at company websites); insider trades; historical price charts (again, something you can usually find for free online); and broker research, recommendations, and earnings projections. One of the London exchange's best services is free: an annual-report service in which the exchange will deliver to you the annual reports of listed companies, including companies from countries such as Spain, South Africa, Sweden, and Switzerland, among others, that cross-list their shares in London.

Exchange sites are generally the place to visit to find a list of brokers operating in a given country, and for links to corporate home pages, since searching for a foreign firm online is sometimes a challenge, particularly in markets where the language relies on letters, symbols, and pictograms not found on your computer keyboard. Moreover, in markets where shares trade in certain block sizes, the "company profile" found on many exchanges will generally detail how many shares you must trade at minimum.

With some exchanges, you'll find you have access to the same research reports that the local brokerage firms are supplying to local investors. At the Singapore Stock Exchange, for example, you can register for free to see thousands of research reports produced by respected firms such as UOB Kay Hian, DBS Vickers, OCBC Investment Research, and others. These reports are frequently posted on the Singapore exchange's website the same day they're published.

Brokerage firms: Once you're signed up with a firm, you'll generally have access to the research that firm's analysts produce or, in the case of online-only brokers, third-party research. This gives you the chance to gauge what the pros think about some company you're interested in. But don't base your decisions simply on what analysts think; they have their own agendas many times and are not always as independent as you might imagine. Still, the reports are a good way to double-check for any trouble spots in an industry or within a company that you might have missed. In many cases these reports aren't in English, but don't instantly discount their usefulness. The Internet is loaded with free services that will translate words, passages, or even entire Web pages into English from a wide variety of foreign tongues. The downside is that the translations are not always grammatically clear and you frequently need to read and reread through the sentences to make sense of what's going on. But that's a relatively small inconvenience for gaining a bit of locally produced insight into a particular company.

One of the better uses of a brokerage firm is the ability to create "tracking books" or "watch lists" that let you keep tabs on the stocks you fancy. Tracking books are almost universal, and most firms have a system to alert you when a particular stock hits a particular price target that you establish.

Also, look for a list of "recommended sites." Not all firms will post this, but many do. The links often lead to quite useful sites germane to that local market, such as local newspapers, share registries, and research and charting services. Through a New Zealand broker, I stumbled across the *Australasian Investment Review,* a lovely online newsmagazine that does a wonderful job of reporting on the business news of Australia, New Zealand, and much of Asia. The firm dispatches both a daily e-mail chronicling news of interest and a weekly e-mail that links to what is essentially a glossy business magazine online. Best of all, it's free.

Mutual funds: I don't own many international mutual funds (my wife's IRA holds the Matthews Asian Growth & Income fund; I have Fidelity's Diversified International fund in my 401[k] plan; and part of my young son's college-savings account is the Japan Fund). That said, I visit mutual-fund websites all the time, and not just those in the United States.

Mutual funds are a great source of investment ideas and even a bit of interesting analysis on occasion.

U.S. mutual funds by law must report to their investors every quarter. In doing so they open their kimono, so to speak, to show you what they own. They list their ten largest holdings (the stocks they like the best, essentially) as well as their full roster of holdings as of some particular date. Those holdings may or may not be accurate at the moment you scan through them, but that's not really the point. What a particular mutual fund does or doesn't own doesn't really matter; the list is simply a starting point for research, in terms of either what companies fit into a specific sector you might be interested in or what companies exist in a certain country where you want to own stocks. You might, for instance, have an interest in bank stocks in Asia, which will benefit over the long haul as the region grows. Reading through the Dodge & Cox International fund report from the third quarter of 2006, you'll come across Kookmin Bank in South Korea, DBS Holdings in Singapore, and Kasikornbank PCL in Thailand. You may not rush to own any of those companies, but you at least have three bank stocks to explore, which through the course of your research will undoubtedly lead to their competitors, which, for you, represent other investment ideas to consider.

Don't limit yourself, however, to the U.S. mutual funds you know. The world is awash in mutual funds that trade all over Europe, Asia, and Australia, and those fund companies and their managers each have their own unique take on the local and foreign stocks they own, giving you a unique, non-U.S. investment perspective. These funds will own all manner of stocks you'll rarely, if ever, come across in a U.S. fund. You can often find these foreign-based mutual funds simply by searching online for "mutual funds" and picking a country. If you don't know what international funds exist in the United States, stop by morningstar.com, the popular purveyor of U.S. mutual-fund data, to screen through the investment research firm's lists of thousands of mutual funds. That service is free. Morningstar also runs a site in Australia where you'll find a list of local fund companies; just turn around and search for those fund companies' websites to search their funds and the list of stocks they own at the moment.

Along with the list of holdings, the funds typically pen a message to shareholders to explain what happened inside the portfolio during the past quarter or year, and usually what the fund managers see taking shape in the countries in which they're currently invested. Some funds provide monthly updates, some a weekly e-mail. But whether quarterly or more frequently, the commentary can be enlightening. Take, for instance, these few sentences from a Julius Baer International Equity Fund II report from November 2006:

> *From a geographic perspective, emerging markets were the main driver of returns. Poland, which we like due to its strong economic fundamentals and steady growth, was the region's best performer. Our holdings in the country are centered on the financial and consumer discretionary sector.*

For investors with an interest in emerging Europe, such sentiments provide a good reason for researching investment opportunities in Poland, and they give you a starting point: financial and consumer stocks.

Some mutual-fund companies even send you the updates so that you don't have to go in search of them. The Matthews funds, for example, dispatch weekly, monthly, and/or quarterly updates and insights into the Asian market, written by the firm's portfolio managers. Such e-mails can be quite useful. In December 2006, Matthews sent out its "Weekly Asia Update," this one a "Postcard from Japan." Now, Japan is an intriguing investment story because the country has struggled through such a long, well-publicized bout of financial malaise, a fact with which just about any U.S. investor is likely to be at least somewhat familiar since news of Japan's economic anemia has peppered the U.S. media for years. As of this writing, Japan appears to be finally pulling out of the funk, again a fact about which many U.S. investors probably have some marginal knowledge just because of the news coverage.

Well, the Matthews missive, a concise 453 words written by one of the firm's portfolio managers, addresses an interesting question: If Japan's economy is moving again, why aren't the Japanese spending their money in the retail sector? After all, when an economy is expanding, people are spending.

Matthews answers that by talking to some average Japanese citizens. Turns out that nowadays, instead of pursuing conspicuous consumption, the Japanese mind-set has changed. "Where is the cash going?" Matthews asks. "In part, to mutual funds (Investment Trusts) and property. As the economy has grown, and bonuses are up, retail sales have actually fallen, and are getting worse. . . . Now retail money is flowing into domestic equities. The average Japanese is getting a lot older, and is beginning to worry about their pensions and retirement. Investment books abound in bookstores. . . . The property market has also sprung to life. . . ."

That analysis is a road map to Japanese asset-management firms, which stand to profit as increasing numbers of Japanese citizens stick their available cash into investments and real assets instead of Coach bags and Gucci shoes. And, as an example of just how easy it is to be a global investor, this is how effortless it is to find asset-management firms to research in Japan:

Step 1: Search the Internet for "Japanese asset management companies." Up pops a link to Japan's Financial Services Agency and a list of 121 such companies in Japan.

Step 2: On a separate Internet page, pull up the Tokyo Stock Exchange (www.tse.or.jp). Click on the "Listed Companies" and then the "Company Search" function.

Step 3: Toggle between the two websites, plugging the name of each asset-management company into the stock exchange's search box to determine if that name, or some version of that name, is a publicly traded stock. The first one that hit for me was Daiwa Asset Management Co. Ltd. (I plugged only "Daiwa" into the Tokyo Stock Exchange, to be as generic as possible, and Daiwa Securities Group showed up.)

Step 4: Go to the Daiwa Securities website. The Tokyo exchange had the link handy for this particular company, though in other instances you'll have to open another Internet browser to search for the company's home page. Also, in this instance, the Daiwa link led to a page entirely in Japanese, with just one available link in blue. Click that link, though, and you get to a home page with an English-translation link in the upper right-hand corner. And in the "About Daiwa Securities Group" you'll see that the company owns both Daiwa Asset Management as well as Daiwa DB Investments, which was next on that list of 121 asset-management companies.

So, just like that, in a span of about seven minutes, you're reading through a mutual fund's dispatch, realizing there's the germ of an investment idea in there, and four steps later on the Internet you're researching a Japanese asset-management company you had no clue even existed moments earlier. I'm not saying Daiwa is the asset-management stock to own in Japan; just that starting your research from knowing absolutely nothing about a country or an industry is not terribly difficult.

Google: Many times to this point I've noted that I hit Google to search for this or that online. One of the skills to learn as a global investor is how to effectively use Internet search engines. You don't have to rely on Google, of course; use whatever engine you're most comfortable with. The point is that the Internet is the reason why international investing is so accessible to average investors these days, and the searches that are necessary to conduct research, find companies, and even locate brokerage firms are an art in themselves because so much of what every search engine uncovers is debris that has nothing to do with your interest.

The trick is learning how to search and what to search for. You can't just search "Asia hotels," for instance, and expect to generate quickly a list of hotel companies like Shangri-La Asia that you might invest in, or an analysis of the Asian hotel industry. Almost assuredly your search engine will assume you're looking for a place to sleep while on business or vacation in

Kuala Lumpur or Bangkok and gin up a long list of travel sites and discount-hotel providers. "Asia hotels investment" doesn't do much better, producing a list of sites aimed largely at hotel owners, real estate brokers, and tourism officials.

Think, instead, of some key terms specific to a good company you'd want to own—maybe something like "Asia hotels China expansion earnings growth." Well, that gets us moving in the right direction, with links to a website detailing the "Closer Economic Partnership Arrangement" between Hong Kong and mainland China and noting that the "liberalization of travel restrictions" means more Chinese citizens are traveling, "which benefits hotels, restaurants, and retail businesses." So we know Chinese will be traveling more (as I mentioned earlier regarding Shangri-La Asia), so let's throw "tourism" into the search mix. What you get (at least what I got in November 2006) is a link—the first link—to chinahospitalitynews.com, noting that Indonesia has a big push to attract hundreds of thousands of Chinese tourists, making it easier for Chinese citizens to get a visa and adding nonstop flights to large Chinese cities.

Now we're finding some string to start collecting. Does Indonesia offer any interesting hotel companies that might make a good investment? I had no clue either. I typed "Indonesia stock market" into Google, looking for the website for the Jakarta Stock Exchange. There, a simple search of "hotel" dug up 11 companies with ties of some sort to the hotel industry. I don't know which ones are worthy of investment at this point, but the exercise shows you just how easily you can begin to research international companies using refined search-engine queries.

ANOTHER MICROSOFT COUP

Some brokerage firms, as well as corporate and stock-exchange websites, do not always work as expected with all Internet browsers. The Jakarta Stock Exchange, for instance, hangs up when Mozilla's Firefox is the browser of choice but works

perfectly fine with Microsoft's Internet Explorer. I say this so
that you don't give up on some site that seems inoperable. Might
be that you just need to switch browsers temporarily.

Foreign newspapers: Every country has newspapers;
thousands are online. Many are printed in English. And most
publish a business section or at least print business news. This
is a primary source of information, though how independent
and objective the news is depends on the country.

Still, newspapers typically have a search function that
allows you to troll the archives for previous stories about a local
company or an industry in the region. Sometimes you'll have to
sign up for free to view the story; other times you won't have
access unless you pay. If you don't want to subscribe (and I
never have yet), pull some key words out of the synopsis or
maybe even the title of the story and Google that. Oftentimes
you'll find the story posted to a blog, reprinted in part or
entirely in an industry publication, or mentioned in some
meaningful fashion in other online material that you can
access.

Many bigger-city papers the world over follow the local
stock market. Thus they generally write about local, publicly
traded companies, providing you a bit of analysis, insight into
issues you might not be familiar with, and, possibly, the name
of local brokerage firms covering those companies that you
might contact to find out if they'll take American investors —
assuming you haven't found one already.

A long list of English-language papers can be accessed at
www.worldnetdaily.com, where you'll find a "Foreign Newspapers" link. Onlinenewspapers.com lists thousands of local
papers from around the globe and notes which ones are in
English. If nothing else, search Google, again, for newspapers
in the particular city or country you're trying to research.

U.S. State Department (www.state.gov): Each year, the
State Department posts an abundance of research on the polit-

ical, economic, and investing climate in scores of countries. Just type the name of a particular country into the search field on the home page to sift through all that the State Department offers. A key document to seek is the Investment Climate Statement, found in the "Investment Affairs" section on the Bureau of Economic, Energy, and Business Affairs' International Finance and Development page.

This is a good, independent take on a country's macroeconomic conditions. One example: The State Department's take on Croatia in an early 2006 report: "Croatia has begun to emerge as an attractive destination for investment. . . . Since 2000, two successive governments have sought to address bureaucratic inertia, red tape, and a dysfunctional legal system that have stymied investment and economic growth. These efforts appear to be bearing fruit."

You probably don't need to worry too much about this type of analysis with big, developed markets such as those in Western Europe and parts of developed Asia. But the State Department's research is particularly handy when investigating smaller, less developed markets such as Croatia and others.

Industry associations: Whatever industry you can imagine, there is an association representing it somewhere in the world. Interested in owning timberland in New Zealand? The New Zealand Forest Owners Association is a repository of data, including analyses of industry issues. Malaysian palm oil plantations? The Malaysian Palm Oil Council has more than you'll ever care to know about the industry for which Malaysia is the center of the universe — and, by the way, as with beer and nylon, consumption of edible oils increases alongside disposable income.

These associations and councils and boards are a fine source of broad industry trends and data. Here you'll typically find the numbers necessary to examine growth in a particular industry and to understand the dynamics responsible for the growth, or contraction as the case may be. Some will list their members, or track the stocks of the publicly traded members, which can be beneficial in the event you see promise in an industry but are struggling to locate the public companies.

Find industry associations the same way you find everything else online: Google it. Just type in something like "Korea bankers association" and the first link is the Korea Federation of Banks.

Foreign financial sites: All over the world you can find websites catering to investors with market-related data, stock charts, and other financial tidbits specific to a particular country or region. The problem is that there's no one, surefire way to find those sites. It's all a matter of happenstance. You'll stumble across one while trolling through some news site, or some brokerage firm will list a couple that you find useful in a list of recommended links. Wherever you find one, bookmark it in your search engine. No matter how strong your memory, when you're reading through dozens and dozens of sites and running a gazillion searches, you will forget where you found that great website.

Here are a few to bookmark:

Yahoo! Finance: Yahoo! runs several websites around the globe where you'll find everything from local columnists writing about the local market to historical price charts to news on local stocks. The "Finance News" link on the Yahoo! Australia site, for instance, lets you search company news specific to particular industries, such as media, pharmaceuticals, and financials. The Yahoo! sites include these in English:

Australia/New Zealand: au.finance.yahoo.com

Canada: finance.yahoo.ca (French Canadian version: cf.finance.yahoo.com)

India: in.finance.yahoo.com

Singapore: sg.finance.yahoo.com (useful for most of Asia)

United Kingdom/Ireland: uk.finance.yahoo.com

And these in various foreign languages:

Argentina: ar.finance.yahoo.com (in Spanish)

Brazil: br.finance.yahoo.com (in Portuguese)

China: cn.finance.yahoo.com (in Chinese)

France: fr.finance.yahoo.com (in French)

Germany: de.finance.yahoo.com (in German)

Hong Kong: hk.finance.yahoo.com (in Chinese)

Italy: it.finance.yahoo.com (in Italian)

Japan: jp.finance.yahoo.com (in Japanese)

Mexico: mx.finance.yahoo.com (in Spanish)

South Korea: kr.finance.yahoo.com (in Korean)

Spain: es.finance.yahoo.com (in Spanish)

Taiwan: tw.finance.yahoo.com (in Chinese)

IRAsia.com: This is possibly the best website for Asia. Inside is a cornucopia of annual/interim reports, press releases, company presentations, and a ton more. There's even a list of stock brokers throughout the region. IRAsia.com also runs a free alert service, shooting to you e-mails when companies announce news and release annual reports and interim financial results or post company presentations online. You'll receive several alerts every day, a great way to simply learn about the companies in Asia and to build an institutional base of knowledge about which ones exist and what they do.

FDIMagazine.com: FDI is the acronym for Foreign Direct Investment. Produced by the *Financial Times,* and though largely aimed at companies expanding overseas, this site is a wealth of information that individual investors can use, providing insight into countries, regions, and the latest happenings in various industrial sectors.

MBendi.com: "Information for Africa" is how MBendi describes itself. From the home page you can search "Exchanges" and "Listed Companies" for stock exchanges and publicly traded companies in Africa.

ArabFinance.com: Devoted to online trading and financial news, this site initially launched in Egypt and spread across the Arab world over time.

Asia Times Online: This news site offers information on regional and global business, political and economic issues. Though English-language, the content is aimed at Chinese readers instead of Western readers, meaning the news comes from an Asian perspective.

The BBC (news.bbc.co.uk): The British Broadcasting Corp. seemingly has correspondents in every remote corner of the globe imaginable. This site is a wonderful resource for news and trends happening well outside the purview of U.S. investors. Its search function is invaluable for digging up stories on all manner of topics.

Google Finance (finance.google.com): Type in a company name and up pops an abundance of news stories from publications all over the world. For instance, search for information on Johnston Press plc, a highly profitable newspaper publisher in Scotland, and news arrives from sources as varied as the *Irish Times* newspaper, Forbes, and Reuters. Google Finance also often provides the company's Web-page link—a surprisingly convenient bonus, given how challenging it can be at times to find many a foreign-company home page.

MSCI Barra (mscibarra.com): This one is run by the folks who compile the multitude of Morgan Stanley Capital International indices that hedge funds, foundations, pensions, and mutual funds the world over rely on to benchmark their performance. The great benefit of this site is that you can find the companies that constitute some particular indices. That can be helpful when you're trying to locate companies that exist in a particular part of the world. You'll have to register for this site, but it's free.

GeoInvestor.com: Run by a former *Wall Street Journal* editorial board member and international correspondent, this site provides a host of links to market, financial, and economic news for roughly 45 countries, big and small.

CIA World Factbook (cia.gov): This site run by the U.S. Central Intelligence Agency isn't just for spooks. Here you'll find basic though useful information on a particular country's economy. This can help you hone in on industries that are big players in various countries. From there, you can begin to search out the industry associations and the local companies that form that industry.

Radio Free Europe (rferl.org): The RFE site provides extensive coverage of issues throughout Central and Eastern Europe, the Caucasus, the Balkan states, and Southwest Asia. It's funded by the U.S. Congress, so the news is coming at you from a democratic, Western perspective.

Latibex.com: "Latin America in Euros" is how this site from Spain describes itself. Latibex is an international market trading solely the securities of Latin America (Mexico to Chile). Not every Latin market is represented on Latibex, and not every security is available from the markets that are represented. This market is in Spain, and though the shares are priced in their original currency (as are the foreign ordinaries that trade back in the home country), they trade in euros. Latibex lists the brokers that have access to this market, and it provides some company research as well.

BusinessNewEurope (businessneweurope.eu): This website reports on business, economics, and politics in Central, Eastern, and Southeastern Europe. BNE does a good job of reporting on issues relevant to investors in markets from Russia down through Turkey, including some real periphery markets such as Kazakhstan, and dispatches a daily e-mail of stories specific to individual countries.

Oxford Business Group (oxfordbusinessgroup.com): OBG dishes up coverage of roughly two dozen emerging markets, with economic briefings on countries ranging from Algeria to Ukraine. The full service will set you back a few bucks, but the free synopses are highly detailed and very useful in their own right.

ETFConnect.com: This is a U.S. site focused on exchange-traded funds (ETFs) and closed-end funds. It's one of the best sources of information on global-centric ETFs and funds.

Institute for International Economics (iie.com): Formally known as the Peter G. Peterson Institute for International Economics, this site produces a host of research and erudite papers on economic issues all around the world. Not all the information here will be of use, but you will find economic analyses of various countries that will help you build your investment profile on an individual country.

Middle East North Africa Financial Network (menafn. com): An excellent source of pan-Arab financial news and from an Arab perspective, here you can find out about IPOs in the Arab world. The "Regional Research" link dishes up data and analysis on 13 countries in the region, from Egypt to Oman and up to Lebanon.

ADR.com and **BNYADR.com**: The two leading websites for research on American depositary shares, ADR.com is run by JPMorgan and BNYADR.com is run by the Bank of New York. Both are key players in the ADR market.

WorldPress.org: Simply put, this site provides news from around the world, all culled from a disparate collection of publications. Business and economic news are only part of this site, and it's not necessarily a site you'd put total faith in. Still, it is useful for gaining local perspective and ginning up potential investment ideas.

Australian Investment Review (aireview.com): This one is by far among the best sources of information on the economies and stock markets of Australia, New Zealand, and Asia. Sign up and you'll receive a daily briefing on the financial news in the region, and a weekly online magazine (a very good one, at that) on issues ranging from the dark side of Australia's economic boom, to meaningful analysis of the global mining sector (since Australia is home to some of the largest mining firms), to useful market insights across the coverage area. Plus, you have access to the archive of past stories. Best of all, AIR is supported solely by advertising, thus your subscription is free.

Economist.com: The website for the weekly *Economist* newsmagazine, which is perhaps the best in the world for covering global events, *The Economist* online runs a particularly useful link called "Country Briefings" (www.economist.com/countries) that compiles all manner of data such as political and economic forecasts and links to recent *Economist* articles about that particular country. Moreover, it slips in a list of other non-*Economist* links that are highly useful. The China profile, for instance, lists links to sites such as the Xinhua News Agency; the English-language newspaper *China Daily;* and articles written on China by the Brookings Institution, an American think-tank.

There are a ton more of similar links. The previous list is just a taste of the vast selection of news, opinion, and data-laden sites that help global investors succeed in researching potential investments. Just spend a bit of time on the Internet and soon enough you'll have a library of online resources to reference when rooting around for stocks around the world.

SO, WHERE DO IDEAS REALLY COME FROM?

While I was researching Croatian investment opportunities, a link popped up with the title "Slovenes and Croats Forge Foreign Investment Path." Oddly, this link was for the Institute on War & Peace Reporting — not exactly the sort of site you'd typically seek out when researching investment ideas.

Nevertheless, I said a few pages back that investment ideas come from just anywhere and everywhere, so long as you're open to them. This is the proof.

The institute's report noted that Slovenia and Croatia, former country mates before Yugoslavia's disintegration and now neighbors, are playing a substantial role in the economy of nearby Serbia, also part of the former Yugoslavia and the site of a violent civil war and ethnic-cleansing campaign under the late Slobodan Milosevic. In particular, the report noted a couple of companies that are investing fairly heavily in Serbia. The Croatian company, the story reported, was privately held; the Slovenian company wasn't. Its name: Mercator. I was immediately interested because Mercator, according to the institute, is in retail—an industry easy to understand and, more important, an industry that benefits greatly as developing nations develop.

A universal truth in developing nations is that they empower a progressively wealthier consumer class to spend. "Wealthier" is, certainly, a relative term. But whether it's a factory-floor worker in Chengdu, China, or a cabdriver in Belgrade, Serbia, people the world over use the increasing amounts of money they earn in generally the same manner: They buy products such as washing machines and cars that make their life easier. They buy beer, higher-quality food, and clothes. They spend on vacations and entertainment to feel better about their life. And they buy brand-name goods to send the message to their peers that they have "made it" and can afford to splurge. Americans may have cornered the market on ostentatious spending and debt accumulation, but it's only because we had a head start.

The report led me to the websites for Mercator (www .mercator.si) and the Ljubljana Stock Exchange (www.ljse.si), which publishes a good bit of useful data—in English—on its listed companies.

Mercator, through rapid growth in Slovenia, Croatia, Serbia, Montenegro, Bosnia, Herzegovina, and Macedonia, is emerging as one of the leading retailers in Southeast Europe for food and household products. The company operates grocery stores, hypermarkets, department stores, convenience stores, discount stores, sports stores, and hardware stores. Mercator's financials look pretty good and the company is funneling profits into additional store growth.

According to Mercator's stock-price history on the Ljubljana Stock Exchange, the trajectory of the company's shares shows that it is a proxy for the Slovenian Stock Exchange Index, called the SBI 20. The two move in near lockstep. Thus, aside from being a strong play on the development of Southeast European economies, Mercator is a play on investors piling into Slovenian shares.

That, though, is the reason I haven't invested in Mercator— yet. The Slovenian market, as the charts and data on the stock exchange's website showed, began to surge in late 2001 and by late 2006 had nearly tripled, notching an average annual gain of more than 23%. Much of that came because Slovenia joined the EU in 2004, and investors began pumping money into the local stock market years in advance of Slovenia's accession, knowing that the run-up to EU membership is as sure a sign as you can find that a country's stock market is set to heave higher as the economic, legal, and political systems improve.

Once Slovenia cools, and it will, just like all markets do, I'll be back to poke around.

The point, however, is not so much Slovenia or Mercator in particular as it is the process that led me to the country and the company in the first place. Sources exist all over the place for finding public companies in foreign markets. Sometimes they're just in really random spots.

CHAPTER 5

CASA DE CAMBIO

What You Need to Know About Currency when Investing Overseas

Anyone who has traveled on holiday outside the United States is, by default, a currency trader.

What's the first item on the To Do list within minutes of passing through customs? Track down the currency-exchange kiosk to convert U.S. dollars into the local money to pay for the cab, the car, the bus, the trolley, or the train into the city. And if you don't need to do that, it's likely because you live in a major city such as New York and you thought ahead and ordered currency from one of the major banks that now offer currency-to-go services.

Either way, at some point during your trip it's almost universal that you begin to notice exchange rates posted in the hotel lobby or on tote boards at shops along the street, and you compare them with the price you originally received and start planning where you'll next exchange dollars to seal a better deal. That's a currency trader. Sure, you're not trading for the same reasons that currency investors do, but you are nonetheless trying to turn your dollars into the most rubles and rupiah you can. In short, currency trading.

By and large, however, foreign currency is not a concept most Americans deal with all that regularly, if at all. Beyond buying currency on those foreign holidays, and maybe collecting a few specimens of the bills we find novel and interesting while traveling, as a nation we really have no reason to think about Mexican pesos, Canadian dollars, British pounds, or Thai baht on a routine basis. I'm willing to bet you have no idea where to find the nearest currency-exchange shop in town — and that's assuming you live in an urban center where currency-exchange shops exist. If you live in most American towns, there simply isn't one because there's not enough demand for the service to sustain the business.

Much of the world is much different. In small English villages, in tertiary Chinese cities, in the farthest crannies of eastern Romania, at the southern tip of South America, in southwestern Siberia near the Kazakhstan border . . . just about anywhere you roam you'll readily find kiosks, shops, and local hotels that will gladly exchange your dollars for the local scrip. Though it has increasing competition from the euro, the U.S. dollar remains king of the world when it comes to currency.

Yet you cannot use your dollars to buy stocks directly on the exchange in London, Budapest, Tokyo, or Windhoek, Namibia (and, yes, as a U.S. investor you can buy stocks directly on the Namibian exchange). When you're trading through local brokerage accounts, you're trading in the local currency. When you're reading stock quotes from foreign exchanges, you're seeing them priced in the local currency. And assuming you're buying stocks overseas directly, the dividends you receive are in the local currency, too. For that reason you need to be proficient with currency conversion, lest you follow my lead and fail to wire the appropriate amount of money to your local broker, as I did with that first account I opened in New Zealand.

This, then, is the money chapter — the basics of understanding currency transactions, as well as the opportunities and risks of investing in currency directly.

THE CURRENCY MARKET

Every minute of every day, except for weekends, currencies are trading somewhere in the world — and I don't mean at those airport kiosks or on the black market; that sort of currency swapping goes on 24 hours a day. I'm talking about the official currency market itself, a vast marketplace where dollars and yen and euros and Slovakian koruny and a vaultful of other currencies move up and down in relation to one another almost 24/7, around the world, as banks and governments and investors big and small buy and sell various currencies for various reasons.

You can begin trading currencies the moment the New Zealand business week awakens each Monday (late-afternoon Sunday in New York) and not stop until 4 p.m. Eastern time the following Friday, when currency trading at the New York Board of Trade ceases. The size of this market is monumental. In 2006 the average daily trading volume on the New York Stock Exchange totaled about $68 billion. Average daily trading volume in the currency market: $1.9 trillion, or 28 times larger. And that reading was as of 2004, the last time the Bank for International Settlements tabulated the data.

But why do currencies even trade? And why do they fluctuate in value from moment to moment?

The short answer is supply and demand, stemming from need.

Let's start with that need.

Toyota Motor Corp. in fiscal 2006 sold 2.55 million cars in North America — the equivalent of nearly 7.5 trillion yen, according to Toyota's annual report for the year. The vast majority of those North American sales happened in the United States. But Americans don't buy cars with yen; those sales were obviously in dollars. Back across the Pacific, however, Toyota doesn't pay dollars to its workers in Japan, where many of the cars were made; they earn yen. Toyota thus must sell the dollars it earns in America to buy the yen it needs in

Japan. Or consider that Saudi Arabia in 2005 produced 26.8 million barrels of oil, according to OPEC, worth nearly $175 billion. Like Japan, the desert kingdom doesn't operate in dollars; its economy is built on riyals. All those oil dollars, then, need conversion into the Saudi currency.

As with oil, much of the world's trade is denominated in dollars, necessitating that governments around the world maintain a supply of dollars so that their citizens and businesses can access the greenbacks required to trade on global markets. You can begin to see the seeds of need for a mechanism that lets governments and businesses conveniently and efficiently trade one currency for another.

That's where supply and demand comes in.

At the most basic level, the value of, say, a Swiss franc depends on the demand for that franc at that moment. It's the same concept as with a share of stock: Supply and demand dictate price. When demand rises, prices rise. When supply rises, prices fall. Beyond that, however, the currency supply-and-demand mechanics get a little screwy. If you want to buy a particular stock, you represent demand for those shares. When you return to the market to sell that same stock, you represent a supply of shares. But in the currency market, you are both the supply and the demand *at the same instant.*

Say, for instance, you want to buy those Swiss francs. Well, the dollars you're trading represent a supply of dollars, while the francs you want represent demand. Expand that single transaction to a global scale and you can begin to see how and why currencies fluctuate. It's not just you who wants to own Swiss francs at some particular moment; there might be tens of thousands or even millions of people like you around the world who want francs in the same general period as well — and in this case, "period" could be the same day, the same month, or the same year, since currency trends often happen over an extended stretch. Likewise, thousands of banks and institutional investors at that moment might be getting out of dollars and into francs as well for whatever reason.

The result: a flood of dollars coming to market, which means dollars are increasingly easy to find, which in terms of basic economics means they're cheaper to buy (the more there is of something, the cheaper that something is). At the same time, there is increasing demand in the market for francs, which tightens the supply of available francs, which in basic economic terms means francs are more expensive to buy (the greater the demand for something, the dearer that something becomes).

Currency, money, is essentially water in paper form: It flows everywhere and lubricates just about anything, and governments, banks, and institutional investors whip it around the world for various needs almost continually through the currency market. Some of this movement is business-related, such as Toyota's need to change dollars into yen; some of it is speculation as investors bet that one currency will move against another. Whatever the case, this supply-and-demand dance that is almost continually in motion is why currency prices fluctuate constantly.

ONE TRADE, TWO CURRENCIES

Unlike stocks and bonds and mutual funds, currencies trade in pairs such as the USD/JPY, or the U.S. dollar/Japanese yen. These pairs operate much like a seesaw: When one side goes up, the other necessarily goes down. If you decide, for instance, you have a yen for yen and want to own the Japanese currency, you are implicitly betting the dollar will fall—you are, in market slang, "shorting" the dollar and "going long" yen.

The vast bulk of all currency trades center around the eight major currencies: U.S. dollar (USD), euro (EUR), British pound (GBP), Japanese yen (JPY), Australian dollar (AUD), Canadian dollar (CAD), Singapore dollar (SGD), and Swiss franc (CHF). You can, however, find quotes readily available on every currency in the world, including Iraqi dinars and North

Korean won—assuming you ever need them. The quotes themselves look like this:

CURRENCY PAIR	QUOTE
EUR/USD	1.29233 / 50
AUD/USD	0.7724 / 4
GBP/USD	1.99650 / 83
USD/CAD	1.1829 / 33
USD/CHF	1.2494 / 7
USD/JPY	121.371 / 91

I won't belabor this point because you won't really use it when trading stocks overseas, but just so you'll know . . . the quote shown in that first example, for instance, indicates that each euro will buy you 1.29233 dollars, but it will take you 1.29250 dollars to buy a euro, the difference being the "spread." If you think about it, it's the same with stocks, only with two currencies instead of one company. When Coca-Cola is quoted on the New York Stock Exchange at $46.53 / 58, the quote tells you that you can sell Coke shares at $46.53 but it will cost you a nickel more per share to buy them, that nickel being the spread. Same concept with currencies.

The pairings are what make currency trading a bit baffling until you're accustomed to the mechanics. Take a look again at that currency chart. In some cases you'll notice pairings such as EUR/USD. Other times its USD/JPY. That's the sneaky fact about currencies. Those are two entirely different quotes, and not because one is euros and the other yen. The first implies "dollars per euro" (or how may dollars each euro will buy), while the second implies "yen per dollars" (or how many yen each dollar will buy). Since you'll presumably be wiring dollars to whatever foreign accounts you open, knowing what that difference means will be helpful—and if nothing else, you'll better understand the quote board at those airport currency-exchange kiosks that can look like a tote board at a Vegas sports book gone haywire.

In a quote where the USD is listed first, a rising value means the dollar is getting stronger; it's buying more yen, for instance. Therefore, the yen is falling in value. With quotes where the USD is listed second, a rising value means the dollar is weakening. The lead currency, what's called the "base currency," in this case the euro, buys more dollars. The dollar, therefore, is losing value, meaning each dollar buys less of that foreign currency. This is what it looks like in practice using simple, round numbers:

- Let's say the USD/JPY pair is quoted at 120 yen on January 1 of some year and 132 yen exactly a year later. So basically each dollar is buying you 120 yen one year and 132 yen the next. Ergo, the dollar has gained 10% against the yen because each dollar now buys 12 more yen than it did a year ago. So if a single piece of sushi at a shop in Tokyo's Tsukiji Fish Market cost you ¥12 that first year (and, no, sushi isn't that cheap in Japan, but go with the example), you'd be able to buy 10 pieces. The next year, you'd be able to buy 11. Your dollar is stronger because it buys more foreign goods.
- Now consider the EUR/USD pair. On January 1, the euro buys 1.20 dollars, and a year later is quoted at 1.32 dollars. In this instance, the dollar has fallen 10% because each euro now costs an additional 12 cents to buy. So if a baguette in a French café costs €1, you'd need to pull $1.20 out of your pocket in the first year, but $1.32 the next year — 10% more. Your dollar is weaker because it takes more of them to buy that baguette.

Now, you're not going to have to worry too much about these currency pairs in your day-to-day, overseas stock-market activities. I only mention this so that you understand how currencies work and how they play against one another, and so that you can see exactly why it is that when the dollar falls in value, assets priced in other currencies are, by definition, more valuable. Your foreign-denominated investments are, in essence, worth more dollars than you originally began with . . . but I'll show you an example of that in a minute.

In buying stocks globally, the currency quotes you'll more regularly pay attention to are those found every day in *The Wall Street Journal* or the *Financial Times,* or continually updated online at a site such as XE.com. There, each quote is just a single number, such as 1.9654 dollars per British pound. If you need £10,000 in your account in the UK, well, you know you must wire about $19,654 from the United States (10,000 × 1.9654). If you needed ¥500,000 when the quote is 121.435 yen per dollar, you know you need about $4,118 (500,000 ÷ 121.435).

> *The rule to remember: When it's "dollars per foreign currency" you multiply; when it's "foreign currency per dollar" you divide.*

More convenient still: XE.com runs a currency-conversion calculator that will do the work for you — though knowing how to do the calculation yourself is beneficial. Sometimes you have to know how the sausage is made to appreciate it.

Since currency-exchange rates change constantly, the quotes you see, particularly in a newspaper, may or may not be the rate you actually receive when converting dollars into another currency, but it's close enough for your purposes. You just want an approximation of how many dollars you need to wire to your overseas account to fund the trades you want to make. And when you're wiring funds around, always overshoot the mark by 2% or 3% to account for currency fluctuations and the possibility that the stock's price edges up slightly while you're moving money between countries.

GLOBAL DIVERSIFICATION THROUGH CURRENCIES

Though some Main Street investors play around in the currency market, for the most part currency trading is not a traditionally popular corner of Wall Street. Exceedingly few currency mutual funds exist in the states, and aside from day-trader types, relatively few individual investors are trading currencies at the online sites providing that service. Nevertheless, owning currencies directly can be a good way to diversify a portfolio because not only do you gain the exposure to a foreign economy, you're expanding your base of assets to another investment class — money itself. And there is effectively no correlation between currencies and the U.S. stock market.

Owning currencies is the purest way to gain exposure to another economy because you own the medium through which that economy functions, its money. Foreign stocks, by definition, provide currency exposure since they are priced locally. Yet with currency itself you lose some of the risks inherent in stocks, particularly stock-market risk and company risk. You are, however, still at the mercy of geopolitical machinations, interest-rate movements, local economic trends, and the bone-headed policy risk of lawmakers and governments imposing knuckleheaded rules that work to undermine the currency.

As with stocks and stock markets, currencies run the gamut from big/stable/developed to small/unstable/developing. The Swiss franc and the U.S. dollar, for instance, are two of the world's bedrock currencies in times of trouble — what you'll hear called "safe haven" currencies. Because of their perceived stability, investors generally flood into dollars and francs the moment the world gets itself into a nasty place. You'll also hear the term "reserve currencies," those for which other nations hold significant quantities — i.e., reserves — in what are essentially gigantic savings accounts. The U.S. dollar is the world's leading reserve currency by a long shot, with about two-thirds of all international foreign reserves denominated in dollars as of 2007. The euro comes in second, though well behind, accounting for about one-quarter of all global reserves. The pound and yen fit the bill, too, but reserves held in these two are both in the low single digits.

Farther down the spectrum are riskier currencies, the small-cap stocks of the money world, so to speak — currencies such as those in many of the emerging Asian, African, Latin American, and Middle Eastern nations. These are currencies that have blown apart over the years because of various financial crises. Brazil's real. Argentina's peso. Russia's ruble. Mexico's peso. Thailand's baht. Turkey's lira. Investors suffered when each of those currencies had a meltdown in the 1990s.

Although currency trading is a pro's game for the most part, individual investors can participate as well. Depending on your temperament as an investor, you can go all out and speculate on the movement of the Aussie dollar against the British pound, or you can play it conservatively with bank accounts denominated in foreign currencies. And you don't necessarily have to leave American shores for these investments.

First up, the potentially riskiest option: currency trading online. Many books have been written on currency trading, and since that's not the overall focus of this one, I'm just going to touch on it here so that you at least have a working familiarity with the concepts.

As with stock trading, the Internet has revolutionized currency trading, with a number of websites having been launched that let anyone with as little as literally $1 trade currencies right alongside the pros. Small-time investors do so for generally one of two reasons: 1) they're prudent investors who understand currency trading and are seeking diversification through conservative currency trading strategies; or 2) they're gamblers, oftentimes neophytes, speculating on currency trends through the use of leverage because they've read somewhere that currency trading is hot at the moment and they don't want to miss out on all those supposedly easy profits. (Free advice: Resist the urge to trade currencies if you're a newcomer to the currency market; you're more likely to lose big than win small.)

Currency trading makes use of leverage so that you can control a much larger stash of cash than your initial investment. With some online currency accounts, you can leverage your money 200 to 1, so that a $1,000 deposit controls $200,000 in currency. The currency market works on leverage because currency movements are so minute. For instance, on Feb. 5, 2007, the Australian dollar moved in a range between

$0.775 and $0.7761 Aussie dollars per U.S. dollar, a spread of just 11-tenths of one cent. If you'd invested US$1,000 at the low end and sold at the high end, you'd have cleared a whopping profit for the day of US$1.42. Remember, don't splurge with your winnings.

With leverage of 200:1, your profit on the day would have been US$283.87, a roughly 28.4% gain. A far superior result made possible through leverage.

On Feb. 5, 2007, the Australian dollar traded in a range between A$0.775 and A$0.7761 per U.S. dollar. Here's what that trade looks like if you invest US$1,000, and what it looks like if you use leverage of 200:1 to control US$200,000:

Open original position at A$0.775 = US$1	US$1,000 buys: A$1,290.32 ($1,000 ÷ 0.775)	US$200,000 buys: A$258,064.52 ($200,000 ÷ 0.775)
Close original position at A$0.7761 = US$1	A$1,290.32 buys: US$1,001.42 ($1,290.32 x .07761)	A$258,064.52 buys: US$200,283.87 ($258,064.52 x 0.7761)
Profit	US$1.42 ($1,001.42 – $1,000)	US$283.87 ($200,283.87 – $200,000)

Of course, in the sometimes Jekyl and Hyde world of currency trading, the benevolent has its malevolent side as well. Had you relied on leverage and invested at the high end, only to sell later at the low end, you would have lost more than US$283, as painful a bite in percentage terms for one day's currency trading as the stock market can be in its worst years.

That's leverage for you, though: a friend, indeed, when the currency markets are moving with you; a nasty little bugger that can suck the life right out of your account when the markets are moving against you. In the worst situation, when you're not paying attention and a currency moves against you dramatically, you could be on the hook for additional money beyond what you've already invested. However, most online accounts geared for individual investors are arranged so that you cannot lose more than the amount of your initial investment. The account automatically unwinds your positions before your losses drop your account value below $0.

You don't have to max out your use of leverage, of course. You can leverage up, say, 10:1 or maybe 50:1. Or you can leverage to the hilt but trade only a small fraction of your account, leaving a large reserve of dry powder to protect yourself against market swings. Your potential profits go down with both strategies, but so too does the potential for an unexpectedly quick exit if the market veers away from you.

So why own currencies this way? Those leveraged returns. A simple savings account in Zurich or London or Santiago isn't going to generate the kinds of returns that a currency-trading account potentially will.

Then again, that savings account doesn't carry the same degree of risk, either. Moreover, foreign-currency savings accounts are an easy option for investors these days. Banks overseas will generally welcome your money just as warmly as do the foreign brokerage firms. I was traveling in Vancouver, Canada, in 2005 and popped into a local bank branch downtown and opened a savings account in just a few minutes with my U.S. driver's license and passport. As I mentioned elsewhere, I opened an account at a bank in Sydney, Australia, by way of e-mails and a letter sent with photocopies of my passport. I was in the process of opening a Chinese renminbi account at the Bank of East Asia's Canal Street branch, in the heart of New York City's Chinatown, before a cross-country move sidelined the process. It really is that easy.

But you don't have to physically travel overseas or e-mail banks in foreign lands to open a foreign-currency savings account. Instead, you can go to Jacksonville, Florida—electronically speaking.

There you'll find EverBank Financial Corp., a thrift holding company that runs EverBank.com, the only online bank in the country (as of 2007) that offers deposit accounts and certificates of deposit denominated in 16 world currencies, everything from the major currencies mentioned earlier in this chapter to the Czech koruna, Mexican peso, and South African rand. You can even open an account linked to the movement in the renminbi. All the accounts are FDIC insured, meaning your account is covered in the event of a bank insolvency, though the value of the account itself can go down if the foreign currency sinks.

Why own currencies this way? A few reasons: You pick up exposure to a foreign economy you want included in your portfolio for diversification reasons; you want to benefit from higher interest rates that might be paid overseas; or you just want to speculate on a weakening U.S. dollar. For example, in February 2007, the average one-year CD in the United States paid about 4.65%. In Australia the rate was 5.13%, while in New Zealand it was 6.25%. That's fairly narrow, though at one point, when U.S. CD rates were at or below 1%, New Zealand CDs were paying in excess of 7%.

A key benefit of this type of currency exposure is that you don't have to worry about the market swinging wildly against you over the course of a single day, wiping out your investment. In fact, with a savings account or CD, your investment will never be wiped out. It may lose a tremendous amount of value in dollar terms over time, but you will always own the currency itself, which will have some value. If nothing else, whenever I'm in Canada I can stop by the ATM and pull out my Canadian dollars and spend them while traveling.

THE SEESAW EFFECT

Several pages back I mentioned that when the dollar weakens, your foreign assets are suddenly more valuable by default. That's the natural result of that seesaw action in the currency market—when one currency goes up against another, that other necessarily goes down. When you don't deal with this on a daily basis, it can be a bit confusing, so consider the following example.

You're just back from a trip to London, where you spotted the Boots the Chemist pharmacy chain throughout the city; you even popped into one to grab some toiletries you forgot to pack and picked up their house brand of shaving gel, Botanics, which it turns out you like a good bit. Back home you're shaving one day, thinking about ways to diversify your portfolio by owning some foreign shares, and you look at that tube of shaving gel and remember Boots. Good products, convenient stores, lots of shoppers. You wonder if it's public. It is. The shares trade on the London Stock Exchange as Alliance Boots plc. So, you buy 1,000 shares at a price of £7.03, on a day when $1 will buy you 0.5088 British pounds. (A brief aside: This is a reciprocal quote, the exact opposite of the £1 = $1.9654 a few pages back. If a pound buys $1.9654, how many pounds will $1 buy? Find that answer by dividing 1 by 1.9654 . . . you get 0.5088.)

Now, it's exactly one year later and you decide to sell those Boots shares, and the stock is trading for the same price at which you originally bought it: £7.03.

From the looks of it, your investment accomplished exactly nothing.

Take a look, though, at where the dollar is trading: one greenback now buys only 0.4579 pence. The pound has gained about 10% on the dollar. Your reality: You pocket a profit exceeding 11%. Here's what that math looks like:

PURCHASE

1,000 shares at £7.03 = £7,030

$1 = 0.5088 pence

So, £7030 = $13,816.82 (£7,030 ÷ 0.5088)

Sale

1,000 shares at £7.03 = £7,030

$1 = 0.4579 pence

So, £7,030 = $15,352.70 (£7,030 ÷ 0.4579)

Profit

$1,535.08 ($15,352.70 - $13,816.82)

Return = 11.1% on your original investment.

Even though the price of Boots' stock flatlined, the U.S. dollar weakened against the British pound. That benefited you because when you sold your shares, those pounds, when turned back into dollars and repatriated, bought 11% more dollars than you originally sent overseas to London to buy Boots in the first place.

Imagine now that even as the dollar fell the price of Boots had increased by 20%, rising to £8.44. Here's what that would mean:

Sale
1,000 shares at £8.44 = £8,440
$1 = 0.4579 pence
So, £8,440 = $18,431.97 (£8,440 ÷ 0.4579)
Profit
$4,615.15 ($18,431.97 − $13,816.82)
Return = 33.4% on your original investment.

That—rising prices for foreign investments at a time when the dollar is falling—represents the best of all worlds. Your international investments work twice as hard for your portfolio.

Of course, the same processes work in reverse. If the dollar strengthens against the currency of a country in which you own stock, the value of your investment can shrink in dollar terms. And if the price of the stock has fallen at the same time, well, then you're a two-time loser, at least on paper. There's no rule, of course, and often no pressing need, to sell a stock just because the price is down and the home currency is weak. I've owned foreign shares through up and down currency markets and up and down stock markets, since both regularly ebb and flow. I've never paid much attention to these cycles, content instead to adhere to a main tenet of Chapter 1: Own good companies. They survive the cycles and grow increasingly more valuable over time.

At the end of the day, you just have to accept—and generally look past—the currency fluctuations that are inevitable and recognize that one of the reasons you own overseas shares, or the currencies themselves, is to diversify your portfolio away from dependence singularly on U.S. investments. Just accept that the currency market does go up . . . and the currency market goes down. And then it goes back up again.

It's all just part of the ride.

MUTUAL FUNDS: TO HEDGE OR NOT?

I mentioned this back in Chapter 2, but it bears repeating in a chapter on the effects of currency trading on global assets: When you invest internationally through mutual funds, pay attention to whether a fund hedges its currency exposure or not. It can have a dramatic impact on your returns.

Those that hedge seek to offset their inherent currency exposure through investments in the currency market that are designed to neutralize any currency movements. If a mutual fund owns Britain's Alliance Boots, for instance, it might use currency contracts to negate any fall in the pound, so that whatever returns the fund earns will be the result of stock-price movement and not currency swings.

That strategy has its pros and cons. On the upside, currency swings will not impact the returns and the only factor that matters is company performance, and you don't face that double-edged pain of falling foreign stock prices as the dollar strengthens. On the downside, you miss out on currency diversification since there's no currency impact, and you do not benefit from the double-edged surprise when foreign stock prices are rising even as the dollar weakens.

Hedged mutual funds are best for investors who want international stock exposure but for whatever reason do not want the currency risk.

Funds that do not hedge leave you wide open to all the currency risk and rewards. These funds are best for investors who want not only international stock exposure but foreign currency exposure as well.

You can usually determine whether a particular fund is hedged or not at morningstar.com. Or, hit the fund company's website; the prospectus will detail how the fund handles currency exposure.

CHAPTER 6

A SLEEPING GIANT

China Awakes

China is like a sleeping giant. Let her sleep. For when she awakes, the world will be shaken.
NAPOLEON BONAPARTE, 1803

That giant has awakened.

Anyone with access to a TV, radio, newspaper, or magazine since the turn of the millennium knows that China is booming. I knew that when I first opened brokerage accounts in Singapore and Hong Kong to gain access to stocks in mainland China and the stocks of companies across Asia that will be long-term beneficiaries of China's expansion.

And then I saw China.

My wife and I arrived in Hefei, in the dead center of China's Anhui province, a few hours west of Shanghai, to adopt a baby girl. We had just flown in from Guangzhou, China, on a noticeably modern and efficient, Boeing-built China Southern Airlines flight that departed from a sparkling new international airport the country had recently baptized, and into which China had poured the equivalent of some $2.4 billion in an effort to appropriately service the tens of millions of tourists and business folk who now visit the gateway to the vibrant Pearl River delta region in southern China.

This was fall 2004. Our hotel (owned by France's publicly traded Accor SA, which also operates the Motel 6, Studio 6, and Red Roof Inn chains in the United States, the shares of which, however, are not available on either the NYSE or the Nasdaq) was near the center of town, overlooking a sculptured park and lake that stretches several city blocks and houses a temple originally built 1,000 years ago to memorialize a local army officer revered for his honesty and strict enforcement of law. I learned this while sitting on a bench in that park one morning; an elderly Chinese gentleman, after moving gracefully, if not artistically, through his Tai Chi choreography, approached me to practice his best broken English. The temple, he said, "is symbol of city's past." If so, then Hefei itself, and in particular the view from our hotel balcony, is a symbol of China's future.

A flock of construction cranes — 17 that I counted, though I only had a view of a portion of the city — towered above the low-rise cityscape, each resizing Hefei's skyline with an ultramodern office tower, apartment building, or shopping mall that stretched up instead of out.

The notability is this: This is Hefei. This is not Beijing; it's not Shanghai; it's not Guangzhou. It's not even Qingdao, a port city that Americans might recognize if only because of the eponymous beer—publicly traded Tsingtao—that's brewed there and that's on the menu of just about every Chinese eatery in the states. Those cities, most along the eastern coast, generally commandeer much of the press when it comes to explaining China's growth. And those cities are, indeed, impressive examples of growth. Storied Shanghai, for instance, was once so morose that Hong Kong residents who flew in to visit family would invite those relatives to stay with them for the day at the famous Peace Hotel—the only hotel of any luxury at the time—for a hot shower. Today Shanghai is every bit as luxurious as Hong Kong, and well-heeled Shanghainese, looking for a bargain on haute couture and jewelry, jet off to the former

British colony for the weekend because prices there are often cheaper than in the designer boutiques back in Shanghai's fashionable French Concession neighborhood and the Pudong district, so futuristic it's reminiscent of the movie *Blade Runner,* only without the dark, foreboding ambiance and Harrison Ford's voice-over. Ten years earlier, Pudong was pastures and farmland. Nearby, sitting amid newly designed and manicured golf courses and landscaped parks and ponds are bucolic developments designed to reflect the colonial, California, and Southwestern architecture in the United States. In the summer of 2006, many of these homes were selling for the equivalent of $400,000 or more.

Hefei is none of that. Of course, the scale is warped in comparison with the United States.

With 1.4 million urbanites, Hefei is a city that, if transported to America, would rival Philadelphia and Phoenix as the fifth or sixth most populated urban center in the states. In other words, a player, home to a professional sports team or three. In Chinese terms, however, Hefei is relatively picayune, a bush leaguer whose population doesn't even crack the country's 30 largest cities. Mention Hefei to Chinese natives and many times they'll gaze at you in that same puzzled way an American would if someone from China mentioned they'd visited Starkville. You've heard of it somewhere, but can't recall that it's in Mississippi. Hefei is a tertiary town — middle America, Chinese style.

Yet Hefei's streets tell the story of an emerging consumer class unfolding from the coastal cities in the east to Chongqing in the southern interior of the country, the fastest-growing city in China and where half a million new residents arrive every year, roughly the equivalent of Albuquerque, New Mexico, relocating to Chongqing annually.

During a nearly two-week stay in Hefei, I shopped with locals in new hypermarkets, where Chinese consumers increasingly buy everything from name-brand foreign foods to Chinese-made air conditioners (Haier, publicly traded in Hong Kong, not only is popular in its home country but is also a low-cost competitor gaining market share in the United States). These were well-stocked, well-designed stores with reasonable prices and buyers in just about every aisle, and service that generally exceeds that found in the United States. Looking to replenish the minutes on my cell phone, I ducked into an electronics retailer several city blocks away that the hotel bellman had pointed me toward. Inside was a scene that fills the dreams of retailing executives. Consumers, several rows deep, circled around a central glass counter, each fingering a vast collection of mobile phones more advanced than those typically found in the states. Some shoppers had under their arms new Japanese and South Korean DVD players and a dozen DVDs.

When I made it to the glass counter, I showed the twenty-something clerk the brand of phone card I was looking for and pulled out my mobile phone to show him the SIM card (the phone's electronic brain) that I was using. For the record, this was a phone I had just purchased, brand new, in New York City three weeks earlier. His comment: "This, old technology," he said with the ridicule of a twenty-something chastising an elder for being numbingly out of step with modernity. "You buy this in states, probably. You way behind, mister."

My point: In many ways, China today — as demonstrated in a third-tier city — is as modern as any place in the world, and its growth track resembles that of America of the late 19th and early 20th centuries — a land of great promise for investors, though a promise packaged with guaranteed risks, assured market turmoil, and the great likelihood of more than one financial meltdown along the way. The challenge for a foreign investor lies in riding out the volatility by identifying the companies built to weather the inevitable storms, those that will ultimately survive for the long term in an economy changing as rapidly as it is growing.

How, though, to find those companies when, as a U.S. investor, you're unfamiliar with China, the Chinese economy, Chinese brands, and China's publicly traded stocks, not to mention the language? You don't have to travel to China to do it. That's what this chapter is all about — researching unfamiliar companies in unfamiliar markets to find worthwhile investments. This chapter and the next one, on Eastern Europe, bring together everything in this book, the case studies to help you see the process in action, from soup to nuts.

Don't be intimidated by the term "research." You don't need an MBA to be a successful stock picker. Ferreting out good companies is much more about basic detective work than it is rocket science or convoluted mathematical calculations. Here's what you need:

- an understanding of the company in which you're interested in investing;
- a feel for the trends that define the company's future growth prospects;
- working knowledge of some very basic financial calculations so that you can determine the degree to which a company has been growing and how it's using the cash it generates, and to ensure that you don't wildly overpay for the assets you're buying.

That's pretty much it in a nutshell. Nothing difficult about it really. And the best part is that everything you need you can find online. The biggest challenge is time, since even at the speed of electrons, researching an investment idea online will likely consume several hours over a few days — a comparatively small ante, of course, when you consider the profit potential of tapping into a rapidly growing company about which most other American investors are clueless.

Be forewarned: Before investing your first dollar in China, you have to enter this country knowing that it is not a short-term investment.

Nor is China a market for investors with a fragile constitution. The country is racing through a litany of economic, political, legal, and social reforms, many of which will take years to fall into place and any one of which can upset investors on any given day, sending Chinese stocks into a tizzy, if not a tailspin, that can last months or even years. The government still makes

pronouncements that routinely unsettle the market as bureaucrats schooled for decades in central planning struggle to
impose restraints on the free market and the currency that naturally want to move in unfettered fashion. Graft and corruption
remain commonplace, particularly at the local and city level.
Corporate governance certainly raises concerns, since the financial statements and managerial motives for some mainland Chinese companies often leave much to wonderment. The legal
system needs reworking to cement in place the rule of law that
will protect the property rights of individuals and companies.

Avian flu and SARS . . . either will have investors fleeing
markets around the globe if a pandemic ever erupts. On a more
localized level, however, a bout of avian flu in Southeast Asia,
and particularly in Hong Kong or China, will drive Chinese
shares much lower.

Perhaps the single biggest risk is the split dividing wealthy
Chinese who can afford European sedans and Western-style
McMansions in the coastal cities, and the poverty-addled peas-
ants in the rural hinterlands who have yet to taste China's new
prosperity. Deng Xiaoping, head of China's Communist party
from the late 1970s to the early 1990s, famously launched
China's capitalism-with-a-Communist-flavor boom by pro-
nouncing that "to get rich is glorious." And while many Chinese are, indeed, gloriously rich these days, the gap between
those haves and have-nots is now one of the widest in the
world, wider even than in the United States. Nothing like a
bout of economic iniquity to boil over into political insurrec-
tion that destabilizes China at some point. If that happens,
investors will fly out of Chinese stocks for fear that a government crackdown will revoke economic and social freedoms, or
lock down assets. This is a risk that will be around for a few
decades at least, until the prosperity redefining coastal China
spreads west into the less affluent provinces.

Scary possibilities aside, Chinese leaders are not blind to
any of these matters. They recognize that for China to morph
into that economic giant of which Napoleon foretold, they must
successfully address each. And they're trying to do so, openly.

The country's 11th Five-Year Plan, adopted in 2006, includes a stated push to drive development from the prosperous south and east into the north and west. The document (found all over the Internet) also has the central and regional governments addressing the rich-poor/urban-rural chasm, as well as wasteful use of resources, environmental deterioration that has happened alongside rapid development, and the corruption that remains all too rife. The fact that China's leadership is even talking about these necessary fixes is a step toward the solutions.

Corporate governance and China's legal system are coming in for a makeover, too, making those but temporary risks. Perhaps more than in any other developing nation, Chinese companies recognize that the imprimatur of a big, respected Western accounting firm provides a comfort level that global investors demand. Many companies, particularly the entrepreneurial companies that did not come out of state industries, are listing their shares in Hong Kong, where financial-market regulations have long met Western standards. Combined, that's giving investors greater confidence in those companies. Meanwhile, the Chinese court system in late 2006 upheld the patent on the world's most famous blue pill, Pfizer Inc.'s Viagra, ordering two Chinese drug companies to stop producing generic knockoffs and to pay Pfizer damages. It's a small step, but a significant one toward the industrialized world for a country where piracy of Western products is a national sport.

To own China means to be a part of all such processes — and the ups and the downs and periods of sideways inactivity — over the long term. And "long term" in this instance describes at least a decade, preferably more. It will take that long for China to work out all the kinks and put in place the necessary rules, laws, and regulations that investors, businesses, and consumers demand; to institute the investor protections that industrialized nations operate under; to right an addled banking system; to bring development and prosperity into the interior of the country; and to remove all currency controls that hamper the renminbi's movements against world currencies. All of this is happening at various speeds, though in every case much too slow for Western governments and investors. But China is what China is, and Western pronouncements and desires will not change China's measured gait, just as European and Asian frustrations with American policies don't prompt immediate changes in Washington, D.C. You want a short-term play on China, go buy shares in Starbucks, which will see its stock pop the first time the company talks about opening its 1,000th store in China. Or take a flyer on the iShares FTSE/Xinhua China 25 index (an exchange-traded fund on the American Stock Exchange) when the market is in a funk over some Chinese policy or event, and then sell when the rebound strikes. Maybe plunk down some dollars to buy Chinese ADRs in New York just as you hear or read that U.S. investors are beginning to turn bullish on Chinese stocks again, as they routinely do from time to time, after some period of bearish worries. That's the way to play China if you're just a punter. But if you're a risk-tolerant investor, the way to play China is to own Chinese shares directly — preferably in China, rather than on the New York Stock Exchange — or to own shares that trade on other Asian bourses of the companies that are operating directly in China.

For the reality of China early in the 21st century is that the country is well along its road to economic success, though it certainly has many more miles to travel. More important, China as a nation wants the rest of the developed world to look upon it as a financial peer, an equal, not an emerging nation. The Chinese populace, meanwhile, wants stable politics (and China is already far more stable than most), a clean environment, and a legal system that protects their rights. And it's all coming, though from here to there remains a lengthy, winding trip.

A middle class — estimated in 2006 at some 66 million people, or about a quarter of the entire U.S. population at the moment — is rising up in part because local and Western businesses, recognizing the opportunities to serve a vast population of buyers, are setting up shop to be part of what China will be. In doing so they're competing for the best and the brightest talents. That always drives up salaries, which in turn naturally leads to disposable income that Chinese consumers deploy just as consumers in Des Moines and Denver do. Even if just 10% of the population reaches middle class — and China is shooting for a much larger percentage than that, given that 5% have already attained that status and the growth is just beginning — the Chinese middle class will about equal the size of the American middle class, meaning China will be running alongside America as the world's largest base of consumers. More likely China's middle class will equal about 45% of the population by 2020, according to Ernst & Young, meaning the Chinese middle class will be gargantuan, the largest group of consumers in the world. Here's why that's so important, aside from being a mother lode for retailers and consumer-product companies: Most emerging-market economies are tied in some meaningful fashion to the United States or Western Europe. If consumption in either of those markets softens, the emerging economies feel it, too, since their consumer base isn't large enough to grow a business beyond a certain size. China, along with India, is of such potential girth that it can escape that tradition, developing a level of consumption that, while still tied to some degree to America and Western Europe, will be self-sustaining.

As for that rural/urban divide so many rightfully fret about, turn it around and it's an opportunity as China's leaders seek ways to bring wealth to the poor, and as Chinese businesses and foreign companies move inland to develop the multitude of interior cities, many of which already exceed a million residents.

Even as all this growth is transforming the country, however, there's no reason to blindly rush into Chinese stocks. The upward bias is a long-term, secular move, with the emphasis on long . . . really long. Yet if Chinese stocks are expensive when you read this, and many of them were very expensive as I wrote this in mid-2007, bide your time researching the companies you want to own, determine a fair price you'd be willing to pay, and wait for those shares to come back to you. That's investing. Chasing a high-priced stock higher simply for the sake of not wanting to miss the train is Russian roulette with multiple bullets: there's far more likelihood of pain if that train derails unexpectedly. Better to buy good companies at broken prices.

And so the question: How do you invest in China, and what's worth owning for the long haul?

FIRST STOP . . .

You need a broker.

Before you start researching Chinese stocks to potentially buy, you must have a way to buy the ones you like. So, start searching the Internet first for Asian brokerage firms that will service a U.S. client *and* that provide access to the Chinese stock markets. Look back at Chapter 3, where, in the early pages, you'll find a template for the short, simple e-mail to dispatch.

The logical location from which to base a China-investment account is Hong Kong because it uniquely straddles the Western world and the Middle Kingdom, providing trading capabilities directly on Chinese exchanges, yet operating bilingually and according to trading and reporting standards not unlike what you're accustomed to at home. As mentioned previously, Boom Securities (www.boom.com) is one Hong Kong brokerage firm that, at least as of this writing, provides direct access to the Chinese exchanges in Shenzhen and Shanghai. But shop around for others that might serve your needs better. The world changes often, and what existed when these words were written may be vastly different from what's available when you're reading these words now—whenever "now" is for you.

THE CHINESE MARKETS

Essentially, you have five stock markets on which you'll find the purest Chinese investments: Hong Kong, Shanghai, Shenzhen, Taiwan, and Singapore.

- The **Hong Kong** Stock Exchange is the principal
exchange for China, and it is a major, Asian financial
capital. It represents the largest, most liquid market in
China; is considered one of the world's handful of
developed markets; and is jockeying for position as the
most important financial capital between New York and
London (assuming, of course, you fly west out of JFK
Airport). It operates under regulatory standards similar to
those in other developed markets, and according to
generally equivalent accounting standards. China's blue-
chip stocks are traded here, though they're known as red
chips (but more on that in a minute), and it is the
exchange to which leading Chinese companies such as Air
China and the Bank of China go to launch their initial
public offerings. Not all the shares listed here, however,
are China-focused. These are Hong Kong companies, by
and large, and while many do have natural ties to the
mainland, not all do. So don't just assume that if you own
Hong Kong companies, you own an investment in
mainland China's growth.
- **Shanghai** and **Shenzhen** are the purely Chinese markets,
where the bulk of Chinese shares trade. Different stocks
are assigned to different exchanges. The regulatory
environment and the financial reporting standards are
not equivalent with what you'll find in Hong Kong and
what you're accustomed to in the United States — though
that is changing and some companies are already up to
snuff. Liquidity can also be an issue. Though these are
Chinese markets, foreign investors can only buy and sell a
select number of Chinese companies, known as B shares,
which I'll explain in a moment.
- **Taiwan,** though an emerging market, is a well-developed
economy. In 2006 the island nation had one of the world's
larger economies and the third-largest store of foreign-
exchange reserves. The country's soft infrastructure —
such as legal, banking, education — is relatively strong in
the region, and Taiwanese companies have been leaders at

investing across Asia. Many companies on the Taiwan Stock Exchange have operations in mainland China, though the risk, of course, remains that tensions in the Taiwan Strait flare up, China exerts some sort of military power over Taiwan, and investors hammer Taiwanese shares.

- **Singapore** is less China-centric than Hong Kong; many of the Singaporean companies are Singapore-focused, particularly involved in local real estate and finance. Others have a strong global bent, offering energy and shipping services. So a China investment in Singapore is a bit removed. Nevertheless, companies with deep, fundamental ties to China do trade here; some Hong Kong companies have relisted their stocks in Singapore, as well. And like Hong Kong, Singapore is considered one of the world's developed markets. The economy, the government, and the currency are some of the most stable in the world. Financial regulations are stringent.

THE CHINESE SHARES: A, B, AND H, AND THE RED CHIPS AND P-CHIPS

This is potentially the most confusing aspect of Chinese stocks. These multiple share classes determine what you're buying or who's eligible to buy it. Here's how it breaks down.

- **A shares**: Chinese companies incorporated in mainland China and, as of 2007, only Chinese citizens can own them (or qualified foreign institutional investors, but that's not us). These represent the vast bulk of China's public companies. Here you'll find everything from bloated, stagnant state industries that have been pawned off to the public in a privatizing campaign, to some pretty well run businesses with a bit of an entrepreneurial spirit. Many are troubled companies; some are quite good. Either way, if you're not Chinese you can all but forget about them . . . unless you happen to find a mutual fund in Hong Kong or elsewhere in Asia that holds A shares, in which case you do have a way in, assuming you want A-share access. **You can always tell an A share because it is priced in renminbi, the local currency.** China is talking of restructuring its share market at some point, a function of which will be to remove the restrictions on A-share ownership, allowing foreigners to trade them, too.

• **B shares**: Also Chinese companies incorporated in mainland China, but these are the Chinese shares that foreigners can own. These trade in either Shanghai or Shenzhen. **You'll always know the B shares because they're priced in either U.S. dollars (in Shanghai) or Hong Kong dollars (in Shenzhen).** Again, you'll find companies that span the spectrum of respectability, with some real dogs mixed in amid some standout businesses. But far fewer B-share companies exist, limiting your opportunity to diversify into sectors and companies you might want to own. Many companies issue both A and B shares, though you'll typically find that the B shares trade at a discount—sometimes a steep discount—to the A shares. That's because the A shares are essentially a punter's playground for China's individual investors who largely see stocks as just another gamble; meanwhile, the professional Western investors who buy into the B-share market do so according to a traditional investor's mentality and do not, by and large, trust the accounting or the regulations by which Chinese companies play. So, they discount the shares to account for the various risks they face. Pay attention to the B-share market and you will find some excellent companies at attractive prices. But B shares can be highly volatile as foreign investors move into and out of the stocks as interest in the China-investment theme comes and goes from time to time. When China completely reforms its financial markets, the B shares will likely convert to A shares.

• **H shares**: Just remember that the "H" stands for Hong Kong. Once again, these are **the Chinese stocks incorporated in mainland China, but they trade in Hong Kong.** H shares are typically—though not always—China's most dynamic companies. The Chinese and Asian mutual funds U.S. investors come across at home almost exclusively limit their China experience to H shares, largely because they are highly liquid and must abide by the far more strict financial-reporting requirements imposed by Hong Kong's securities regulators. These are all priced in Hong Kong dollars. Again, a key consideration: Relatively few H-share companies exist compared with the A-share firms inside China. That is changing as increasing numbers of Chinese companies seek H-share status, for the credibility it confers and the access to global capital that a listing in Hong Kong provides. Indeed, the largest initial public offering in history (at least through 2006) was a Chinese H share, the Industrial and Commercial Bank of China, ICBC, which raised roughly $19 billion in October 2006.

• **Red chips**: A lot like the H shares, only their place of incorporation is different. Red chips are **Hong Kong–incorporated companies whose assets are largely Chinese.** They trade on the Hong Kong Stock Exchange, priced in Hong Kong dollars. Why red? In China, red symbolizes prosperity and good fortune—which, if you think about it, is a better image for investing than America's famed blue chips, which got their name from gambling's blue poker chips.

• **P-chips**: The truly private sector, from which comes the "P" designation. These are the **private, entrepreneurial companies incorporated outside of China, but which conduct the bulk of their business or hold their assets and investments inside China.** Whereas all the other share types often have some form of ties to the state, P-chips are independent of the state, and thus investors generally put more faith in these companies' financials and their corporate governance— though P-chips are just as capable as others of misrepresenting reality. These stocks trade on the Hong Kong exchange.

CHINESE SHARES BY THE LETTER . . . AND COLOR

China shares	A shares	B shares	H shares	Red chips	P-chips
Place of incorporation	Mainland	Mainland	Mainland	Outside of China	Outside of China
Listing exchanges	Shanghai Stock Exchange; Shenzhen Stock Exchange	Shanghai Stock Exchange; Shenzhen Stock Exchange	Hong Kong Stock Exchange	Hong Kong Stock Exchange	Hong Kong Stock Exchange
Trading currency	Renminbi	US$ in Shanghai; HK$ in Shenzhen	HK$	HK$	HK$
Who can trade	Mainland residents; qualified foreign institutional investors	Foreign investors	Foreign investors	Foreign investors	Foreign investors

WHERE TO BUY . . .

The obvious answer is China, and I'll get to that in a moment. The not-so-obvious answer is "all over Asia and around the Pacific," since countries from New Zealand to Japan to Chile are feeding the beast that is China's bulging economy.

You can take that a step further, to Europe, since a number of European firms have China ties as well. Carrefour, the French retailing giant, operates an expanding base of food markets across China. Nokia, the Finnish mobile-phone firm, has seen a sharp profit increase thanks to growth in China. And Kingfisher plc, a UK retailer that runs the B&Q do-it-yourself home-improvement chain (think The Home Depot or Lowe's), has plans for 100 stores across China by 2009 to benefit, the company hopes, from the rapid escalation of home ownership in the Middle Kingdom.

In short, companies far removed from China are rushing to capture some of the growth there, while China, because of the speed at which its population is urbanizing, has no choice but to look to international companies to satisfy its need for resources and its citizens' desires for consumer items.

There's a shortcoming, though, with this backdoor approach. Generally speaking, the further removed you are from China itself, the less pure your exposure. To pick on Starbucks yet again, while the coffee chain will certainly have a big klatch of shops in China, it will still be a U.S.-based company. China will certainly add incrementally to Starbucks' earnings, but the country won't define the company—just as China won't define Carrefour or Nokia.

A savvier backdoor strategy is investing on China's periphery through Asian neighbors, since so many Asian companies have so much to gain from being so close to China's threshold. For many of these companies, sales inside China represent the bulk, if not all, of their business, as is the case with a cracker maker in Singapore known as Want Want Holdings Ltd., which books nearly 90% of its sales inside China. That's much closer to purity than owning companies a world away that benefit only on the margins from China's growth.

These are just some of the industries you might think about: Taiwanese glassmakers supplying the windows going into all those high-rise towers; Japanese heavy-industries firms making the construction machinery clearing the land and raising the towers; Australian mining companies digging all that copper and other metals out of the ground that China is consuming with all the cars it's making and the homes, office complexes, and retail centers it's building; Hong Kong and Singapore retailers and banks catering to the expanding mass of Chinese citizens who have the discretionary income to both spend and save; Hong Kong natural-gas companies that are piping the smelly commodity into many of the new homes and businesses that are springing up all over the place; agribusiness companies around Asia, but particularly in Malaysia, Thailand, and

Indonesia, that are supplying China with everything from edible oils (think palm oil) and rice crackers to dairy products and canned fish. (By the way, anything you might want to know about Chinese food trends is packed into a 68-page report from the U.S. Department of Agriculture's Economic Research Service, which you can read for free at www.ers.usda.gov; look for the report titled "China's Food and Agriculture: Issues for the 21st Century." One idea based on this report: Companies producing fertilizers, oilseeds, and grains face a bright future. China must import all of those in large numbers.)

But be cautious: Although there are certain areas where China has no choice but to buy from outside its borders, such as its need for, say, copper and other industrial metals for which it does not have big internal capacity, the country is ramping up productivity in other industries, such as glassmaking, that will one day pressure the outside firms.

INVESTMENT RESEARCH

Much of this is covered back in Chapter 3, and those same strategies for uncovering the facts and figures and future prospects for various companies and industries work just as well for China investments as they do for other global markets you might be interested in. But there are a few sites specific to Asia and China that will help:

• **Xinhuanet.com**: This is the official Chinese news agency, so the news has an obvious Chinese-government bent. But it is considered one of the world's premier news agencies nonetheless. The stories are fairly thin and without much analysis, though the site provides information useful to investors doing China research, and it often names other publications you'll find online to help you round out your research.
• **ChinaNews.cn**: Another news agency, though one not tied directly to the government.

- **ChinaDaily.com.cn**: The Web version of China's English daily newspaper. Some stories it runs are reprints of Xinhua News Agency and other wire-service stories, but it also has its own staff of reporters offering writing with a bit more analysis.
- **People's Daily** (english.peopledaily.com.cn): Another English-language Chinese news site, similar to *China Daily*'s, with wire-service and staff reports.
- **Association for Asian Research** (asianresearch.org): A nonprofit, nonpartisan, nongovernmental, independent research institution writing to enlighten a Western (read U.S.) audience about the social, economic, cultural, environmental, and political affairs throughout Asia. The "Trade & Economics" section offers very detailed, analytical takes on various topics from whether the Bank of China is overvalued to revaluing the renminbi. Basically, a very good current-affairs e-zine for Asia.
- **China Center for Economic Research** (en.ccer.edu.en): A bit threadbare, this site, run by Peking University in Beijing, nevertheless posts useful pieces on the Chinese economy that offer investors a unique, Chinese insight into the country's economic issues.
- **European Institute for Asian Studies** (eias.org): A Brussels-based research institute and think-tank, largely sponsored by the European Union. Much of what's on offer requires a pricey membership. Some analysis, however, is gratis, and it provides a European perspective to balance out the U.S./Chinese perspectives that both can be too extreme at times.
- **U.S.-China Economic and Security Review Commission** (uscc.gov): A U.S. government commission that monitors and reports on the national-security implications of America's trade with China. This free site posts some detailed, excellent analysis on a variety of economic issues that have direct impact on industries you might be interested in owning in China.

WHAT TO BUY . . .

The answer to that question varies from day to day, month to month, year to year as market conditions change, as company finances improve or deteriorate, as stock prices fluctuate, and as various sectors of the economy move into and out of fashion with investors. Telling you what to buy in 2008 wouldn't mean much to a reader in 2012, when so much is likely to be so different. But there is a simple way to consider China for the long haul: Whatever China needs, own it.

Think about what it means for an economy to grow. Actually, think about what it means for your family to grow. Families are economies in microcosm: As they grow in size, they need more infrastructure — a bigger car, a bigger house, more insurance, more food; as they grow in income, they have more money to spend on disposable items and consumer goods — electronics, higher-quality food, vacations. The Chinese economy will mirror that, writ large — really large. So, spending will be an overriding theme for several decades as Chinese consumers, businesses, and governments spend to propel the country into the ranks of the industrialized world. That means spending on:

- Infrastructure — roads, bridges, airports, ports, sewerage, water-treatments plants, housing developments, skyscrapers, malls, zoos, electrical plants, stadiums, hospitals.
- Leisure — air travel, hotels, cruises, restaurants, movies, bowling alleys, casinos, sports equipment, retail shopping.
- Consumer durables — washing machines, dryers, dishwashers, microwave ovens, refrigerators, furniture, cars, audio/video equipment, computers.
- Consumer staples — milk, beer, soft drinks, medicines, food, clothes, natural gas, automobile gasoline.
- Financial services — banking, insurance, mutual funds, brokerage firms, investor services.

Those represent a few of the areas where you want to begin searching for long-term investments in China. You won't find all of them as publicly traded companies at the moment, since some of these areas are too immature. But they will appear over time. **Don't fall into the trap of regarding China as purely a play on global outsourcing and cheap labor for Western companies to exploit.** That's not the China of tomorrow. If China were to succeed singularly as the cheapest place on the planet to manufacture widgets, then the country would see itself as an utter failure. China is increasingly an incubator of homegrown companies, many of which are becoming multinationals themselves, striving to create their own local and global brands.

Indeed, in 2005 China National Offshore Oil Corp., the country's mammoth energy company, tried to buy American oil firm Unocal, while in 2006 ChinaMobile, the country's leading cell-phone firm, went shopping for new business in Asia, Africa, and Latin America. That same year, Nanjing Automobile set out to become the first Chinese automaker to build a production plant in the United States. Or consider Top Victory Electronics, a Hong Kong company that serves as an original-equipment maker supplying liquid crystal displays to electronics giants the likes of Dell, Sharp, and Sony. Yet Top Victory is one of the largest makers of LCD televisions inside China, where it has a substantial share of the consumer market. The company has also begun to market its brand overseas, including inside the United States, under the name Envision. Or just think Lenovo, the Chinese electronics firm that bought the IBM computer brand and now markets the name around the world. Even Chinese grocery chain Lianhua Supermarket Holdings (more on this company in a moment) has talked of expanding into Europe with its own branded retail stores.

As an investor in China, then, you have to look beyond manufacturing and outsourcing to find the companies that will be the belles of the ball years from now.

How do I know all of this? None of it is secret information. You don't need contacts within a Chinese brokerage firm or an economic think-tank to figure this out. All of it is based on reading and analyzing publicly available data. So, in keeping with the overarching message of this book—that owning foreign stocks directly is easier than you think—let's dig into some research. Again, none of the companies mentioned are specific investment recommendations; they're just examples of what companies exist, how to think about an expanding economy, and where to go in search of stock ideas to meet the themes that you ultimately determine are worthwhile.

ALL ABOARD . . .

Take a look at the news item below. It comes from the *Financial Times* of Apr. 26, 2006 —a tiny blurb that ran in the World News Digest. Small, yet with big implications. The headline says it all:

CHINA TOURISM SPENDING TO SOAR

China will grab the world's second largest share of global travel and tourism spending after the U.S. by 2016, an industry body said in a report published this week.

"We're all running very fast to keep up with the changes that are taking place," the World Travel and Tourism Council (WTTC) quoted its president, Jean-Claude Baumgarten, as saying at the launch of the group's report three years after its last one.

The WTTC report forecast that China's tourism demand would grow an average 8.7 percent a year between 2007 and 2016. Reuters, Beijing.

Here it is that China, according to this report, "will grab the world's second largest share of global travel and tourism spending after the U.S. by 2016." An investor with a long-term bullish bent on China should read that and immediately think: What travel-industry companies will win?

I mentioned Hong Kong hotelier Shangri-La Asia in Chapter 4 and explained the rationale for buying the company's shares when I did several years ago. Shangri-La is likely to be on the list of long-term winners. But it isn't the only hotel chain with a meaningful presence in the region. A cursory search of the Internet offers up other possibilities, including Mandarin Oriental International Ltd., the Singapore company behind the eponymous chain; Hong Kong and Shanghai Hotels Ltd., which operates the luxurious Peninsula Hotels brand; and Regal Hotels International, another Hong Kong–based chain. In late 2006, Shanghai-based Jin Jiang International Hotel Co. listed its shares on the Hong Kong exchange; Jin Jiang owns more than 200 hotels across its home country, everything from five-star luxury hotels, including Shanghai's famed Peace Hotel, to budget-priced inns that dot the country. All of these chains are worthy of at least a few minutes of rudimentary research to determine whether any would make a decent play on China's long-term travel trends.

Beyond hotels, there are the airlines that ferry tourists into and out of China. Inside China are several carriers that, while they compete to a certain degree, tend to be regional in their coverage. Air China is the big national airline and is publicly traded in Hong Kong. Of the regional carriers, Shanghai's China Eastern Airlines and Guangzhou's China Southern Airlines are the largest and fastest-growing. Outside of mainland China is Hong Kong's Cathay Pacific, routinely rated one of the world's best airlines, a fact you'll find plastered all over the Internet with minimal search effort required. Cathay itself has limited exposure to direct flights into and out of China (serving only Beijing, Shanghai, and Xiamen), but the carrier in 2006 snapped up Dragon Air, a top-flight Hong Kong carrier that serves roughly a score of Chinese cities daily.

Of course, airlines are a notoriously risky lot, particularly in the United States, where price competition is intense among long-standing carriers that have overlapping route structures, and because of the high costs of equipment and fuel. Overseas airlines must manage similar fuel and equipment costs, but the price competition they face isn't of the same intensity. For that reason, you'll find that foreign carriers sport far more muscular profit margins than U.S. carriers. Cathay Pacific, for instance, reported a net profit margin north of 8% in 2005; Singapore Airlines posted profits above 9%; Air China approached 10%. U.S. carriers were generally 5% and below. In case you care, that same year Brazil's Gol Airlines (profit margin of 23%), Ireland's Ryanair (22%), and Panama's COPA (17%) were three of the strongest carriers in the world financially, and all are publicly traded. All this information, by the way, you'll easily find at the International Air Transport Association, which publishes a variety of industry data on its website, www.iata.org.

Casinos represent another tourism segment poised to benefit over many years. The Chinese are big on gaming, and Malaysia and Macao are their destinations of choice. Macao, the former Portuguese colony that reverted to Chinese control in 1999, is home to the largest number of casinos in Asia, while Malaysia is home to the biggest casino, Casino de Genting, run by Resorts World Berhad, a Malaysian casino-gaming company traded on the Kuala Lumpur Stock Exchange. And who's making all the slot machines and other games the casino patrons are playing? Look south to Australia and Aristocrat Leisure Ltd., which announced in its 2005 annual shareholder presentation that, among other things, "Macau remains [a] standout performer."

All of that from a three-paragraph blurb in a pink-hued newspaper? Well, yes and no. Yes, because that's the kind of blurb that leads you to research companies in some industry that seems poised for expansion. No, because it's not just that little blurb that had me thinking travel. Over the months leading up to that blurb, I'd clipped several other articles noting the boom in Chinese travel. In one, U.S.-based Expedia.com, the world's largest online travel company, had announced plans to upgrade the Chinese travel website for which it was majority owner on expectations that China's army of travelers will balloon in coming years. An *Economist* magazine piece noted that "a record number of Chinese tourists traveled around their own country during a seven-day national holiday . . . and spent record amounts of money," and that the prospects for continued growth of the tourism market inside China and out into the Asian neighborhood "look promising." And in just one issue, *Travel + Leisure* magazine (again, anything can be a source of investment inspiration) noted that 1) the United Nations World Tourism Organization projects that outbound travel from China will grow at an average annual rate of 13% for the next 13 years; 2) that China is in the midst of a campaign to build 48 new airports by 2010; and 3) that Macao is remaking itself in the image of Las Vegas, with numerous ostentatious hotel-as-theme-park projects, all in an effort to woo the Chinese, who, again, love their gambling.

That blurb? It just added to the preponderance of mounting evidence leading a rational investor to conclude that China's surging middle class represents many years of profit opportunity in the travel sector.

GOT MILK?

The land of tea has never been much for milk.

But the milk mustache is appearing with greater frequency among the increasingly prosperous Chinese populace. Consider this entry from www.foodsolutionschina.com, an online site for international suppliers to link up with China's food industry:

> *As China perches on a phenomenal wave of economic expansion, the Western world has been lit up in anticipation of the doors opening up to consumerism. But one industry has already slipped over the threshold and made itself very much at home, without the need for great universal logos or zealous pomp: the dairy industry. For years, dairy products have been a foreign commodity in China, but alongside the country's new prosperity has emerged an undeniable thirst for milk.*

How would an investor even know to research milk, or come across something as arcane as Food Solutions China? It goes back to thinking about what consumers want to buy when they have more money.

One of the basic truths of economics is that when you have more cash at hand you upgrade your life, not just your home and clothes and car but also your food. People the world over want to provide themselves and their family with better, more nutritious food. Instead of chicken necks, you buy legs and breasts, or you go for beef every now and again. Instead of the rotgut distilled by a neighbor, you buy beer. Likewise, you start to shop in the dairy case. Milk, like beer, is an upgrade in a developing economy. That bit of 30-second analysis leads you to search "China milk consumption," and up pops the Food Solutions China website. It turns out that milk consumption at the moment is a largely urban affair in China — since that's where the country's consumer cash is concentrated — and that the Chinese consume per-capita about 11 kilograms of milk annually, far below the world average of roughly 98 kilos. In short: There's a lot more room in the Chinese belly for the dairy industry as tens and hundreds of millions of additional Chinese consumers grow into milk drinkers.

The added benefit of that online story: It mentioned by name two Chinese dairy companies, Yili and Mengniu, which, even though they are up against world-class competition from the likes of Nestlé and Danone, have rapidly gained market share. Both are publicly traded (Yili Industrial Group Co. on the Shanghai Stock Exchange; China Mengniu Diary Co. on the Hong Kong exchange). Plug those names into your search engine and you'll unearth a *Business Week* story from late 2005 about Mengniu (pronounced a bit like muhng-nyoo) sponsoring one of China's astronauts, what the magazine labeled a "marketing savvy [that] has helped Mengniu rocket into the ranks of China's best-known brands since its founding" in 1999. The report adds that research firm ACNielsen shows Mengniu is China's leading dairy brand, with 22% of the market.

Mengniu operates its own website, and quite a good one at

that, for English-speaking, investment-minded folks. A couple of minutes poking around the company's investor-relations pages (www.mengniuir.com) and you'll quickly find Mengnui's stock code on the Hong Kong exchange (2319) and a wealth of financial data showing that the milk maker's finances are growing seriously fat off moo-juice. All good reasons to keep a dairy maker based in Inner Mongolia on the radar screen.

On a related front, Western-style supermarkets are gaining traction across China, in part because of the SARS scare, in part because of the increasing consumerism and the demand for prepackaged, ready-to-cook foods that are synonymous with supermarkets. This fact comes across in a 2005 USDA Foreign Agricultural Service report on the northern coastal city of Dalian that I stumbled upon while researching industries that might benefit from the SARS worries that are pervasive in China. That report noted:

> *Similar to many cities in China, as the economy and consumers have matured, traditional wet markets are disappearing. Today, consumers shop at supermarkets, seeking higher quality, consistency, sanitation, and convenience. During the last few years, Dalian's food retail sector has undergone radical transformation given the rapid rise of supermarkets and hypermarkets. These retail formats have extensive dry and frozen goods, fresh and frozen meat and seafood, fruit, vegetables, prepared food, and food service sections. Many of these outlets are located in mall settings or a shopping destination for the whole family with restaurants, theaters, fashion boutiques, sporting-goods stores, and other specialty shops.*

Shopping as entertainment? Sounds an awful lot like the United States, and helps explain why foreign hypermarket retailers such as France's Carrefour, the UK's Tesco, and our Wal-Mart are making such a concerted push into China.

Yet you don't have to venture outside of China itself to find the country's biggest player in supermarkets, hypermarkets, and convenience stores: Search for Lianhua Supermarket Holdings Co. on Yahoo! Finance and you will have found the leading grocery retailer in China—with plans to expand into Europe. Dig only slightly deeper in your search and you'll find a Harvard Business School publication attributing Lianhua's success—expanding from a small Shanghai-based company with a few stores in 1991 into a national superstar with more than 3,600 stores in more than 100 Chinese cities—to its adoption of information-technology systems. You'll also find industry commentary in a variety of places discussing Lianhua's expansion plans and its rapid financial growth.

The build-out of a supermarket retail sector across the vastness that is China still has many stores to go before slowing growth is a concern. And milk has many—many—more gallons to sell before the Chinese market is saturated.

GOT WATER?

As I've said—and shown—global-investment ideas leap at you from all over the place, so long as you're attuned to what's flowing in.

Consider this: In China's Tenth Five-Year Plan, the country's quinquennial outline of development strategies for all parts of society, the economy, and the environment, this one for the period 2001–2005, water was a central theme. The government vowed increased efforts and increased finances to ensure the safety of urban water and to control water pollution, among other water measures.

Water is a huge issue for China, as any rudimentary research will uncover. It may be the ultimate supply vs. demand struggle that the country (and, actually, the world) faces. This from the *New Agriculturist,* a British online publication (www .new-agri.co.uk):

. . . by far the most serious environmental issue that the Chinese urgently need to resolve is that of water. The

country is facing increasingly frequent and desperate shortages . . . insufficient water is already limiting industrial and agricultural output in some areas and threatening to curb China's high economic growth rate . . .

China Daily (www.chinadaily.com.cn), China's English-language daily newspaper, meanwhile, reported in 2004 that more than 400 of 600-plus Chinese cities "are short of water." Or how about this, from Wen Jiabao, at the time China's vice-premier when he made this comment in 1999: "The survival of the Chinese nation is threatened by the country's shortage of water."

How, though, to benefit from this need?

It's readily apparent that any company that can help China manage its water challenges will define "long-term winner" for investors. Water is the antithesis of luxury; it is the epitome of a must-have purchase, not just for consumers but for the businesses and industries China wants to lure. You can't rely on polluted river water to sustain a population much less a company, as Mr. Wen's statement above hints at. And the greatest traits about water—at least for investors—are that water is a commodity without a single substitute and that it's unaffected by economic or geopolitical conditions. Water, not money, makes the world go round, a fact particularly relevant in a country where demand for clean, potable water is taxing local abilities to deliver it and threatening the economy.

Water, though, is one of those areas where you'll have to look outside of China for investment possibilities, given that China doesn't have the technology or water-management skills necessary to handle a problem of this magnitude in-house. The world is awash, however, in water companies of one sort or another, including France's Veolia Environment and Suez Lyonnaise des Eaux, the two leading water companies in the world. Both have large-scale projects under way across China. RWE, a German utility company, is heavily involved in Chinese water projects as well.

Look around the Asian neighborhood and you'll find companies closer to China that also stand to prosper from this ultimate Chinese water torture.

Just across the Sea of Japan, for instance, Kurita Water Industries Ltd., traded in Tokyo, is setting up water-treatment facilities in China. Sekisui Chemical Co., also in Japan, has set up a pipe-fabrication facility in China to help supply the country with the conduits necessary to meet the needs of the expanding water infrastructure. And I mentioned in an early chapter Singapore's Hyflux, which, you'll find at the People's Daily Online, is working with China to build Asia's largest seawater desalination plant in the northern Chinese port city of Tianjin. Singapore's stock exchange is also home to several other water-service companies such as Sinomem Technology, DarcoWater Technologies, Asia Environment Holdings, and Asia Water Technology, all of which are addressing China's water issue in some fashion.

You can find all of these companies and more by simply searching for "China water Singapore," "China water Japan," "China water (fill in a country's name)," or just "China water desalination." Broad searches such as that will gin up more links than you'll ever care to peruse, but reading through a handful will begin to help you narrow your search to specific companies, specific government agencies and their reports, or specific industry analysis that will help you determine how best to invest.

INSURANCE, BANKING, AND CREDIT

"Nowhere are the changes in Asian banking practices more evident—or more sweeping—than in China." That comment comes from one of a series of special reports published from time to time throughout the year by Matthews International Capital Management, the San Francisco shop that runs the various Matthews Asia-focused mutual funds. It's a report that goes to all shareholders, but, more important, it's one that's also available online for anyone with an interest in Asia to read.

This particular report was labeled "The Banking Issue" and focused in large part on China. For China investors, it's good reading. Here are a few of the observations:

Under the Communist system, China's banks were nothing more than an arm of the state — banks in name only — that served to dole out government financing for projects. Even as the country emerged from Communist control, its banking system remained rudimentary . . . China's reforms of 1999 were intended to give the banks a fresh start with fresh capital. But when the banks continued to lose money, the country's leaders realized they had to make fundamental changes in the way the banks did business . . .

In 2003, the government stepped in to recapitalize the two biggest banks. This coincided with a massive reform program, led by the government, encompassing almost every aspect of the banks' operations, management and governance . . . Market deregulation and privatization have compelled banks to become innovative to compete and survive . . .

The biggest driver of change is growing consumer affluence and market demand. Branches have been redesigned to better accommodate retail customers, and banks are moving quickly to expand electronic banking capabilities. Consumer banking is widely viewed as the leading factor in the growth and profitability of China's banks. By some projections, China's total banking assets could double by 2010 compared to 2004 . . . Consumer credit is viewed by some observers as having the potential to transform Chinese society fundamentally.

What's obvious here is that after years of catering almost exclusively to the state, Chinese banks are now refocusing their business on the consumer, and as a result not only is consumer banking surging in China, but it also has a long way to go before it matures as tens of millions of Chinese migrate into the cities, where banking, borrowing, and credit services are increasingly necessary.

A similar future awaits China's nascent insurance industry — as well as credit-card purveyors, brokerage firms, real estate agencies, and asset-management companies, among others. Indeed, just about any financial-services business has many years of growth in front of it. Simply put: Though China is millennia old, its financial-services industry is immature and about to hit a major growth spurt. Little wonder, then, that in December 2006, Carlyle Group, one of America's biggest buyout firms, tag-teamed with Hong Kong's Dah Sing Financial Group to buy a quarter of Chongqing City Commercial Bank in one of China's fastest-growing cities. Earlier, Citigroup grabbed nearly 86% of Guangdong Development Bank, while Newbridge Capital, another U.S. buyout firm, snapped up a significant piece of Shenzhen Development Bank.

Overall, foreign financial firms have invested billions of dollars in China's financial-services sector in what you might call the mother of all deposits. Those firms made — and continue to make — these investments for one reason: the profit potential that's plainly visible as Chinese by the millions seek services ranging from simple checking and savings accounts to credit cards and life insurance.

Consider a few facts from a report you can find online from U.S. consulting firm Booz Allen Hamilton:

- China is set to become Asia's third-largest life insurance market by 2010.
- In 2003, 83 million Chinese took out private health insurance, a market that has been growing at 30% a year.
- China is set to become the world's third-largest market overall for financial services by 2015, trailing only the United States and Japan.

You can smell the money.

Without a doubt, you run headlong into various worries when you own Chinese financial-services companies, most notably banks. Chinese banks have a sordid history littered with lax lending standards, fraud, and risk-management practices that make a night with malarial mosquitoes seem sane. Bank officials have been convicted for accepting bribes to approve loans, which helps explain in part why nonperforming loans across the industry are magnitudes greater than with Western banks.

To be fair, banking regulators in China these days are imposing improved standards and warning systems to bring Chinese banking up to par with that of the industrialized world, though that process will certainly take time. In the meantime, even crime and mismanagement don't stop demand for services that Chinese citizens increasingly see as beneficial to their lives. From an investment standpoint, the trick comes in finding the service providers operating within the bounds of propriety and the law. Some you will find in China itself, such as China Minsheng Banking Corp., the country's first private bank and a custodial bank for China's emerging social security system (as of late 2007, Minsheng traded on the off-limits A-share market in Shanghai but was approved to list its shares in Hong Kong, making them available at some point to foreign investors). Many others you'll find along the fringes of the mainland. Hong Kong's Bank of East Asia and Singapore's DBS Bank Ltd. have made great headway into China and are building branch networks that will grow alongside China's economy. Shinkong Life Insurance, traded in Taiwan, is in a joint venture to hawk life insurance in China.

The industry is still primitive by Western standards, and scores of companies inside China and out are running in too many directions to count as they look for ways to exploit the exploding market for financial services. Some will succeed. Some will stumble along. Some will undoubtedly fail. So, again, there's no need to immediately rush into any one particular stock or industry. You have time to do some research and find the companies you want to own at the price you feel comfortable paying.

HOME IS WHERE THE PROFIT IS

A fast fact from the U.S. Department of Commerce:

China expects to build between 5.2 billion and 5.9 billion square feet of floor space annually in the first 20 years of the 21st century.

In square miles, that amount of space would consume New York's Manhattan island . . . nine times. Basically, China is erecting the equivalent of nine Manhattans a year—for 20 years — for both commercial and residential use.

Yes, there's a chance the country overbuilds and drives prices south for some period of time, a concern that rears up frequently among the media and analysts tracking this stuff. But there's no questioning the basic volume of new demand, particularly when you consider:

- The population shift under way is sending millions upon tens of millions of rural Chinese into cities, all of whom need a place to live.
- Improving standards of living are allowing apartment dwellers to upgrade to better apartments or even single-family homes.
- All the new businesses started by locals and the businesses flooding in from foreign lands to be a part of the economic growth demand office or retail space to serve all the millions of consumers and businesses.

All of this means billions and trillions of renminbi flowing toward property development as well as housing purchases. That's a profitable future for the architectural and construction firms designing and building the office towers, apartment buildings, and residential neighborhoods (and many of those will also be infrastructure plays), as well as the property-management companies that own, lease, or manage office buildings, apartments, and retail centers. This would include companies the likes of China Vanke Co., Beijing North Star Co., and Shui On Land Ltd., among others. All own vast tracts of property in various parts of China upon which they're building, combined, tens of millions of square feet of commercial and residential space. Their stocks weren't necessarily cheap in 2007; both Vanke and North Star had posted a strong surge to that point, and Shanghai's Shui On had just listed its shares on the Hong Kong exchange a few months earlier and thus didn't have a long track record yet as a public company.

But since you're not likely to find it very easy to buy and own a home or apartment directly in China, property-development and management companies like these represent the best opportunity to participate in China's long-term real estate expansion. Shui On, for instance, owns nearly 90 million square feet of office, residential, and entertainment space in Shanghai, Hangzhou, Wuhan, and Chongqing — all major cities. That's just four cities, though. Think about what these companies see when they spread out a map of China on their boardroom tables. Remember Hefei, from the beginning of this chapter? There are dozens of Chinese cities like Hefei, each with more than a million residents, where property-development and management companies have yet to tread to any real degree. The takeaway: Immeasurable growth opportunities exist throughout the country, and only the tiniest sliver has so far been tapped.

Beyond property development and management, growth in real estate, particularly on the residential side, will have impacts on the many products that homeowners buy, from furniture to appliances to fixtures. The beneficiaries are consumer-product makers such as Haier Group, the Chinese maker of freezers, washing machines, televisions, water heaters, air conditioners, and microwave ovens. Hisense Electric Co. Ltd., meanwhile, is China's most recognized consumer brand, making household items ranging from TVs to DVDs to refrigerators and air conditioners. The company, traded on the

Shanghai exchange as B shares, also owns a big slug of Hong Kong–listed Kelon Electrical Holdings Co., another major appliance maker in China.

As with everything else, you'll have to navigate potholes investing in Chinese real estate as it matures. Unlike the United States, China has no truly developed secondary market for residential real estate. No Multiple Listing Service (MLS) that Realtors tap to help clients locate suitable properties. No way to compare prices for sales of comparable properties. The mortgage market is underdeveloped, and real estate and zoning laws are just evolving. And, of course, prices have run wild in many markets, owing partly to speculation. With so much inventory being erected, investors face the real risk of a bubble bursting at some point. That would soften home prices as well as the share prices for public companies in the housing sector.

None of that should warn you away from the profits that will flow from China's real estate sector, but it should prompt you to choose your entry points with an eye toward value. The best returns in real estate come when investors are down on property ownership and prices (for properties or property-management stocks) are relatively cheap.

INFRASTRUCTURE

Several pages back I mentioned that *Travel + Leisure* magazine reported in one issue that China aims to build 48 new airports by 2010. And as reported in a *Washington Post* newspaper article found online at the Chinese Embassy website, Beijing has announced that it plans to "connect all the nation's major cities with a 34,000-mile highway grid second in length only to that of the United States."

That's infrastructure — on a mammoth scale.

So much fits into this theme that the topic of infrastructure investments in China could probably consume its own book. It all follows the same line of reasoning: China's growth means the country must shovel billions upon billions of dollars into the big projects that make life better, easier, safer for its citizens. Companies, too, are spending wild sums on various projects that fall under the rubric of infrastructure. That means China is seeing not just a rash of new airports and roads but also new water-treatment facilities, as mentioned above, and the necessary pipelines; hydroelectric dams; traditional and nuclear power plants and the transmission facilities; and bridges and tollways. China is increasingly warming up to natural gas as a cleaner alternative to other fossil-fuel sources, or so says an online report from the U.S. government's Energy Information Administration, which projects that demand in China will grow by nearly 7% a year. For comparison's sake, consider that here in the United States, where investors are all agog over natural gas and the promise of increased consumption, demand through 2030 is expected to increase at barely more than 1% a year. For China, which must import natural gas, that means a big ramp-up in liquefied-natural-gas terminals and untold miles of pipelines as companies run natural gas into homes and businesses.

Look around your hometown: What's being built? Shopping malls, office complexes, hospitals, new schools, new universities. Stadiums. Government complexes. Apartment buildings and single-family homes. China is building them all, en masse. The beneficiaries of this activity are all over the world, though some will benefit much more than others. They include metals miners, glassmakers, and cement concerns. Construction and engineering firms, and the companies making the heavy-duty machines that tear down and build up. Pipeline companies and those making the pipes. Chemical companies churning out PVC. The list of opportunities stretches for days. Companies such as Hong Kong's HKC Holdings Ltd. are the type that stand to rack up increasing revenues from China's expansion. HKC is one of Asia's leading engineering and construction firms and is strategically focused on what it terms on its website "the exponential growth that exists in the property, infrastructure, and alternative energy sectors in China."

The risk with infrastructure investing is that companies and governments will sometimes pursue speculative projects, the "build it and they will come" philosophy of economic growth. Only that philosophy is not necessarily true. As an online report from the Asian Development Bank warns, "High-quality infrastructure on its own is rarely the major factor in developing resources, attracting investment, and stimulating economic growth in a county, city, region, or country."

The message: If you're going to invest in infrastructure in China, do your research to be sure that you're investing where unmet demand currently exists.

CHA-CHING!

That sound is the reason so many companies are so interested in the promise of China: consumerism on a scale seen only in one other place — the USA.

China represents retailing's nirvana, and Chinese consumerism may well prove to be the single most-profitable trend over time. It's hard to name any consumer item the expanding middle-class and wealthy Chinese are not consuming in increasing quantities. Cars, clothing, cell phones, air conditioners, washers, dryers, refrigerators, couches, computers, DVD players and DVDs and the TVs to watch them on, restaurant meals, digital cameras, shoes . . . this list is essentially endless and could just as easily bleed over into many of the industries mentioned in previous pages, such as dairy products, housing, financial services, and travel. All are driven by consumers with more renminbi to spend.

Brand awareness, never much in the Chinese consumer consciousness before, is now front and center. Walk the streets of Shanghai and brand-chasing is blindingly apparent. BMW, Mercedes, Ferrari nameplates on cars. True Religion, Seven, and Levi's riveted to the blue-jeans-wearing rear end of pedestrians. Ralph Lauren and Nike. Adidas. Coach. Gucci. Evian. Marlboro. Hennessy. They're everywhere.

This brand consciousness isn't, however, concentrated exclusively on foreign names. Just as China is out to create its own multinational companies, it's out to create recognized consumer brands as well. Just consider Li-Ning Co. Ltd. The Hong Kong–traded maker of sports apparel in late summer 2006 signed American basketball superstar Shaquille O'Neal to endorse its line of athletic shoes, a clear sign Li-Ning aims to compete not only in its home country but on a world stage with the likes of Nike and Germany's Adidas.

Don't overlook the seemingly random ways that rampant consumerism in China — and the developing world in general — will benefit publicly traded companies. PT Akr Corporindo, traded on the Jakarta Stock Exchange in Indonesia, is the world's second-largest producer of sorbitol. If that product sounds vaguely familiar, go check your toothpaste tube; it's a leading ingredient in many brands. Hygiene improves as the bank account gets bigger. So, more tubes of toothpaste are in China's future. India, too. Thus, more profits are likely headed toward Akr's bottom line over time.

But with "Cha-ching," I'm specifically referring to retailers — the stores that will benefit as a nation of chronic savers starts spending its money. China has never been much for organized retail. Brands have traditionally had little intrinsic value, and stores are often ill-stocked and dingy. Shopkeepers haven't typically paid a tremendous amount of attention to merchandising. That's now changing as the bazaar mentality fades in favor of strategies that successful Western merchants use — namely, appealing, well-lit stores, well stocked with quality, branded goods.

This retailing revamp is reshaping a variety of sectors. I've already mentioned Lianhua Supermarkets above, but there are also retailers such as Gome Electrical Appliances Holding and Yongle Electronics, two well-known electronics chains; Wu-Mart, one of China's biggest retailers; and Convenience Retail Asia, which runs the Circle K chain in Hong Kong and China. Speaking of convenience stores, 7-Eleven Japan Co. has plans to open several hundred in China by 2010, while Taiwan's President Chain Store Corp., Hong Kong's Dairy Farm Group, and Thailand's Charoen Pokphand Group are all battling for convenience-store market share in southern China. Again, the numbers speak volumes. Search the Internet for "investing in China's retail industry" and you'll find an April 2006 report of that same name from PricewaterhouseCoopers, noting a couple of fairly staggering statistics:

Some 70,000 new supermarkets opened outside major cites in 2005, while the Beijing municipal government expects to see around 600 new convenience stores and supermarkets open in its suburbs in 2006 alone.

Clothing chains, department stores, and discount retailers are likewise taking hold. Hong Kong's Giordano International Ltd., a fashion retailer, has nearly half its retail operations in China now. Shinsegae Co., one of the largest retailers in South Korea with both department and discount stores, has begun invading China. So, too, has its home-country competitor, Lotte.

And then there's beauty. Water Oasis Group Ltd., a Hong Kong company with exclusive distribution rights to the -H_2O+ line of skin-care and beauty products, operates a chain of specialty retail outlets in Hong Kong, Taiwan, Singapore, and China. The Chinese operations are now driving the company, or so says Water Oasis's 2006 interim report, which announced to shareholders that China in 2007 "should overtake Hong Kong as the group's prime source of income." Or there's Beauty China Holdings, a Singapore company that operates more than 1,100 Colour Zone outlets in China. From 2000 to 2005, Beauty China's sales grew by a compounded 39% as all those Chinese women with growing paychecks spent part of their income on cosmetics. Think about: branded cosmetics for sale . . . inviting retail outlets dedicated to beauty . . . a land with more than half a billion women. The possibilities aren't hypothetical. In the summer of 2005, the University of Pennsylvania's Wharton School of Business held a China Business

Forum focused on the rising purchasing power of the Chinese middle class (available online with a free membership to Knowledge@Wharton, knowledge.wharton.upenn.edu). An executive from global cosmetic giant Clinique noted that China is second only to Japan in the Asian cosmetics market and that the high-end market for cosmetics is growing rapidly.

For retailers, then, the math adds up to stunning numbers in China. Just be sure that for the retailers you invest in, China has a meaningful impact on their revenues and earnings. Even if a global chain opens 1,000 stores in China, the ultimate impact might be muted if that chain already has thousands upon thousands of stores elsewhere in the world. Better it would be to own a local or regional company for which those 1,000 stores represent half or more of the company's operations.

Without question, China must confront a number of issues: political freedoms, environmental degradation, a vast social divide between the classes, a currency that does not float on world markets yet, an urban-rural chasm, a legal system in need of reform, corruption at the political and corporate level. Each of these presents varying degrees of risk to an investor. But they are not risks that should keep you out of China. At worst, they are short-term annoyances, though just how short "short-term" is isn't knowable. Over the long term, they're certain to be addressed in some fashion.

And, if you think about it, those risks aren't terribly different from what European investors considered more than a century ago when they sent their cash across the Atlantic to invest in an upstart America — a young, brash nation with tremendous potential; that pursued what was best for itself, not what others thought best for it; troubled by political assassinations and a relatively recent and destabilizing civil war that threatened to cleave the country apart; which had struggled through currency crises; absent an established rule of law; seriously lacking in corporate accountability; and home to an equity mentality where buying stocks was more gambling than investing. No one will argue, moreover, that America's industrial revolution was a bastion of environmental purity. Steel mills coughed all manner of mucus into the sky and waterways, lumberjacks felled vast plots of old-growth forests, textile mills and manufacturers spit a caustic menu of chemicals into lakes and rivers, animals were driven to extinction — all in the name of economic progress and building a country into a global, economic power. Yes, as a people we understand far more today about our symbiosis with the environment than did our industrial-age ancestors. Far wiser it certainly is to preserve the environment as a way to preserve ourselves. Still, faulting China for every misstep on its path to national prosperity is wildly hypocritical.

At the end of the day, China is on a road that, in a matter of a few decades, will have it competing for global economic supremacy with the United States. That road is destined to be bumpy. There may be a wreck or three to contend with. Detours may take you in unexpected directions. But for investors who own the stocks of companies and not stocks as lottery tickets, China presents an opportunity few generations ever see: that rare chance to participate in the growth of a soon-to-be global leader. The last time this opportunity came around, America blossomed into the greatest financial power the world has ever known and her stock market has been on an upward bias ever since.

A new giant is now awake.

CHAPTER 7

THE OLD DERVISH AND THE CEE

New Opportunities in the Old World

On the road from Atatürk International Airport into old Istanbul, there comes a sweeping bend in the four-lane highway where the view stretches out across the Sea of Marmara, across to the Asian continent, and you'd swear that, aside from all the minarets needling the sky, you're driving along a stretch of California's famed Pacific Coast Highway. It's an appropriate vision given that, just as California is a vibrant young economy helping propel the United States, Turkey represents the vibrant young economy that could ultimately propel Europe.

That is, if the Europeans don't screw it up.

Turkey — a nation that straddles the divide not only between Europe and Asia but between Christianity and Islam — is on the list for potential inclusion in the European Union. But driving toward that goal puts Turkey on what might just be the most difficult road to navigate on the continent. Europe is largely Christian; Turkey is largely Muslim. And millennia of Christian/Muslim tensions, hatreds, animosities, and distrust stand in the way of the EU making one of the smartest financial decisions it will ever face — welcoming Turkey into the club.

Either way, any global investor has to pay attention to what's happening in Turkey. Because no matter the ultimate outcome of the efforts to join the EU, and despite the assured turbulence along the way, Turkey will emerge with a stronger economy, an enhanced legal system, companies that are more transparent and investor friendly, and a stock market that is higher than it was in the summer of 2007.

In this section, I'm going to make the case for Turkey as an investment, just to show the sort of macro thinking that goes into putting your money to work in what is certainly a risky market. Below, in a section on Central and Eastern Europe, I'll detail exactly how to put this thinking to work in terms of locating the industries and specific companies in which to invest.

THE DERVISH

In many ways, Turkey is the answer to one of Europe's most pressing problems: the continent's aging demographics. As with the clot of baby boomers bulging through the U.S. population, the same problem in Europe promises to create a socioeconomic maelstrom as tens of millions of workers retire and put increasing financial pressures on the various states to foot their bills. Consider this: Eurostat, which produces European community statistics, reported in 2006 that growth in the EU's population through 2025 "will be entirely due to foreign migration" because deaths in EU countries will outnumber births. After 2025, Eurostat projects, the EU population will begin to contract. Not a good sign for governments seeking new workers to fund all those costs of a population that is not only aging but living longer, too. Thus, just as the United States needs an injection of young workers to support the ever increasing number of retirees milking the Social Security and Medicare system, so, too, does Europe need an injection of youth to help support its own horde of approaching retirees. That's Turkey.

Inside Turkey reside some 73 million people, roughly 17% the size of the current EU. The average age in 2006: 28. A quarter of Turks are under the age of 14; 70% are younger than 35. Under EU rules, this mass of young Turks would be allowed to freely roam the continent, seeking higher-paying jobs from Leipzig to London to Lillehammer. That would put more workers on the tax rolls across the EU, generating income for governments that will sorely need the money. Those 73 million Turks also represent a vast, new base of consumers for European companies to profit from, and a large supply of highly skilled, lower-cost workers that EU companies can tap into as they relocate manufacturing and production plants to Turkey.

Yet instead of looking for ways to help Turkey fast-track its entrance into the union, EU leaders are throwing up numbing roadblocks that are frustrating the process and that ultimately will hurt Europeans more than they'll ever hurt Turks. Because the irony is that no matter the outcome of the accession vote, Turkey wins. Certainly, European rejection would be a blow to national pride in some quarters of Turkey (a reason to rejoice in others), but the history of EU accession shows conclusively that success comes from the journey, not the destination. In other words, even if the EU ultimately denies Turkey's admission, the process leading the country toward EU eligibility will mean a great deal to Turks, and investors in Turkish companies, than will inclusion itself. For that reason, you have to be bullish on Turkish stocks.

As with China, though, investing in Turkey won't be a smooth ride. Turkey is a developing nation with immature financial markets, buffeted on occasion by the ill winds that roar through emerging-market stock exchanges and currencies with hurricane-like intensity.

In some ways, Turkey is riskier than China, and substantially riskier than Eastern European markets. Where the Middle Kingdom is nearly ethnically homogeneous and politically stable, the land of Homer is riven by a secular/Islamist divide politically and socially. Kurdish separatists routinely harass the Turkish government with bombings and other maliciousness as they try to establish their own political authority. Such harassment is likely to continue until the Kurds are appeased in some fashion. And certainly not least, Turkey sits atop the powder keg that is the Middle East, bordered to its south by some of the region's most troublesome characters: Iran, Iraq, and Syria. If the Middle East ever explodes into regional violence, Turkey will be dragged in as it tries to protect its own interests.

Moreover, while China husbands the world's largest stash of foreign-exchange reserves (the equivalent of more than $1.3 trillion in mid-2007, a surplus that exceeds the annual economic output of all but the world's largest economies), Turkey is a debtor nation that struggles through financial crises on occasion. A banking blowup in 2000–01, for example, singed global investors badly.

And yet if you look at Turkey, you see the long-term possibilities as the country navigates all the hoops needed to join the EU, likely between 2012 and 2014—assuming accession happens at all. Regardless of what comes with European negotiations, though, global companies have begun courting Turkish firms, particularly in the financial arena, where European and American banking giants have grabbed stakes in a number of Turkish banks in recent years. They're doing so for several reasons. One is the fact that the country's economy and its judicial and political systems are improving as Turkey takes up the reforms necessary for potential EU inclusion. Another stems from those 73 million Turks: Global companies want to tap into that consumer base as the middle class expands.

The reality is that while Turkey is a Muslim nation, it has historically had its face turned toward the West, not the Middle East. Though average Turks are divided on whether joining the EU is good, bad, or indifferent for their homeland, Turkey's business community is strongly behind the push, recognizing that EU membership would propel the Turkish economy, cement political stability, and continue the economic reforms that are making business quite the attractive venture for local and foreign companies. And business leaders often have a way of steering politicians in a particular direction.

Like China, Turkey has a long history of trade, so it's not as if the country is late coming to capitalism, like some of the Eastern European nations that were hidden behind a Communist veil for decades. The Ottoman Empire once controlled the spice trade between East and West, and for centuries Turkey served as the crossroads between three continents—Africa,

Asia, and Europe — a place where merchants naturally congregated and negotiated deals. Though widely viewed as a bridge between Europe and the Middle East, the more important reality is that Turkey is a bridge between the West and numerous former Soviet states, many of them energy rich and looking to build stronger economic links to Europe and the United States. Turkey serves as the logical base for that trade because it's in the neighborhood.

Today, nearly a century after the Ottoman Empire faded, Turkey is a modern economy, more modern in many ways than some of the Eastern European countries that are already part of the EU or that are pressing for entry. Istanbul's business district of glass towers recalls Dallas or Miami or Atlanta. The Sea of Marmara is awash in freighters, while all of the world's largest shipping lines make call in the Mediterranean port of Izmir, as they have for half a century. The Istanbul Stock Exchange, though small, is set upon a leafy modern campus and is entirely electronic. Housing demand is booming and credit is emerging alongside an expanding consumer industry. Turks are well educated and skilled, recognizing they need a degree to land a good job. Turkish auto plants meet or exceed the quality coming out of Western plants. Ford Motor Co., for instance, named its Otosan joint-venture plant in Turkey the best in Europe four consecutive times. The business community is as sophisticated as in some European capitals. Online banking is rampant and local investors can even buy and sell shares of stock and mutual funds through bank ATMs. Indeed, unlike in China, where the locals invest in stocks more for the thrill of the gamble, an investment culture is emerging in Turkey with the introduction in 2002 of a private pension system similar to the ubiquitous 401(k) plan in the states.

As it stands in 2007, the short term in Turkey — that is, the next five to seven years — is certain to be rough sledding because of the uncertainty with EU negotiations, and the geopolitical and financial risk of Turkey and its general neighborhood. Turkey has budget issues to deal with, inflation to battle, and a currency sharply overvalued in relation to major world currencies. Any or all of those can cause a nasty upset at some point.

Over a longer horizon, however, Turkey is a stock market where patient investors will prosper. But as an investor, you want to invest in a market like Turkey prudently. That means waiting for the next big downdraft—and it will come—when some exogenous event spooks emerging-market investors, either in Turkey directly or in some other market that has spillover effects elsewhere. Then, you step in amid the carnage and snap up the companies either that will thrive on the growth of the Turkish consumer or that will benefit from EU-mandated reforms.

What might you consider snapping up?

The Turkish banking sector is benefiting from increasing demand for retail banking and a variety of financial services ranging from credit cards to auto loans to home mortgages. Mortgages, in particular, are an emerging product with vast potential. Remember, Turkey is a very young country moving into its home ownership years. And it's an urbanizing culture. Home ownership will grow with both trends. Moreover, the economic reforms required of EU membership will continue to strengthen the economy and the banking system, making banks increasingly more attractive companies to own. The major Turkish banks, all of which have a Western partner somewhere in the mix, include names like Akbank, Işbank, Garanti Bankasi, Türkiye Vakiflar Bankasi, and DenizBank. Smaller banks trade publicly as well.

As for real estate, the Istanbul Stock Exchange is loaded with real estate investment trusts, or REITs. Many are off-shoots of the local banks, some aren't. Either way, the property market will grow more valuable alongside the expansion of the Turkish economy. Eastern European countries such as Romania and Bulgaria saw property values surge because of EU accession. Turkey will be no different. Local REITs include the likes of Yapi Kredi Koray, Akmerkez, Ihlas, Nurol, and Alarko, among others. As an aside, real estate is often the best way to diversify a portfolio because it is the ultimate in local investing. After all, what happens in Los Angles or London has no real pull on rents in the office towers, retail centers, and apartment complexes in Istanbul or Ankara. In addition, because REITS own or manage property that is generally subject to contractual leases that generate monthly income in good times and bad, REITS tend to be a stabler investment when stock markets are volatile, though there are certainly exceptions to such a rule.

Consumer spending is a huge category easily sliced into a variety of specialties such as everyday staples like groceries to infrequent purchases like cars and TVs. But they all fall under the same general rubric of growth in the sheer number of consumers and the growth of those consumers' disposable income. On the Istanbul exchange you have everything from Anadolu Efes Group, a beer and soft-drink maker; to Turkcell, the national mobile-phone provider; to Migros, the largest retailer, with stores ranging from neighborhood convenience stores to hypermarkets; to Arçelik, the home-appliance leader in Turkey.

Though airlines face mountainous obstacles such as treacherous competition, energy price spikes, horrendously large equipment costs, and, of course, the threat that another airborne terrorist attack idles jets once again, they can be good investments when you think like a contrarian and buy the stocks when other investors loathe the business. Because of horrendous service, travelers once derisively referred to Turkish Airlines as They Hate You, a play on the company's Turkish name, Türk Hava Yollari, or THY. The carrier, however, has raised its game and is one of Europe's fastest growing, adding planes and passengers, new destinations, and expanded cargo service.

There are certainly other winners in Turkey. Insurance companies will pick up lots of new business as consumers save more money and need to protect their lives and the homes and cars they're buying; construction firms will prosper because of all the infrastructure additions and improvements that are making life safer and easier for Turks; manufacturers will benefit from Western European firms that are continually setting up lower-cost plants in Turkey; electricity providers will have increasing numbers of clients. The list goes on.

The point is that no matter where you look in Turkey, the same picture is emerging: Turkish companies have a tremendous future just beyond the horizon — that horizon being the years-long European Union accession preparations. Investing in Turkey, though, means you must have the temperament to stomach volatile times without rushing to flee when unexpected hiccups upset the market.

More than any other type of investment, frontier economies require patience and fortitude.

A VIEW OF THE CEE

Easy it would be to spout off a bunch of reasons why Central and Eastern Europe is a promising region for investors. I've traveled through parts of the region — particularly Romania, Russia, Hungary, and Turkey — and I've seen the changes reshaping the economies. I've talked to the locals who are bullish on business in their homeland, excited about the future. (Technically, Russia and Turkey are not part of Central and Eastern Europe, nor are the emerging former-Soviet states such Belarus, Ukraine, and Georgia, but I lump them together under the so-called CEE banner for the sake of simplicity here.)

My observations, though, mean nothing. As a skeptical reporter, I don't take the word of everyone who tells me how great some investment is, so I don't expect you to take my word. You might read facts much differently than I do and come away with an entirely different analysis of the same situation. Instead, I'm coming at this — my view of the CEE and one country in particular — from solely an Internet perspective. The purpose: To show you how to begin building the research mosaic necessary when investing in a region or a country you've never visited and for which you have no historical knowledge base to draw upon when it comes to the local companies, industries, and economies. With this type of information, you can formulate your own theories and analysis, instead of relying on the theories and analyses of others.

Everything below is pulled from Google searches that include various iterations of: Eastern Europe, Central Europe, investing, advice, equity market, stocks, economy, individual country names, various sectors, company names that pop up during the research, investment review, workforce, central bank, and so on — basically any word combination that relates to business and industry, the economy, and stock markets. I'm not going to cite every Web address from which come these comments, since many are too long. But I will note the organization responsible. Moreover, although all the commentary is verbatim, in many cases I've edited down the text to the most salient points for the sake of brevity.

My basic research on the CEE comes from two reports — both found online — from well-regarded consulting firms: a 2006 analysis of the region by Deloitte Touche Tohmatsu; and a 2005 report from KPMG titled "Of Tigers, Dinosaurs and Gazelles: Defining competitive business models for manufacturers in the New Europe." Substantially more research exists, and I typically use a wide variety when analyzing countries and regions. But I don't want to weigh down this section with a bunch of research statistics and factoids when these two pieces serve to point out the ease with which you can quickly and easily find substantive, relevant information to help you begin to establish an investment thesis.

In the briefest of fashion, here are some of the key bullet points from those reports that would lead a rational investor to think, "Hmmm, I need to be investing in Eastern Europe." Some of this is verbatim, some is paraphrased.

- Central Europe is becoming a major part of the European and global business environment, and many CEE countries have sharply slashed their tax rates to attract foreign investment. That's one of the driving factors behind the relocation of manufacturing and service-oriented business activities into the region.

- The CEE has undergone dynamic developments since the fall of communism, and economic growth is much higher in comparison with Western Europe, a trend that is expected to last for many years.
- By and large, the region is maligned or misunderstood by foreign investors, generally because the CEE isn't China or India, and the bloated, inefficient bureaucracy of the Communist past remains a fresh — albeit wrong — image even today.
- The reality: Strong business performance is generating a positive strategic outlook across the entire region, including all industry sectors and all geographic locations; increasing levels of competition in the region and consumer choice are forcing companies to respond by increasing their product quality; homegrown companies have looked throughout Central Europe to find growth opportunities, and have done so, even against multi-national competitors, by picking their battles effectively.
- Local companies are experiencing strong growth, but not at the same levels as their multinational counterparts. They are, however, clearly achieving greater improvements in their productivity.
- Regional companies represent the up-and-coming stars for Central Europe. Many have been heavily restructured or have risen phoenixlike from the ashes of previous existences, and have learned to cash in on their profound understanding and knowledge of the region. Some, such as Czech pharmaceutical producer Wallmark, are entrepreneurial upstarts in the right place at the right time to be able to fill some of the many voids that appeared in the defunct marketplace that emerged after the fall of the wall in 1989. As a group, the regional companies are the most impressive, are achieving the fastest growth rates, and have demonstrated the highest overall productivity.

- Compared against the 800-pound gorillas of the emerging-market world — Brazil, Russia, India, and China — Central Europe seems decidedly dainty. Yet taken as a whole, the region has a population 90% the size of Russia but almost 30% richer in terms of GDP (this calculation does not take Turkey into account). Its proximity to Western Europe makes the region a much better place for producing and exporting bulkier, higher-value-added goods to key markets in the EU. It's also stabler politically and economically. Perhaps most important, though, is profitability. To date, achieving overall profitability has generally been easier in Central Europe than in China.
- Some of the risks of investing in the CEE: Issues remain with excessive administration, bureaucracy, and corruption despite EU membership; companies have had difficulties attracting sufficient staff and training them; infrastructure can be a hindrance to development given that, in Poland, for instance, there are only a few two-lane roads that connect the major cities and development has been obstructed due to difficulty in the purchase of land, corruption, and a lack of interest from investors; and in some cases, such as with Hungary, ratings agencies have expressed concerns over unsustainable budget and current account deficits.

So, from just two reports — and, again, many more exist on the Internet — you begin to build a pretty good profile of what's taking shape in the CEE, and that despite the risks that certainly exist, the eastern half of Europe offers some real opportunities for investors with the gumption to venture beyond the borders of Western countries.

But you come back to this question: How does the average, individual investor translate this analysis into action?

At this point, the process centers on drilling down into the individual countries to ferret out the industries and companies that meet your specific investment criteria. Let's make an example out of Romania, for no other reason than that I visited the country on a reporting trip in 2000 and, based on all that I saw taking place, told myself I'd like to invest there someday.

One of the largest countries in Europe, Romania entered the EU on Jan. 1, 2007. The stock market, as I noted in a previous chapter, had already moved dramatically in recent years in anticipation of EU accession. Does that mean, though, that Romania is already played out? Or do opportunities still exist for investors who want to own a piece of the Eastern European growth story?

The logical approach is top-down: a macro view of Romania, an analysis of the leading industries, and then honing in on the successful or promising companies in those industries. Here's a truncated, split-page example of the research I built. The left side is the research, the right is my brief back-of-an-envelope analysis of how I see the research. You may well see it differently, and that's fine; my conclusions' only purpose is to get you thinking about the meaning behind the comments you read when conducting your own research.

A BRIEF DIGRESSION ON EU MEMBERSHIP . . .

Several times in this book, and particularly in this chapter, I've mentioned Eastern and Central European countries acceding to the European Union. Here's why that's relevant.

The EU is essentially a United States of Europe—a single economic bloc, larger than the United States, in which citizens and goods can move just as freely across borders as a Floridian can move into Georgia and then South Carolina. The EU shares a common currency, the euro, though not all member countries use it just yet. Most of Western Europe has long been a part of the club. In 2004 the EU admitted ten new members from Central and Eastern Europe, most of those former Communist nations, and in 2007 the union welcomed Romania and Bulgaria. That still leaves a small number of countries—largely the Balkan States in southeastern Europe and several former Soviet republics—that have yet to join, though most want to.

To enter the EU, countries must abide by a certain set of political, economic, and legal rules, the so-called Copenhagen Criteria. That's where the benefits as an investor begin.

Among the variety of requirements, accession forces countries to hew to the ideals of a democracy; strengthen legal and judicial systems by acting in accordance with the rule of law and respecting property rights; respect human rights and indigenous minorities; and retool the local economy to ward off inflation and allow a market economy to flourish where state-controlled economies often reigned.

Basically we're talking about democratic and economic revitalization—the equivalent to some degree of a city stepping in to revitalize a run-down neighborhood. The investors who buy into that neighborhood before the gentrification is complete often buy at depressed levels and profit when the value of their property escalates as the neighborhood becomes increasingly popular.

With the EU, all of this revitalization must happen before a country becomes a member state. Preparations begin years in advance, and as countries undertake the measures necessary to join the EU, their economies bloom. As economies bloom, local companies prosper. As local companies prosper, the local stock market rises. As local stock markets rise, foreign investors tend to flood in, growing the economy even more. All in all, a benevolent cycle that benefits investors who find their way into countries that are pushing for EU inclusion.

To date, the countries that have begun EU accession efforts have seen their stock markets improve dramatically during the run-up to union inclusion. There's little reason to doubt that won't continue to happen, since countries make fundamental political, economic, legal, and financial changes that can't help but benefit stock markets.

Certain kinds of companies typically benefit the most as a country progresses toward EU accession: banks and finance companies, since they are economically sensitive; infrastructure companies that profit as a country builds up its roads and sewers and such amid a stronger economy; property investment firms, since land prices and buildings tend to rise in value as Western European companies come looking for buildings and land to expand into a new, growing market.

Countries currently in line to potentially join the EU include Croatia, Turkey, and the lot of Balkan nations, among others. Croatia's accession is all but assured, by most accounts, but how many more join the party remains questionable, given that EU leaders have begun to grouse about the size of the union (27 member nations as of Jan. 1, 2007) and the quality of some of the countries that have joined in recent years.

ROMANIAN MACROECONOMICS

Source: U.S. Department of Commerce (April 2007)

Romania is a country of considerable potential: rich agricultural lands; diverse energy sources (coal, oil, natural gas, hydro, and nuclear); a substantial, if aging, industrial base encompassing almost the full range of manufacturing activities; an educated, well-trained workforce; and opportunities for expanded development in tourism on the Black Sea and in the mountains.

This is good stuff already. If the country is rich in coal, oil, natural gas, and other energy sources, then there are obviously investment opportunities in a sector for which much demand exists globally, particularly in Europe. There's also likely to be burgeoning tourism along the Black Sea coast, and the country is a good source of workers for Western businesses looking to the region.

Foreign capital investment in Romania has been

My kind of factoid: Although the stock market has moved, foreign increasing, but remains significantly less in per-capita terms than in most other transition-economy countries in Eastern and Central Europe.

The country made substantial progress in the energy sector in 2005, completing or launching numerous privatization projects. Four of the country's eight regional electricity distributors have now been privatized, and the government is continuing the process. Privatization of natural-gas distribution companies also progressed with the sale of Romania's two regional gas distributors, Distrigaz Nord (to E.ON Ruhrgas of Germany) and Distrigaz Sud (to Gaz de France). Further progress in energy-sector privatization, however, has been delayed as the government reconsiders its strategy on the Rovinari, Turceni, and Craiova energy complexes.

Source: The World Bank (Country Brief 2006)

Romania is now a visible and attractive destination for

investors aren't focused on Romania to as large a degree as elsewhere in the region, giving Romania a bit of a contrarian play, often the best way for patient investors to generate long-term profits.

Natural gas is an industry to research. Western Europe clamors for access to natural gas; Romania is a supplier. Buyout potential for other publicly traded gas providers. Government considering privatizing other providers.

This is just a minor note from the World Bank, nothing substantive.

international investors as a result of better sovereign ratings and improved access to international capital markets.

Still, it's a vote of confidence from a generally nonpartisan organization in a position to know a great deal about the financial and economic backdrop of a particular country.

Source: Romanian Business Digest (report by ING Bank, a Dutch banking giant)

The macroeconomic fundamentals [of Romania] shape up an economy that, if it still cannot match the absolute figures of its European colleagues, is certainly working toward convergence at a historically accelerating rate.

At a big-picture level, the Romanian economy might not be improving at the same speed of other European nations, but it is catching up a quickening pace. Essentially, being part of the EU is improving Romania's business/investing climate.

With the entry of Romania into the EU, pension funds will contribute to the rally on the [Bucharest Stock Exchange]. The effect will be mainly coming from foreign pension funds that will access the equity market in Romania as an "EU" branded market, and at a later stage the effect will be amplified by new local pension-fund [legislation].

This news of local pension-fund legislation is particularly interesting, since it implies that local workers will have some sort of access to a new pension program, and that the program is expected to bolster the local stock exchange. That's certainly worthy of additional research — the next entry.

Source: European Commission (Report on Romania, January 2007)

The second pillar [of Romania's pension reform] — the private-managed compulsory

Romania is instituting a new private pension system that is mandated to hold a certain percentage of the assets in equities.

pensions — will be implemented starting January 1, 2008. The main consequence . . . is the redirection of a certain part of the contribution [to private pension funds]. The contribution to these private funds will be mandatory for the entire population under 35 years and voluntary for those aged between 36 and 45. The allocation of the assets . . . will be 70% in government bonds, 15% in equity, and 15% in [cash] deposits.

That's great news. It means some level of continual support for Romanian shares, since some level of individual Romanians will begin to have a vested interest in their country's stock market, drawing more of them in with their own cash over time. Think of the U.S. 401(k) market, which started as a novelty but now has millions of families in the stock market. This local-investor support also means that the Romanian market will increasingly be less dependent on institutional investors. It also means investment opportunities in companies that will be providing pension accounts and services to workers, à la our own Fidelity and Charles Schwab.

ROMANIAN INDUSTRY ANALYSIS

OK, we now have a little taste of some basic information about Romania, enough to at least recognize that the local economy is strengthening in the wake of EU membership (obviously a good sign), and that increasing numbers of everyday Romanians are likely to find themselves involved in their country's stock market because of the new pension legislation. It's not as deep and detailed an analysis of Romania as you'll ultimately build, but, for the sake of this exercise, it's enough to know that this frontier market is on the right track, and for me to want to poke around in some of the industries.

Source: PMR Publications (Polish consulting firm), March 2007

Following its accession to the European Union, Romania is attracting increasing attention from companies in the construction sector . . . which will very positively affect the future growth of the construction market in this country. However, local firms will not be able to handle the completion of large infrastructure projects, hence the expected expansion of international construction enterprises in that market.

Common sense tells you that building stuff is big business in an emerging economy. Romania's contractors, though, aren't of a size to handle the work alone. That means they will instead be brought in as subcontractors or consultants, or they'll be acquired by outside firms. However it happens, whatever publicly traded Romanian construction firms exist are in a good position — though multinational construction companies elsewhere in Europe will benefit as well, and are worth a few minutes of research, too.

In particular, modern commercial space, including hypermarkets and shopping malls, has the best growth prospects.

This comment stands out because it speaks to growth in another industry — retail. If there's growing demand to build hypermarts and shopping malls, it's clear there's demand from consumers. Thus, a comment in a report on construction leads to another industry to research: retail.

Over two-thirds of the total length of the roads are in need of renovation [and] the Romanian government has drawn up ambitious plans [to build thousands of kilometers] of new

This gives scope to the size of some of the construction work that needs to be done and, if you're an investor who believes in the infrastructure-investment opportunity, should point you toward those companies focused on

motorways [through] 2013. The majority of large infrastructure projects will be implemented by large international consortia or construction enterprises, which will engage Romanian firms as local contractors.

bridge and road work. It also bolsters the earlier point about foreign firms coming into Romania and partnering with the local companies, a good sign for the locals.

You might be wondering how I decided to research the Romanian construction market. I didn't. I plugged into Google the phrase "Romanian economy stock market analysis 2007" and high on the list was the PMR Publications report.

All of the snippets below come from an online blurb for Oxford's *Emerging Romania 2007* report. The report itself is $180; these factoids were all free.

Source: Oxford Business Group (London, economic and political research)

Banking: Though some worry that the country has become overbanked, the sector is set to perform strongly over the medium term.

Insurance: Growth is exceeding all expectations in the Romanian insurance industry; the sector has also seen major regulatory reforms; penetration rates reveal plenty of room for further expansion in what is turning into a fiercely competitive field of business.

This is the kind of treasure trove you seek. Certainly, none of this is deeply specific, and you definitely would not base an investment decision on a couple of snippets. Nevertheless, these teasers do just enough to whet your appetite. Banking is set to do well; insurance sales are obviously surging; opportunities exist in energy-company privatization as the government sells assets into the public market; tourism is still sleepy, but sleepy industries in an emerging economy can be a great place to make big profits; mobile telecom has continuing growth

Energy: Restructuring with a view towards privatization has been the trend in the energy sector, with the country's biggest oil company being sold in 2004. Natural gas companies should also be completely out of the government's hands in 2007 as per EU requirements.

Tourism: Romania is a corner of Europe that remains off the beaten path for most international tourists. In recent years, even Romanians have preferred to visit neighboring countries, feeling services at home are not up to scratch. But plenty of potential for development exists . . .

Telecom: Telecoms [have] leapfrogged to a point where industry players are now focusing more on value-added services and diversification. The incumbent fixed-line provider is facing increasing competition from alternative carriers, while mobile providers work to increase rural penetration.

Retail: With a large population, fast-growing

opportunities in the rural marketplace; and retail, always one of my favorites in places where locals are increasingly wealthy, is still underdeveloped, telling me that demand among consumers is huge. All of these are industries that an investor in this part of Eastern Europe would want to spend time investigating. You might not find any worthy investments in some of these, particularly tourism, but, then again, you just might. If nothing else, you're building a base of knowledge that will help you with future investments in Romania or the CEE.

GDP, and currently underdeveloped retail [opportunities], Romania is now attracting large-scale foreign investment. Developers are speedily constructing malls, hyper-markets, and cash-and-carry outlets to exploit the opportunities.

Source: Mindbranch (U.S. market-research firm) — Report on the Banking Market in Romania, 2007

Like the Oxford information above, this is part of a report that, in this case, sells for more than $2,000. But the blurb is free, and it not only offers useful data on the banking sector but even dishes up a specific bank name to research.

The number of bank outlets [as well as ATM and point-of-sale networks] has increased in 2006 by several hundred. Many banks have also upgraded their remote channels (Internet, call centers) to improve their service level and reduce costs of transactional operations.

The mid-term prospects are very good. Growing wealth of individuals, very low unemployment, and [the] good condition of enterprises fueled by record foreign direct investments will convert into additional

For free research, this is pretty good stuff. It's apparent from the growing number of branches and ATMs, and the growing wealth of consumers, that there's a big appetite for more convenient and better banking services. And where there's increasing demand, there are increasing profits over time.

Moreover, EU accession has made Romania a more robust environment for banking, and it's attracting outside players, i.e., foreign banks moving in to buy local banks to own instant market share. (Note also the otherwise parenthetical comment "as it happened in other accession countries." Pay attention to such demand for banking services. The EU membership and higher market transparency is likely to attract to Romania new banking players and financial services specialists, as it happened in other accession countries.

During 2006 some rising stars have changed significantly the [order of the] top banks. Most dynamic bank: Banca Transilvania jumped from #10 (2004) to #5 (3Q 2006), breaking the myth that banks having foreign investors grow faster than local ones.

comments when you see them. If this is happening in Romania, and it has happened in other EU ascendant countries, then it's likely to happen to future countries—Croatia, Turkey, others—that join the EU, meaning you already know where to look for investment ideas there.)

Perhaps the most important point is that this blurb gives you the name of a local bank—Banca Transilvania—that's obviously on the move. So that's our starting point . . .

ROMANIAN COMPANY ANALYSIS

With just the three reports above, we have numerous industries to research. But I'm going to concentrate on banking and Banca Transilvania since that last paragraph made a compelling case that this is a rapidly expanding bank in an industry where consumer demand is on the rise. If nothing else, it's the first company name we've come across, and even if it turns out Banca Transilvania isn't a stock to own, researching it will certainly unearth other names to consider.

So, let's see what else we can find about a bank from a part of the world most people associate with a particularly bloodthirsty Bram Stoker character.

WHEN IN ROME, SEARCH AS THE ROMANS DO

Here's a tip for researching: Use local and regional search engines.

When you research Romania through Google.com — or other search engines to which you naturally gravitate in the states — the engines typically return search results that have a decidedly U.S. bias. You'll certainly find several foreign websites in the mix, but you're largely looking at a foreign market through the prism of an American search engine.

Go native instead and your search results will change demonstrably.

Google has sites all around the world, and every market has its own local search engines. Use them. Google.co.uk (the British site, and a good place to start searches because London is the epicenter of global investment research) returns a different set of results. Google.ro (the Romanian site) offers up yet another set, though those results are primarily in Romanian and you'll need to find a Web-based translation site to help you navigate.

First, the most basic question: Is Banca Transilvania publicly traded? If it's not, then there's little use researching it, since you can't buy shares anyway.

You'll find the answer at the Bucharest Stock Exchange home page, where the English version of the "Companies Directory" shows that Banca Transilvania is indeed a public company in Romania, traded under the symbol TLV. The share price in the summer of 2007 was about 0.85 Romanian lei, in the middle of its high-low price range for the year.

Now, to find out what we can about the company.

Banca Transilvania posts in English on its website (www.bancatransilvania.ro) an "Investor Relations" link that provides three years of annual financial results, reported according to International Financial Accounting Standards and audited by KPMG. Banca Transilvania has had a good run.

Based on the four years of data ending in December 2006, the bank:

- grew assets to more than 8 billion Romanian lei from just over 1.4 billion — the growth that pushed Banca Transilvania into Romania's top five banks in terms of market share;
- lifted net profits, the proverbial bottom line, to more than 108 million lei from roughly 31 million;
- expanded the number of bank branches under the BT banner to 341 from 71, and grew the base of ATMs in operation to 528 from 157.

The various financial documents and bank commentary posted on the site help build the profile of what Banca Transilvania is all about. Here's what you'll learn about a bank most Americans, including me, have never heard of until now:

- began operations in 1994;
- has 16% of the market for small- and micro-sized businesses, making it Romania's #2 bank for that segment, which is BT's core competency;
- has nearly 900,000 bank cards — both credit and debit — in circulation among retail clients, where BT is making a concerted push to gain market share;
- ended 2006 with more than 706,000 total, active clients, a 75% increase from 2005;
- operates subsidiaries under the BT name that engage in insurance, leasing, consumer finance, and asset management, among other endeavors. The bank's investor-relations page even offers a link to BT Securities, an online brokerage where Americans can open an account and begin trading Romanian stocks for the equivalent of $6.58 per trade, based on currency exchange rates in the summer of 2007;
- for 2007, the bank's objectives included growing the total customer base to at least 1 million; increasing debit/credit

cards in circulation to about 1.05 million; expanding the asset base by nearly half; opening more than 100 new branches; building 5 regional centers to train the growing base of employees; opening a call center; and launching several credit-based products aimed at core business.

In short, BT is a bank on the move and trying to grow itself into a national brand across its home country. That's good. But that's according to the bank. What do others think about Banca Transilvania, and what other news is available?

- Several large European financial institutions, including the private-sector arm of the World Bank and the European Bank for Reconstruction and Development, decided in November 2006 to invest some €60 million in BT through a loan, money aimed at helping a developing-market bank "sustain [its] substantial growth and ambitious development plans" (www.ebrd.com, website for the European Bank of Reconstruction and Development). The organizations put up the money to help develop financial services in a formerly Communist nation, to increase competition in the Romanian market, and to help BT bring banking services to the small- and micro-sized businesses that promise to expand the Romanian economy.
- AEGON, the giant Dutch life insurance and pension company, teamed up with BT in early 2007 to begin building a jointly owned company that will hawk pension-related products and services to consumers when Romania's mandatory pension-investment system launches in 2008 (www.banknews.ro, English version). BT will market the products through its bank branches and agents at its insurance subsidiary, BT Asigurari, and aims to position itself among the top five providers of pension-plan investment assistance (www.zf.ro). My interpretation: BT is gaining the expertise of a global leader in pension products, and it will be a bank at the epicenter of

what will be government-mandated demand for accounts, which naturally leads to increasing demand for investment options and advice from millions of Romanians. Being one of the fastest-growing local bank brands means BT is in a favorable position to win a fair share of business, which will give the bank the opportunity to cross-sell its banking, lending, and credit-card services to people who might not yet be BT bank customers.

- In recapping the Romanian equities market in its 2006 annual report, Intercapital Invest (www.intercapital.ro), a Romanian brokerage firm, noted that BT— along with Banca Carpatica — "remains a take-over target." Certainly, investing based on takeover potential is a crapshoot at best, and generally not the most effective way to build a portfolio. However, we're talking about an emerging-market here, one in a part of Europe that is rapidly moving into conformity with its Western counterparts; one that has a growing mass of both retail and commercial consumers; one that naturally is appealing to outside firms looking to gain a toehold in the local market. In these situations, multinational and regional competitors sit like hawks on the periphery of the market, waiting to swoop in and pick off what they perceive as the best and brightest local prospects. That gives the takeover-target talk some credence worthy enough to factor it into the overall mosaic you're building. Moreover, you would expect a local brokerage firm to have a good read on the most promising companies in Romania, so, if nothing else, Intercapital's comment is at least a vote of confidence in BT's future. (As an aside, takeover talk also explains why the stock's price-earnings is elevated — 26, fairly high for bank, though not out of line with BT's growth trajectory. Investors are buying into the company and holding on to the shares on the expectation that the bank will be bought out at a much higher price by a bigger, European peer.)

- Speaking of BT being a takeover target, the *Business Standard* (www.standard.ro), a Romanian newspaper, in early June 2007 posted a report in which the general manager for the Romanian unit of Dutch banking giant ING states that in order to meet its growth goal ING might acquire several smaller, local banks, such as Banca Transilvania and Banca Carpatica.

- Hotnews.ro, a Romanian news site, reported that same month that, according to new research, Banca Transilvania has the sixth most powerful Romanian brand name, having jumped four spaces, which makes it the fastest-growing brand name as well. Though not a major piece of the overall research, this nevertheless is a good indicator of growing consumer awareness for a regional bank trying to build a national brand — and it appears to be working.

- In a banking-market research report, Intelace, a Polish market-research firm (www.intelace.com), lists Romania as "one of the most promising banking markets in Central and Eastern Europe." Though not directly specific to BT, the rapidly expanding demand for retail and commercial banking services in Romania is certain to reflect in profit and asset growth at Banca Transilvania, given what we already know about BT's burgeoning asset growth and its brand awareness among Romanians.

All that within the first eight pages of Google links that popped up. Certainly, this is not all the information you need to fill in all the blanks on Banca Transilvania and its potential worthiness as an investment. There's substantially more to the BT story you must suss out, including an analysis of the bank's financial results. All of that is online, but that sort of necessary financial minutia is beyond the scope of this book.

At the end of the day, however, you have the beginnings of a useful analysis about Romania, the industries with promise, and the potential for one particular stock — Banca Transilvania. And you built all of it from online sources.

That's how easy it is to go global with your greenbacks.

Epilogue: I noted at the top of this section on the CEE that any rational investor would come to the conclusion that "Hmmm, I need to be investing in Eastern Europe." Prior to writing this section I had no investments and no brokerage accounts in the region, though I did have a long-standing interest in the CEE. Because of all that I learned—and, again, I've detailed only the highlights—I opened an account at Vanguard.ro, an online Romanian brokerage firm, which, in keeping with my preferences for those matryoshka doll-like firms, offers trading not only in Romania but in Bulgaria and Austria as well, and, as of this writing, Croatia and Ukraine soon, with other markets potentially on the way.

DON'T LET THE BIG BOYS
SHUCK ALL THE OYSTERS

I opened this guidebook with an anecdote about a dishwasher. Let me now bring that story full circle.

Prior to the fall of 1995, I knew absolutely nothing about Fisher & Paykel Appliances Ltd. Nothing. Not even the fact that the company existed. I first happened upon the name while reading the *New Zealand Herald* newspaper online, searching for local, publicly traded companies in the news that had some ties to Asia and that might be worth investigating. Fisher & Paykel had just reported its half-yearly results and the company made note of its growth and its future prospects in Asia. I found the company's website and shot off an e-mail requesting the last three years of annual and semiannual reports, which arrived a couple of weeks later in my mailbox. After due diligence, I invested in the company—though that was contrary to the advice of Ted the Broker in New Zealand, who, when I told him to buy Fisher & Paykel shares for my account, politely suggested that I temper such stupidity since the appliance maker was quite the lackluster pick. His firm, he reported, had a long-standing hold on this dog.

More than a decade later, in 2007, I still owned those shares.

In that time, this lackluster appliance maker had indeed grown in Asia and, unexpectedly, had become an American consumer brand as well, a popular upgrade in high-end kitchen renovations with a product called the DishDrawer, a dual-level machine that operates as two separate dishwashers. The lackluster stock, meanwhile, had escalated sharply, and the company had spun off to shareholders a highly profitable health-care division. The value of those original shares had quadrupled, and Fisher & Paykel had paid along the way a stream of dividends and special distributions that cumulatively have exceeded my original cost by more 40%. All told, the investment in those Fisher & Paykel shares has gained more than 17% a year, on average. Not so lackluster after all.

For all the years I've covered the financial markets for *The Wall Street Journal,* I have routinely heard the investment industry counsel that investors without $100,000 to invest should stick to mutual funds, not common stocks. That may be true if you have no interest in actually finding common stocks to own, but if you are the type of investor who wants to own companies, not mutual funds, and who sees the work involved as part of the enjoyment of investing, then Wall Street's argument is hollow. You do not need tens of thousands of dollars to open accounts, either here in the United States or in foreign markets. That New Zealand account began with just $5,000. Even today, I routinely wire as little as $1,000 at a time to the various accounts when I need additional funds to make a purchase. Moreover, very few overseas firms I've communicated with through the years impose an account minimum on foreign investors. If they do, it's generally small.

Wall Street's machine nevertheless argues that owning individual stocks, much less individual foreign stocks, is not a game small investors like you and me should play. Many of these pros, though certainly not all, argue that individual investors should avoid fording the oceans on their own to invest anywhere overseas because they — the individual investors — haven't the necessary skills to analyze unfamiliar companies in unfamiliar lands, operating in unfamiliar industries, and according to unfamiliar accounting rules and governmental policies. While Wall Street experts certainly agree with the need to diversify your assets internationally, they insist it's best, instead, to stick your money in a mutual fund or ETF here in America and let the big boys do all the heavy lifting. If you're really adventurous and you promise not to hurt yourself, they might suggest you deploy a little "play money" in some of the big-name ADRs.

Given that I own six accounts outside of America, and have been successful in all of them, you have all the information you need to determine where I stand on the pros' logic. Investing directly overseas is an investment strategy at which individual investors can succeed using basic common sense and the tools readily available on the Internet. Besides, despite the MBAs and the Chartered Financial Analyst designations behind the names of many a mutual-fund manager and stock analyst, the pros get it wrong with great regularity.

Why did Enron happen? Why did Parmalat happen? Why was the stock market dumbfounded by revelations that Merck's Vioxx drug was potentially linked to fatal heart problems? Why did Bristol-Myers Squibb fall out of bed when a Canadian competitor, *which the pros knew about,* announced a generic rival to Bristol-Myers' blockbuster drug Plavix? And what of the technology bubble in the euphoric 1990s — why were pros famously, if not drunkenly, predicting $1,000 price targets for stocks with no hope of ever reaching such oxygen-deprived levels? How could the Street's wisest mavens, all paid big dollars to ferret out the good from the rotten, ride stocks down to single-digit prices — and even into bankruptcy — that months before had been expensive market darlings?

That doesn't mean these people are bad at their job. Many are quite skilled at what they do. Some aren't. Either way, the point is that no investor and no analyst can ever know all the demons that might emerge to sink a company's stock. But you, the individual investor, have something the pros don't: the freedom of time.

I once interviewed — briefly and by fax — the greatest

investor of modern times, Warren Buffett. And while I do not pretend to be Warren Buffett, I fully subscribe to the style of investing he once summed up quite neatly by noting that "Much success can be attributed to inactivity. Most investors cannot resist the temptation to constantly buy and sell." More specifically, he wrote, "Lethargy, bordering on sloth, should remain the cornerstone of an investment style." I am that lethargic, slothful investor. I buy foreign companies because I want to own the business long-term, not because I'm looking to trade in China one day, then dive out to buy in London the next. Of all the foreign companies I've bought in the past dozen years, I've exited only two — one because it crumbled and essentially paid me to leave by returning what capital remained; the second because I misread a tender offer and ended up selling my shares to a firm looking to build a stake in the timber company I owned. I pocketed a nice profit, but had I been paying the slightest bit of attention, I would have refused the tender offer and reaped the rewards as the stock moved higher during the commodities boom.

During the dozen years since opening that first account in New Zealand, I have been part of up markets and down. I've had companies such as Aristocrat Leisure, the Australian gaming-machine maker I mentioned earlier that is supplying casinos across America and the pachinko parlors that the Japanese are nuts about, struggle mightily through a management scandal. I've seen Bank of East Asia and Shangri-La Asia side-swiped by the SARS scare. While many managers where diving out of these stocks, and while analysts began distributing reports voicing concerns over these companies' operations, I stood pat, confident that these businesses were not going away and that they would emerge on the other side of the crisis intact and stronger. They did, and they've gone on to rack up nice triple-digit gains.

So what if Shangri-La Asia's earnings stumble because of SARS or an avian-flu outbreak? Does that mean travelers will never again visit Asia? Or might it just be a temporary blip on a longer road to prosperity? After all, once the crisis passes,

Asian travel will resume its booming expansion alongside the growing wealth inside China, Shangri-La will continue to be a leading hotel brand among the value-priced and luxury travelers, and the company will continue to add hotels inside China. So the stock price hits a downdraft from an exogenous event. That has no meaningful impact on the long-term success of the company.

In such instances, the pros are quick to pull the trigger and ask questions later, assuming they care to ask any questions at all. They have to react this way. They need to look brilliant every three months, when mutual funds post their quarterly results and the public companies that the analysts follow report their finances. They rightfully want to look smart for all those clients who are paying for sage investment guidance, and it doesn't look so swift when the companies a manager owns or the stocks that analysts are high on tank for whatever reason.

For an individual investor, such times can certainly be challenging. But you're under no pressure to do anything. If you're really confident about a company, you might even wade in to snap up some additional shares that everyone else is dumping in a panic. Then all you need do is practice a little sloth, as Mr. Buffett advises.

The simple fact of foreign investing is that you, the average U.S. investor, can succeed in buying stocks directly overseas. You can succeed in locating brokerage firms and banks that will gladly work with you. You can succeed in wiring money overseas and managing the niggling little headaches that inevitably arise. And you can succeed in finding and researching companies that today you don't even know to think about. Even if you've never set foot out of this country, and even if you never intend to, you can globe-trot with your greenbacks to take advantage of opportunities that the vast bulk of American investors will never realize exist, or that they will never pursue because of unfounded fears that putting your money to work directly overseas is somehow the height of risky behavior— though they'll eagerly pursue the next hot stock fad here at home and watch their investments shrivel when they realize too late that the fad had already begun to fade before their dollars even arrived.

Global investing is not a hard game to master. It certainly takes time, but, then again, anything worth its payoff requires some investment of time, even if it's just researching international mutual funds in the United States to find out which ones hedge their currency exposure and which ones don't.

The world really is that clichéd oyster. The pearls really are there. All it takes is a desire to venture beyond lower Manhattan and to open your portfolio to the opportunities awaiting you right now in London, Tokyo, Helsinki, Santiago, Bangkok, Auckland, Johannesburg, Shanghai, Cairo, São Paulo . . .

At the end of the day, and despite the risks and challenges along the way, the dollars you bring home are all the same shade of green, no matter where they come from. Enjoy your travels.

ACKNOWLEDGMENTS

My first recollections of the world outside America are as a ten-year-old sitting in a German pub in Frankfurt, in 1976, with my single-parent mom, one of her girlfriends and some guys they'd met while out drinking one evening — toting around a child, no less. My mom worked in the airline industry for Saudi Arabian Airlines at the time, and, at that point in aviation's history, we could fly free to any destination my mom fancied. And she often fancied any destination. So we would frequently hop on a plane and alight in various points in Guatemala, India, Chile, Argentina, Germany, the United Kingdom, the Bahamas . . . and the list goes on.

That night, I learned a German drinking phrase that I still recall, and learned to flip a stack of coasters off the edge of a table and catch them in my hand before they scattered into a giant mess. More important, I learned that life beyond American shores is no different than life within America's borders. People the world over do the exact same things we do at home, they just do it in a different language (generally, speaking), and in different stores yet often with similar products.

The many experiences I accumulated while traveling with my mom opened my eyes to the fact that America is little more than an island in a much larger sea of humanity. They made me a citizen of the world, though I have never yet lived anywhere but the United States. These days, they shape my beliefs that to truly be a global investor, you have to be, well, truly global — a belief that compelled me to venture directly into foreign stock markets at a time when doing so wasn't terribly easy and was looked upon by others as foolish, if not downright perilous financially. But over the years my returns in global markets, my encounters with foreign brokerage firms and banks, and the research I've done on companies from China to Romania have done nothing but reaffirm my belief, instilled so long ago by a mom choosing to show her son the wider world, that oh, so many opportunities exist when you think and act globally.

For all of that, the greatest thanks imaginable go to my mom, who taught her son that the world is a wonderful place.

Thanks also to Jim Rogers, of *Investment Biker* fame. I've interviewed Jim many times for *The Wall Street Journal,* and he knows the impact he's had on my life as an investor. But just to formalize it in print, Jim's original journey around the world on a motorcycle to chronicle the global investment climate, forced me out of the comfort zone of the New York Stock Exchange that so many American investors slide into and never escape. Jim's words and experiences and analyses allowed me to see the investment opportunities that lay behind the experiences I'd picked up when traveling the world. It was after reading *Investment Biker*—twice in the same month—that I began the search for my first overseas brokerage account in 1995. And I've never looked back. John Mahaney, my editor at Crown, was a believer in this book from the beginning, able to see what others couldn't: That direct investing globally, though available to the financially intrepid for more than a decade, is finally beginning to dawn as a viable investment strategy for mainstream American investors, and that those investors need a guidebook such as this one, to help them on their journey. John was a fan of the project from the start and I appreciate that greatly.

I also need to thank several people at *The Wall Street Journal* who have supported me and tolerated my book-writing exploits over the years. Roe D'Angelo, the *Journal*'s books-project guru helped shepherd my proposal through the system, while my editors, Bob Sabat and Larry Greenberg, earn thanks for putting up with yet another book project.

Thanks to my wife, Amy, who is forever supporting my need to write yet another book only weeks, it seems, after finishing the last one. She picks up the slack I, inevitably, leave behind, and I love her for that.

Last, but not least, is my friend, Debbie Darby, who did a wonderful job reading, editing, and proofreading my book along the way. Thanks to her, you, the reader, have far fewer colons and semicolons to deal with. Thanks; Deb.

INDEX

ABOUT THE AUTHOR

JEFF D. OPDYKE has been a reporter for 15 years, covering Wall Street and personal finance for *The Wall Street Journal*. He is also the author of four books, including *The Wall Street Journal Complete Personal Finance Guidebook*. He began investing directly in overseas stocks in 1995, and today he operates from bank and brokerage accounts in countries stretching from New Zealand to Romania to Canada. He lives in Baton Rouge, Louisiana, with his wife, Amy, and their two kids.